Since winning the BBC New Comedian of 1996, Marcus Brigstocke has emerged as a major talent in comedy, writing and acting. Most recently, he has shelved his stand-up microphone to play both King Arthur in *Spamalot* and Mr Perks in the award-winning production of *The Railway Children* at Waterloo station. Marcus has hosted his own live topical show on BBC4, *The Late Edition*, and has also appeared on *Live at the Apollo*, *Have I Got News for You*, *QI*, *Would I Lie to You?* and *Argumental*, as well as contributing to Radio 4's *The Now Show*. Marcus is currently writing a new show for the Edinburgh Festival in 2012, which will be followed by a nationwide tour.

God Collar is based on Marcus's sell-out show of the same name.

www.transworldbooks.co.uk

GOD COLLAR

Marcus Brigstocke

CORGI BOOKS

TRANSWORLD PUBLISHERS
61–63 Uxbridge Road, London W5 5SA
A Random House Group Company
www.transworldbooks.co.uk

GOD COLLAR
A CORGI BOOK: 9780552164474

First published in Great Britain
in 2011 by Bantam Press
an imprint of Transworld Publishers
Corgi edition published 2012

A CIP catalogue record for this book
is available from the British Library.

Addresses for Random House Group Ltd companies outside the UK
can be found at: www.randomhouse.co.uk
The Random House Group Ltd Reg. No. 954009

The Random House Group Limited supports The Forest Stewardship Council
(FSC®), the leading international forest-certification organisation. Our books
carrying the FSC label are printed on FSC®-certified paper. FSC is the only
forest-certification scheme endorsed by the leading environmental organisations,
including Greenpeace. Our paper-procurement
policy can be found at www.randomhouse.co.uk/environment

Typeset in Granjon by Falcon Oast Graphic Art Ltd.
Printed and bound by CPI Group (UK) Ltd, Croydon, CR0 4YY.

2 4 6 8 10 9 7 5 3 1

This book is dedicated with love to my friend James.
Wherever it was you went, this is for you —
I'm sorry it has no spies or soldiers in it . . .

Acknowledgements

There are a great many people I need to thank for helping me to create this book. To my beautiful family – Sophie, Alfie and Emily – thank you for being so loving, so wonderful and so very patient while I disappeared into this project.

Thank you to the many comedians and friends I have debated and discussed ideas of faith with late into the night – Andre Vincent, Carrie Quinlan and Robin Ince in particular. Sincere thanks to the very brilliant Nick Doody who helped me hammer out the ideas for the original stand-up tour of *God Collar*. Carey Marx, Alun Cochrane and Richard Lett who maintained a spirited and lengthy defence of alcohol and narcotics in the Alps. Mitch Benn, Daniel Kitson, Simon Evans, Andrew Maxwell, Rufus Hound, Josh Howie, Tim Minchin, James and Siobhan Bachman, Bill Hicks and Tim Vine (who wrote one of the funniest jokes about God I've ever heard).

To all the people I know who appear in the pages of *God*

Collar – my parents, my in-laws, my wonderful brother Henry, my friends, safari guides, vicars, atheists and Jesus – thank you and I hope you understand . . .

Thank you to Joe Norris, Danny Julian, Flo Collins and all at OTK for touring my show with me. Thank you to Sam Buntrock who directed *God Collar*, and who clarified and simplified it where he could and encouraged me where I wouldn't let him.

Sincere thanks to Jo Cole who knows where I'm supposed to be when, what I'm supposed to be doing for whom and what to say to whoever it is I'm meant to have done something for but haven't quite yet.

Needless to say there are many writers whose extraordinary insight and clarity have inspired and informed me. Thank you Professor Richard Dawkins, Christopher Hitchens, Sam Harris, Alexander Waugh, David Eagleman, A.C. Grayling, Jonathan Sacks, Philip Pullman and Karen Armstrong – may each of you find in yourselves the spirit of Christian forgiveness for my many-layered misunderstanding of your works.

Thank you to my friends at the Hay-on-Wye literary festival where thought, enquiry, debate, hilarity, humility, pride and freedom of expression ping off every tent pole in a field in Wales, and where I am delighted to launch this book. Peter Florence, Andy Fryers, Paul Blezzard, Hannah Lort-Phillips and the Hay family, you have lifted my aspirations.

Thank you to Malcolm Grimstone and Andy Bird without whom I'd be madder, sadder and ever so much more alone.

Thank you to my wonderful and talented friends who I

toured *Spamalot* with while I wrote much of this. Your gentle enquiries as to how 'the book' was going meant a great deal to me. Graham, Todd, Robin, Simon L, Samuel, David, Kit, Tim, Philip, Paul, Jodie, Amy, Rachael, PJ, Claire, Chris, Simon B, Dean, the band and the crew. Thank you to Hayley for 'onion rings' and the motivation to write the next line.

Thank you to my agents at United – Simon Trewin, Hannah Begbie, Olivia Homan, Arthur Carrington and Kitty Laing.

Thank you to all at Transworld for your faith in me and for your hard work – Madeline Toy, Mari Roberts and Larry Finlay.

Grovelling, huge and immensely grateful thanks to my editor Sarah Emsley for your calm patience, understanding and encouragement.

To all who have read this, thank you and if you know where God is, please tell him I was asking after Him . . .

1
There's probably no God

THERE COULD BE ONE BUT I'M PRETTY WELL CONVINCED there probably isn't. Certainly some people seem very insistent there is a God and that the consequences of suggesting to the contrary will be painful and very lengthy but if anything this makes me less inclined to believe there is a God; or if there is one then He's probably not my sort of chap. It's possible that there was a God and He's hiding or has grown bored with us. Maybe He's sulking or just plain forgetful, perhaps He's dead or He's gone on a really long holiday. There are infinite possibilities as to where God might have got to if he exists at all but it seems to me He probably doesn't. The God I'm fairly sure there probably isn't is the same God that many people are absolutely convinced there is. There might be another God entirely that none of us has considered but the God I am almost totally persuaded doesn't exist is the one

9

described variously as bearded, bathed in light, lives up in Heaven, has a staff of angels, created Heaven and Earth, destroyer, judge, receiver of prayers and half-hearted hymnal dirges, prefers Jews to any of the other tribes, Jesus' dad, He who dictated Al Qur'an to Mohammed in a cave, the fella with the booming voice, one third of the Holy Trinity, Jehovah, Allah, Almighty Father, Yahweh, the God they call Love, He whose name is jealous – the God of Abraham. The God of the Jews, the Christians and the Muslims. He probably doesn't exist. At least, I hope He doesn't . . .

I am an atheist . . . well, I think I am; or I was. I might be a lapsed atheist, having a crisis of whatever the opposite of faith is – facts? I'm having a crisis of facts. My atheism is quite wobbly at present. I haven't watched a David Attenborough documentary for months and I don't have a pop science book on the go. These seem to be the modern standard for non-believers and I'm failing in my irreligious observance. Forgive me, Secularism, for I have sinned, it's been six months since my last confession. I've had thoughts of a spiritual nature and I recorded *Masterchef* over the Professor Brian Cox documentary . . . I'd like to be comfortable with my atheism. It would be good for me and probably a relief for my family if the absence of a God in my life made me feel happy, but it doesn't.

My best friend died a few years ago and it broke my heart. The sudden and tragic loss of James, who was in his thirties, shifted a lot of my thinking and changed the way I felt about the world. It didn't stop me being an atheist – in some ways it galvanized the suspicion that we are alone in the universe and there is no plan – but it made me think a lot. I'm a dad and a husband and I try to be funny for a living. I feel sad and frustrated quite often. I miss my friend and I wonder where he is.

I had a God given to me when I was little. A family heirloom handed down through the generations without much thought as to His relevance or value. I'd have taken my God to *The Antiques Roadshow* and sold him if I'd had any strong feeling about Him being worth something. I'd be curious to see the face of a believer as they were told to insure God for only two to three hundred pounds. It wasn't really my God in any case, it was just borrowed. I also had an uncomfortably prickly teddy that I was given at around the same time and felt much the same way about. I kept God and my teddy until I grew out of them both and became embarrassed to be seen snuggled up with either of the prickly little buggers. I lost God and the bear at some stage between seven and eleven years old, I think. I didn't put them in the bin or anything like that, I just left them behind somewhere and I'm very literally damned if I can remember what happened to them. I found the bear when my parents moved house about ten years ago but there was no trace of God at all. The movers might have had Him . . .

I spent a few awkward years as a teenager being Godless, then a new God was given to me by some good friends who were worried about me when I was in my late teens and early twenties. We became close for a little while, God and I, but

11

like so many relationships at that tender age we lost contact with each other and we haven't spoken since. I didn't start seeing other Gods or anything slutty like that, it just fizzled out. We had different interests, I was a goth, God liked 1980s pop. I was without God for a long while and that seemed OK. I didn't miss Him, He didn't smite me, it was all right. Then I started to wonder whatever had happened to the God I'd known as a youngster? I began to notice other people's beliefs and I became interested by what they were saying about their God. Some of it angered and confused me. Do they believe in the God I was at school with? He's changed, or if He hasn't then it turns out I didn't know Him nearly as well as I'd thought. It's a bit like seeing the photo of the murderer the police are searching for on the news and realizing he used to share a locker with you at secondary school. 'Bloody hell! I'm not sure but I think that's the God I grew up with who just sent thousands of very heavily armed children into Iraq!'

I'm not sure what I believe at present. I know I feel strongly about religion and its ideologies and communities. I am suspicious of religion's past and nervous for its future but in terms of knowing what God is for or against, whether he's kind or unkind, or if there's even a shred of evidence to support the idea of His ever having existed, I'm not nearly as certain as I was two years ago. This book is about embracing that uncertainty and searching for something without really having the first clue as to what it is. This particular theological haystack might well prove to have a needle or two in it but until I've pricked my finger I won't know if that's what I was searching for in the first place. I need to find out if rummaging through the hay to see if that's where God's lurking is anything more than a waste of time given that I think there's probably no God in there, or in Heaven or anywhere else.

If you're confused then, for goodness' sake, don't expect me to lead you anywhere: I'm as lost as you are. My aim is not to tell anyone what to believe. I don't know myself, so it would be an exercise in breathtaking arrogance to suggest I might have any answers for anyone else. I'm a comedian, I'm not an academic, though I do have a BTEC in performing arts so don't dismiss me entirely. I'm in search of a thing that feels like it might be missing. I make no claim other than genuine curiosity as to my suitability and qualifications to guide myself or anyone else on an ambitious spiritual quest. At the first sign of danger I'm likely to cower behind the safe rocks of sarcasm and derision. Where there are forks in the road I'll sit and ponder, take one path, change my mind, try the other, then go back a few steps and see if there's an easier way round. I am to theological exploration as Eddy 'the Eagle' Edwards was to ski-jumping – massively under-prepared, dangerously over-confident and highly likely to fall on my arse to the amusement of the crowd. I'm doing it anyway, and if you're inclined to explore the feeling of precarious uncertainty with me, then I'd be glad of your company.

The truth, as I see it, is that I would rather stay in a place of confusion amongst similar restless souls shuffling about in the hope there might be a sign pointing in one direction or another, than leap aboard whichever bandwagon looks like it's got some momentum behind it and a confident driver. We might find God. We should probably have a plan for that in case we startle Him and He goes for us. I don't mind if we don't find Him. I'd be just as happy to discover that whatever road this is that I'm on, I'm not walking it alone.

2

A bus ride to Hell . . .

WE KNOW THERE'S PROBABLY NO GOD BECAUSE IT WAS written on the side of a bus. That's one of the ways you can know things. You can read books, watch telly, see if there are still any libraries to look something up in, Google it, tweet it, ask your mother or wait until a bus comes by with 'There's probably no God. Now stop worrying and enjoy your life' written on the side of it. If it's written on the side of a bus, you can probably trust it. Unless it says where the bus is supposed to be going, then you should treat the message with some caution. Buses are not like trains. Bus drivers have free will. Buses are large, usually red and often move about in packs, occasionally at high speed, so writing on the side of one takes time and effort. This is why you so rarely see a Banksy art-work sprayed on the side of a bus – they pull away without warning and the incredibly famous anonymous graffitist

G
OD COLLAR

would probably tear his stencil, a particularly nasty injury in the graffiti-ing world. I work on the basis that if a person has gone to all the trouble of writing a thing on the side of the bus, you'd be a fool not to consider it.

You can learn a lot from the side of a bus. I learned that if a startled-looking woman made of plastic rubs a special type of cream into her startled plastic face, it should be taken as proof that she's 'worth it'. Worth what exactly? I'm not certain; whatever she's worth, I'm sure she's earned her place on the side of a bus. Last spring I learned that it was 'Creme Egg season'. Creme Eggs are highly seasonal on account of the Creme bird only laying one egg per year somewhere near a till. She performs this ritual just before Easter (a religious holiday in which we remember the agonizing cross-based death and resurrection of Jesus Christ by telling children that a secretive bunny rabbit shits eggs all over the garden. It's one of the central messages of the life of Christ). Thanks to a bus, I learned that I probably 'Should have gone to Specsavers'. (I walked into the bus.) I learned that I could get 'Cash for Gold' which, without wishing to be obtuse, is the very least I'd expect for gold. Thanks to bus messages I know there is a website that compares the websites that compare the websites of comparable insurance companies, and I know there's 'Probably no God'.

The story of the bus campaign began in 2009 when Ariane Sherine wrote a piece for the *Guardian* newspaper about some Christian adverts running on London buses. The advertisements featured the address of a website which stated that non-Christians would burn in hell for all eternity. This information isn't new, it's been accepted as a threatening fact by Christians for a long time. This was an explicit reminder to anyone who had forgotten that all non-Christians would burn in Hell for ever – that's an awful lot of burnt souls. One presumes they mean everyone who isn't Christian as well as a few people who are essentially Christian, but due to an unfortunate miscommunication have chosen to be the wrong type of Christian. Historically there seem to have been some divisions and the odd spot of tension regarding which type of Christian one is supposed to be.

The list of candidates for the fires of Hell would include lots and lots of children. Sons and daughters of people born in places where the teachings of Christ have not been received. Those non-Christian children will burn in Hell for ever. Them and all of us who, for whatever reason, are put off joining in with such kindly and sweet-natured people, with the love of Christ in their hearts and a pious smile on their faces, gently and lovingly spreading fear, violence, judgement and retribution. We will burn in Hell for all eternity. Ariane Sherine will burn in hellfire for all eternity and probably slightly longer too if the staff in Hell can organize the roster for overtime. Ariane wasn't keen on the idea of hellfire, for herself or anyone else, and felt that this was a rather nasty thought to be driving about on the sides of buses. So she set her mind to coming up with something more benign. She suggested that people reading her article could, if they wished, each donate £5 to a fund that would be spent on a more reassuring counter-advert. The simple aim was to cheer people up after all the unpleasant talk of burning children, which, let's face it, can make you a little bit glum.

Political blogger Jon Worth had read Ariane's article and liked her proposal very much. He took the idea a step further by setting up a pledgebank page so people could donate money to the campaign. Eight hundred and seventy-seven people soon pledged £5 each. A very promising start indeed and suggestive of an enthusiasm for the atheist community to have a public face. I'm not totally sure that atheists can be described as being a community. I don't even know if there's a collective noun for a group of atheists. A smug? A damnation? A rationality? Things really got moving when scientist and famous secular rationalist Richard Dawkins generously agreed to match all donations made to the site. He's a brilliant scientist and exceptionally bright so he quickly and sensibly revised this offer and set a cap on it of £5,500. For a man descended from an ape, he's no fool. The mention of the campaign on Professor Dawkins's website soon set the naturally selected, evolved monkey-cage of atheists a-buzz. Dawkins's website is a hub for the lonely secularist seeking the spiritless joy of communion and mutual approval of other non-believers, and it has many thousands of visitors who soon picked up on the fundraising effort. The hope had been that they might be able to raise as much as £5,500 but in fact the immoral and Godless dug deep into their hell-bound pockets and found amongst the lint, sweet wrappers and despair a grand total of just over £150,000. A lot of people, it seemed, wanted to make an affirming statement on behalf of the life we know we have and reject the idea of living for the next one. This rejection of God and of the teachings of His son Christ would represent a whole lot of eternal burning for God to see to. I hope he's got plenty of firelighters. The unexpectedly large number of donations was enough to pay for the campaign to run not only on London buses but all across the UK, with adverts also on the London Underground and an animated version on two screens in Oxford Street. For those fortunate enough not to know, Oxford Street is somewhat akin to Dante's vision of hell, only with more carrier bags and tourists.

So it was that, on a cold January day in 2009, a bus whose belief system until then had been very much its own business departed Hyde Park proudly bearing the message: 'There's probably no God. Now stop worrying and enjoy your life.' The statement was bold, funny and challenging. It was refreshing to see an intellectual notion promoted alongside the endless crap we are encouraged to consume in the name of 'growth'. I've no idea how much the passengers inside the bus felt part of the message their irreligious double-decker was spreading – there's every reason to suspect they felt no more moved by the provocation they were sitting within than they would have been had there been an advertisement encouraging people to sit on a sofa they wouldn't have to pay for until next year, eat a McFlurry or go to see a film featuring a man shot mainly in silhouette who has stubble and a gun. Perhaps the passengers didn't care at all – perhaps they hadn't noticed the message of theological scepticism emblazoned on the bus they were riding about in. Perhaps they were distracted by the jaw-grindingly irritating R&B played through the tinny 1cm speaker of a shiny mobile phone clutched with pride in the hand of a thoughtless, dead-eyed 'statistic' in a baseball cap. Often I've wished I could direct a bank of speakers some 30 metres across at a faceless hoodie with a fistful of Nokia dance beats and literally pin them to the back seat of the bus with 1,000 decibels of Jenni Murray and the *Woman's Hour* team on BBC Radio 4 whilst screaming, 'Not everybody's tastes are the same as yours, you feckless desert of empathy and hope. Learn something, you dumb-proud hate crime!' But that's me – I'm not much for the R and the B and I get a bit tense on public transport.

Regardless of who within or without the bus cared, the message went out there for all to see. Only a few actually did see it; the rest read about it in the press and got cross or excited or both. A challenge, 'There's probably no God', and then an affirmative invitation to do something positive, 'Now stop worrying and enjoy your life.' This seemed a particularly good combination to me. 'We have no lasagne. Now why not go dancing?' 'There's no such thing as unicorns. Honey is delicious and extraordinary, eat some.' 'Everything that is living dies. Give someone you care about a dirty great orgasm.' 'There's probably no God. Now stop worrying and enjoy your life.' It's a clever message and it captured the spirit of a way of thinking I felt excited to see thunder past me as I clung nervously to my bicycle to prevent myself from wearing the bus as a jazzy new four-wheeled death hat.

In truth, I'd read about the campaign long before I saw one of the Godless buses drift across the cycle lane without so much as a cheeky wink of its indicator. It was only when I saw it first hand that I realized I hadn't actually been worrying and I had been enjoying my life, and since then I've slipped into a sort of existential crisis bordering on a depression. But nonetheless it was an interesting and thought-provoking idea to put out on the streets of Britain and I hope it succeeded in providing reassurance to some who might have been concerned by the whole 'burning for all eternity' suggestion. In any case, it made me feel less alone for a while.

The appeal was copied by other humanist and atheist groups all over the world. The secular community took a huge lurch forward, and then shuddered to an awkward stop again while an anxious-looking atheist fumbled for the correct change to ride the Godless bus to enlightenment. I felt the bus pull away; I'd got on early and nabbed a window seat. It seemed exciting to be on board and I began to scour the bus for faces I knew. There was a good deal of chatter and much ambitious discussion about how far we might take this bus. As an atheist used to a courteous discretion on matters of belief in public discourse, I felt a mixture of pride, vindication and just enough nervousness to make me tingle. This felt like a movement. This was atheism for the mass market. Hallelujah, let the word go forth that we are alone in the universe . . . Ooh, and look, it's Creme Egg season again. I thought it must be because I've just put the Christmas decorations away.

I don't know how well received the message was elsewhere in the world but if there's a bus driver idling at a set of lights in Tehran, Jerusalem or Houston, Texas sporting the same slogan, then I take my hat off to you. I'm sure your hat will come off too, quite possibly with your head still in it.

One curious upshot of the British Humanist Association putting their message out there was that some Christian organizations replied. A perfectly reasonable thing to do – their faith had been challenged, so they responded. What I liked about it was that their responses were also written on the sides of buses. Ha ha! Who says the church is humourless? Well, me actually – but this I liked. You wait for a message about God on a bus and then three come along at once. For a few glorious weeks in 2009 there were atheist buses being overtaken by religious buses and vice versa. Sweaty, nonchalant drivers leaning over their giant steering wheels shrugging at each other as they battled out questions of theology, belief, existence, creation and hope. Is there a God? What better way to settle this age-old question than with a game of bus chicken? Determinedly revving their giant red proclamations in a deadly joust with no less at stake than the answer to the very purpose of mankind. Could a scene set at the lights by Chicken Cottage in Tooting be more dramatic? I imagined God playing dice with the outcome as he looked on (the trouble with omnipresence is you can never look away even when you're being dissed, denied or royally slagged off), mumbling to himself, 'Right then – if the atheist bus reaches the third Carphone Warehouse on the left first I'm abandoning mankind for all time.' Then he'd have to wait for the lights to change. Powerful he may be, but you don't mess with Transport for London.

I like the idea of the great theological debate of our times being carried out via the medium of public transport. I look forward to seeing a tram with 'Buddha was a twat' written on the side of it, or boarding a train to hear the announcement crackle with static, then: 'Welcome aboard this 15.00 service from London Paddington to Bristol Temple Meads. We'd like to remind passengers that the only way to the Father is through His son, our Lord Jesus Christ. There are currently engineering works just outside Didcot Parkway. So, in a very similar fashion, the only way to Bristol is also via the medium of prayer, thank you.'

The Christians' bus messages were more confident and assertive than the Humanists'. One of them read, 'There *definitely* is a God. So join the Christian Party and enjoy your life.' Definitely? It seemed a big claim to me, but then given the stories explaining what God does to non-believers, if I were Christian I'd want to look like I was absolutely certain He was out there. I presume they wrote 'definitely' because as Christians they're tired of being questioned on the subject and wished to draw a line under it once and for all by saying something stupid in public. Since it was written on a bus you'd have to be a pretty confident atheist to challenge it with anything much other than an irritable tut and shrug of the shoulders as the multi-storey testament to the existence of a monotheistic creator screeched by you. It's a bus. What are you going to do? Challenge it to a fight?

There were a great many complaints made to the Advertising Standards Authority about the Humanist Association's 'There's probably no . . .' campaign. It made the top ten most-complained-about advertisements. However, there were many more complaints made about the unsubstantiated Christian Party's 'There's definitely . . .' That really got up people's noses. The complaints were registered and the result was so oddly pathetic it fell into that category of realizations that mean you have to retreat to your 'mental safe place' for fear you will do something publicly unacceptable and unsettling like shout at the sky or watch *Deal or No Deal* all the way through. It transpires the advert had been placed there by the Christian (political) Party, so, according to the Advertising Standards Authority, they, as a political party, are uniquely allowed under advertising regulations to . . . how best to put this? Well, they are allowed to . . . lie. Or if not actually *lie*, then at least to promise things for which there is no evidence at all. That's the ruling on political advertising. You can talk crap and no one expects any different. Good-oh.

The Advertising Standards Authority ruled against the many complaints about the Christian Party ads, saying they were an 'expression of the advertiser's opinion and that the claims in it were not capable of objective substantiation'. They can say, 'There definitely is a God' because, as a political party, no one realistically expects them to deliver on statements made before they rise to power. It's so utterly bizarre and perverse it's brilliant. 'Vote Labour – we will give you the power of flight.' 'The Conservative Party – we have mastered the science of alchemy.' 'Support the Lib Dems – we might win!'

Having done my research, I don't want to join the Christian Party, even if there definitely is a God. I've read up on them and I think they're horrible. I deeply resent their choosing to revel in biblically selective bigotry. If only they were just unpleasant, but to be honest their manifesto is distinctly odd as well. They are very clear about what is needed to improve education. They would *allow schools to elect to use supervised corporal punishment*. These are the words grown-ups use when they want to hit children. 'Supervised' means that other adults can watch the children being hit in order to make sure that child is being hit properly by the adult who is hitting the child. Improper hitting of a child by an adult would mean the hitting of the child would have to be done again, maybe by a different adult, or by the same one after he or she has attended the Christian Party course on how to hit children. Hitting children is usually promoted by men who say things like 'never did me any harm' – when quite clearly it did; the tell-tale twitch in the left eye or private weekends spent wearing nappies are the usual giveaways. Sometimes they say, 'Made me the man I am today.' Sadly this is probably accurate, a childhood spent in awe of the power one person can exert over another if the circumstances allow can turn most people into psychopathic bullies in rose-tinted, tear-stained glasses. Never once have I heard those phrases spew their frothy way out of any man's mouth I didn't suspect was in fact a colossal pervert.

I don't like hitting. I've never been in a fight, although I have been hit. I was hit as a child, not by my parents, but by bigger kids and a few teachers. On one occasion I was given six of the best with a cricket bat. They said it was 'of the best' but it didn't feel like the best of anything much to me. I felt degraded and bruised. I grew big quite quickly as a child so it wasn't long before I became one of those children you'd think twice about before hitting in case I hit you back or ate you. I don't intend to hit anyone any time soon. I really don't like violence. It sickens more than scares me, though I do wonder sometimes how far I might go if I ever really lost it. I'd be very disappointed to discover that I was one of those psychos who is able to beat a man to death with just my hands. I don't hit my children, but if you hit them, I'll hit you. Hard. I send my children to school to learn things; none of those things is calculating how long it will be before they're too big for anyone to assume that hitting them is anything other than abuse. What it is that children are supposed to learn at school from being corporally punished I don't know.

So, hitting children then ... What else would a Christian Party government deliver for this country? They would: '*Seek sanctions for schools that refused to comply with their obligation to assemble pupils for an act of daily worship. Such acts of worship should be Christian.*'

Secular or non-Christian children will soon find that being hit by an adult will help them to understand what Christ's teachings were all about. Perhaps the sanctions would mean that bigger adults would be allowed to come and hit the teachers if the school failed to gather the children together for their act of daily worship. Attendance in any school should be an act of the profoundest worship anyway. The worship of knowledge, the joy of understanding, the communion of shared exploration of ideas, thoughts and freedom of expression. Children should clamber and leap with unbridled enthusiasm over the hills and valleys of what there is to be discovered. Their indiscriminate trampling through ideas and theories should leave a mess of intellectual debris that only need be assembled into anything resembling a thesis once formal education is done with. Sure, you could line the children up in sombre rows with heads bowed in reverence, you could have them mumble meaningless and exclusive prayers they don't understand to a God they are told they should fear. You could make this happen every morning in an act of daily worship, but frankly I'm not convinced there's time. There's so much to achieve before adulthood comes along and ruins that ability to absorb new ideas and meet each one without fear. You could make the children read their star signs and give the Sagittarius ones Wednesdays off because Russell Grant says they're expecting turmoil and should look to their laurels, but there are books to be read and great and interesting ideas to discuss.

The Christian Party would: *'Ensure that proper balanced teaching and debate occurs in schools around the concepts of "Evolution" and "Creation/Design in the universe".'* This one I don't mind at all, as it should only take around five to ten minutes for any decent teacher to explain that creationism was once a justifiable way of explaining the world (in the absence of the data we have now collected, verified and understood) but that now creationism is just a made-up story and to suggest that it serves any purpose other than to preserve the power of the organizations who claim it as the truth is predictable and dull. The evidence for Darwin's theory of evolution continues to flood in, on an almost biblical scale. 'Now then, children, who wants to colour in this picture of a dinosaur and then post it to the Pope?'

The Christian Party would: '*Call for the end of the promotion and teaching in schools of homosexuality as a family relationship.*' Yeah yeah yeah, evil queers, Adam and Eve not Adam and Steve, God Hates Fags . . . so far so hateful, and then . . .

'*Raise the motorway speed limit to 90mph.*'

Pardon? 90mph? Why? What's that got to do with anything? And then . . .

'*Enact a speeding fines amnesty in cases where fines were more a matter of revenue collection than road safety.*'

What? Forget the queer-bashing rhetoric for a second. This is interesting stuff. I've cross-checked this with the Bible and even the complete King James has depressingly little to say on donkey speed limits, sandal tread restrictions and camel congestion around the eye of the needle. The biblical speed camera consisted of a slave with some papyrus hiding crouched in a yellow box on a pole near the road to Damascus (27 DEATHS LAST YEAR! REDUCE YOUR SPEED!). The slave would draw, as fast as his papyrus and charcoal would let him, any speeding hoofed mammals as they trotted by. Even the most knackered ass could amble brazenly past before he'd had time to draw the vaguest sketch of the beast or get a peek at its number plate. In any case, a lot of the yellow boxes didn't even have a slave in them. They were just there as a deterrent.

The Christian Party seem very keen on matters relating to drivers and how they're treated in the UK. One suspects that in spreading the word of God with this level of enthusiasm some of the members may have had to attend the National Speed Awareness Course to explain themselves . . .

'I was caught doing 37mph in a 30mph limit outside a school. No, I'm not ashamed – the work of Jesus cannot be restricted by arbitrary, secular, traffic-calming measures. "Godspeed" is around 90mph – fact. God is omnipresent but only because he isn't limited to the draconian and punitive anti-driver legislation this country has become obsessed with over the years.'

Fail.

It's not just how fast the Christian Party want to be allowed to get where they are going. They've also given real thought to the serious issue of what to do with their car when they arrive for their afternoon of child hitting or whatever it is they do.

'Limit fines for overstaying in car parks to a maximum of the cost of the day rate for parking in the facility.'

This is in line with mainstream Christian values in this country. I think. Or if it isn't, it's in line with the experience of whichever child-whacking, science-phobic, gay-hating dolt put together the manifesto for the Christian Party; a man I suspect has a statuette of the Stig hanging from his rear-view mirror.

The Christian Party (18,621 votes in 2010 General Election

– God help us!) would make abortion illegal, halt stem cell research and seriously toughen laws around assisted dying. They would, as they say, 'Challenge the culture of death by seeking legislation which confers the full protection of the law on all human life from the conception until natural death.'

It's true that there is a culture of death here on earth. There's a little-known statistic that every human being who has ever walked the planet has at some time or other dabbled with death. Shocking. We can change that. Like all good Christians, they value human life as a God-given and beautiful thing, to be treasured and respected and loved.

They would also: 'Maintain a well-resourced military with a nuclear deterrent.' In case it turns out that life isn't as special, sacred or important as they thought. Turn the other cheek? Well, yes, you could do that, or you could invest in a weapons system that would indiscriminately kill every man, woman, child, animal and plant it came near. Force other nations to play a deadly game of catch-up, leaving their people without sustenance, education and sanitation in order to keep spending on the latest weaponry, and hope the dominoes never start to fall. Turn that life-respectin'-cheek, bitch!

Hmm, I wonder what Jesus would do?

The Christian Party sent out their double-decker proclamation 'There definitely is a God', and if there is, I'm sure He was pleased that the argument was settled in his favour once and for all ... on the side of a bus. The Christian Party is not to be confused with a Christian party – I went to one of those once and was asked to leave after I accidentally dunked the body of Christ in some hummus. It's odd how much the body of Christ looks like a Pringle. Also, if you're looking up 'The Christian Party' online, take a look at Christian Party Games, which includes Biblical Bingo. Match a row of ways in which God has killed people and win a bishop's hat!

The Christian Party's 'There definitely is a God' retort to the Humanist campaign looked like it might excite further debate. Had funds allowed, it could have led to an enjoyable to and fro on the buses between the forces of God and the atheist rabble. Advertisements changed on a weekly, daily and then hourly basis as the exchanges heated up.

'Yes, there is.'

'No, there isn't.'

'Is!'

'Isn't!'

'There is a God!'

'I'll get you, Butler!'

'Prove it!'

'You claim there is one – you prove it, you gullible hump!'

'That's it, you Godless bastard, I'm going to hit your children.'

The Trinitarian Bible Society – which publish Bibles – took the view that the best way to preserve their lucrative business would be to place advertisements quoting from Psalm 53.1. The slogan read 'The fool hath said in his heart, there is no God'. It's an insult, it's childish, it's factually doubtful and yet because it's straight from the pages of 'The Good Book' it carries weight. It is, let's face it, a massive diss. I'm no fool. And the part of my body that tells me there is no God is my brain, not my heart. I tend to use my brain instead of my heart when it comes to deciding on the important stuff. My brain is flawed, jumbled, logical and illogical all at once. My brain has looked at the facts as they are and has said there probably is no God. This isn't foolishness. Ignoring information is foolishness. Research, thought, discussion and debate seem reasonable to me. What is a fool? Well, to quote President George W. Bush: 'There's an old saying in Tennessee I know . . . it's in Texas – probably in Tennessee, that says – Fool me once . . . Shame on . . . um . . . Shame on you . . . Er, a fool . . . Me, you can't get fooled again.' That's what a fool is.

Looking at the Trinitarian Bible Society's marketing plan, you can at least say they are consistent with the best traditions of why many people believe in God. It's the 'give 'em a good old scare' approach. There's a reason why many people describe themselves as God-fearing. He's a scary bastard. If I thought He really was up there, I'd be God-fearing too. It's believers I fear the most at present, but if there was a God I knew existed I'd be never-leaving-my-house, hiding-under-the-table-shaking-like-a-leaf, pissing-in-my-pants God-fearing. The Trinitarians quote from the Bible and make it clear in slightly fancy language that any questions you might have regarding God have already been answered. Well, not answered exactly, but it feels like they have if you stop asking them, and the book that has been the number-one bestseller since before even Bruce Forsyth was born takes a dim view of such questions anyway (and I do mean dim).

I'm sure they needn't worry, people will still keep buying Bibles. Even the most foolish amongst us recognize how important a book it is, and funny too. There are passages that make me laugh out loud, some that can make you cry and lots that should anger anyone who has even the vaguest care for humanity. There's a Bible in almost every hotel room in the world, thanks to the Gideons. To date the Gideons have deposited 1.7 billion Bibles in top drawers of hotels, theatres, businesses and libraries all over the world. The Gideons are a group of enormously forgetful Christian businessmen who never travel without a Bible and almost always forget to take it with them when they leave. Occasionally they leave other items behind too, but it's usually a Bible. I once found a pair of socks in a drawer in a Travelodge saying 'Placed here by the Gideons'. As a touring comedian I stay in a lot of hotels and I've been collecting Bibles from each one I stay at. I assume they're like the biscuits, soap, dressing gowns and kettle that you're allowed to take with you when you leave. I've got thousands of Gideon Bibles. Enough to construct a Pagan temple, as it happens.

There were some atheists who pressed for their message to read 'There is no God' without the 'probably' – I for one am glad they failed. However unlikely the existence of a deity is, we don't yet know for sure that there isn't or never has been one. Why insist on an absolute position when you don't know for sure? Dismiss at will the absurd, offensive, destructive, oppressive and dishonest, but this more than qualified as a 'probably' statement in my view. It's quite possible that the 'probably' inspired more thought and debate than the 'definitely' anyway. 'Occam's razor' is a brilliant and important principle to apply here: discard that which overcomplicates the answer and has to travel the longest route in its attempt to arrive at plausibility. That principle shouldn't mean we refuse to reconsider that which we are *sure* of. The sun will rise tomorrow . . . probably. I think, therefore I am . . . probably. Courgette plants cannot hear the approach of a hungry gardener with a knife . . . probably. Simon Cowell produces cynical, lazy, bland records and he's a grasping, vapid twat . . . some things we can be pretty certain of.

The Christian Party will have enjoyed the divinely assured confidence of the definite statement and the secular community will have enjoyed with pride the open-minded nature of scientific enquiry . . . probably. The key, it seems to me, is to remain open-minded, unless to do so hinders further enquiry or should be dismissed because the matter at hand has been satisfactorily demonstrated to be wrong. I strive to be open-minded on all things. That said, I'm not eating Cheestrings no matter what my children tell me about how yummy they are. They are an affront to cheese and a vile blight on the good name of variously rotted milks.

I recognize that I am not open-minded on a great many matters. I try to be but I'm just not. A fully open mind seems to me as dangerous as a closed one. Who knows what rubbish might pour in and, worse still, what might ferment into an opinion and come back out. On religion I have decided that none of the ones I've read up on so far are for me. On faith, though, I'm not so sure. I'm not depressed, but my lack of belief doesn't make me happy and I sometimes wonder what I might have to impose over the blank page in order to be content.

Open-mindedness is a difficult state to maintain (so is North Korea, but for very different reasons). Not when you're young, obviously. When you're young, open-mindedness comes as easily as a young person does. The fickle gift of being fickle is enjoyed without question by most young people, who wake up vowing undying love for Stephanie from class 4b and listening exclusively to N-Dubz, and by bedtime everything's changed: they are now definitely going to marry 'weird Mary' who sits on the wall outside the Spar shop and have replaced their N-Dubz posters with those of Justin Bieber. This joyful, guiltless freedom of thought lasts until the day you wake up and find a squashed can of Tango has been inserted into the hedge in front of your house, and suddenly you are dreaming up severe and violent penalties for pretty much anyone younger than you are. Perhaps the Christian Party could drive a large car at speed towards whatever child shoved the partially squashed drink can into the hedge as the ultimate corporal punishment. These uncompromising views come with age. I'm pretty liberal, which is to say if you put me in a room full of people of a similar age, the odds are that I'll be the one wearing the most corduroy. It can't be a coincidence that as I get older I find that my position on the question of the voting age is that it should be whatever age I am at the time the election is called. A fixed and conclusive view of the world has a mysterious magnetism that seems to get quietly stronger as each year rolls by. A settled and certain viewpoint on what is absolutely right or wrong in the world almost always serves to make us unhappy as we are very unlikely to find the world willing to bend itself to fit our position and yet, give most of us a chance to attach ourselves to this or that 'take on life', and we are like chewing gum in a plait.

The Humanist bus campaign won't have changed that (or much of anything else, I suspect), but the use of 'probably' at least encourages the idea that we should keep on considering all the possibilities.

One driver refused to operate the Humanist bus. Mr Ron Heather from Southampton told his employers that as a Christian he was 'shocked' and wouldn't drive the bus while it suggested he might be wrong to believe in God. Why he was shocked I don't know. You'd have to have your head shoved pretty far up your own belief system not to notice that some people hold a different view to your own. I doubt anyone would seek to associate the driver with what's written on the side of his vehicle anyway. Certainly when I see a floppy-haired driver in a Mini with 'Foxton's Estate Agents' written on the side I almost never think to myself: Wow, look at that – a man with only two GCSEs with a job, a car and fat knotted pink tie. Mr Heather took his job as a Southampton bus driver before the Humanist ad campaign started so in some ways his seemed a reasonable position. I say this with caution as there seems to be an endless stream of sanctimonious dullards who whine in the press, 'I can't do my job because it offends my religious beliefs.' The press are forever finding simpletons who think that having faith in something unprovable confers on them some special rights. I don't know where they get these ideas from but perhaps the House of Lords could ask the bishops who automatically get a free seat in there if they could look into the issue . . . Oh I see. If your employer says don't wear a crucifix to work, then don't wear a crucifix. Especially if it's full size. There was a long and tedious row about this concerning a British Airways employee who wanted to wear a crucifix to work. If you don't trust engineering and science but you think a crucifix will keep you safe at 32,000 feet then you probably shouldn't work for an airline. Jesus almost certainly didn't care what the BA staff wore to work. He almost never flies anyway, what with the whole walking-on-water thing. If you're a Muslim or a Jew, why go for a job at 'Mr Porky's Rib 'n' Pig Bits House of Non-Halal Pork'? If your beliefs prevent you from working at one place, then go somewhere else. It's really pretty simple.

Mr Heather had held his job for a while and even if it shouldn't have, the arrival of this challenge to religious belief represented an unusual state of affairs and a quandary for the devout Mr Heather. In principle, Mr Heather's stand is one I support. I think it's silly, but I can see where he's coming from, and not just because he's in a big red bus. As it happens I'd like to see more people put up a fight when they are asked to carry a sponsor's message as part of their work. I wouldn't wish to wear a T-shirt emblazoned with 'McDonald's – I'm lovin' it' to my place of work, particularly if I worked at McDonald's where I imagine 'lovin' it' would be so far from my reality that I'd end up bobbing for apple pies in the deep-fat fryer just to focus the pain. If Mr Heather believed in God and that was important to him, why should he have to spend his entire working day casting doubt on that and dealing with the looks from strangers and colleagues as he drove his passengers from Southampton Central to the sixth circle of Hell, or wherever it terminates? You could argue that he should drive his passengers wherever the bus is supposed to go, but the fuss he made was minimal and he seemed to enjoy a day and a half in the newspapers. In the event the bus company said he would only have to drive one of the Humanist buses if no others were available. Mr Heather seemed content with that compromise and I'm sure God would see it his way once it had been explained by St Peter that there simply weren't any buses proclaiming God's love for man.

Most of the time we passively consume advertising messages without considering the effect they have on us – I'm sure that's why advertising works so well and the industry is worth so many billions of pounds. I don't even know for sure what 'Ronseal' says on the tin but I'm absolutely certain that it does it. If I wanted to 'Bang' off some dirt I'd turn to 'Cillit' for a really effective dirt banger. No M&S food is just normal food – it's special M&S food and is therefore more full of sex than Paris Hilton staying at the Paris Hilton with the express aim of filling up on sex. When a statement comes along that seems to step outside of the meticulously researched subtleties of the usual advertisements ('It's Creme Egg season'), it is striking and it makes you think. Regardless of what offence the Humanist Association's campaign may have caused, I am absolutely convinced that intellectual provocation is beneficial to us all and that offence is best taken in very small doses with a spoonful of sugar and a good book. This relaxed view of offence is, of course, much easier to lay claim to when you agree with the provocation in the first place and are therefore not offended.

Doubtless some would-be passengers refused to board a bus denying the probable existence of God, choosing instead to wait for the next one with something less challenging on it, like an advert for BP, which now stands for Beyond Petroleum, Burst Pipe or Big Polluter, according to taste. If a bus pulled up claiming, 'There's probably no climate change so stop worrying and don't use this bus', I'm quite sure I'd wait for the next one, or go home and get my bicycle . . . Or perhaps a taxi . . . Or, failing that, one of my cars. I'm no better than anyone else and considerably worse than some. Those passengers are free to choose and immensely fortunate that we live in a country where another bus is likely to arrive fairly soon with something entirely different written on it. As long as that something isn't 'Out of Service' then it should all work out fine and our ability to usefully discriminate between what we are OK with and what we are not is to be celebrated with a return ticket to the swimming baths, please, driver.

I spotted one of the Humanist buses on a Sunday morning

in London. I was out for a walk and the bus was stuck in heavy traffic outside a church. I saw the 'There's probably no God . . .' message and was already enjoying the irony of it being held up outside a church when I noticed that on the front it read 'Sorry, Not In Service'. A bus that was clearly suffering from some post-religious guilt complex. Defiant but still somehow ashamed of its lack of faith. Struggling to let go of the sense of emotional devotion to a set of ideas it had intellectually abandoned years before.

I wish there were still buses whizzing about with theological provocations on the side of them. It was all so refreshing and different. This was my church coming together, not to worship, but to say that your church was wrong to worship. It was, let's face it, in the very best traditions of religious practice. 'You're wrong!' 'Nope, screw you, you're wrong.' The idea of it excited me and I wanted there to be a row and a fuss and for someone to get cross and say something daft on Jeremy Vine's BBC Radio 2 show: 'I think the bus drivers should be arrested' – that sort of thing. Perhaps a strongly worded and overtly intolerant letter to the *Daily Telegraph*, to include the words 'disgraceful', 'moral decline', 'traditionally Christian nation', 'tolerance', 'string 'em up', and something about 'not fighting in World War Two so that these sorts of people can say what they want and put squashed Tango cans in my hedge!' I like a bit of a furore; it helps to clarify where people really stand. A few people stand in the most appalling positions on these issues, but I feel it's preferable to have everyone's views out in the open so we can discuss them. I am capable and guilty of zealotry and am unashamedly prejudiced (all based on research and debate, of course). I hoped that the provocation of the Godless, no matter how upsetting for some, would lead to greater honesty in the end. Rather that than the sort of passive approval or cursory dismissal most of us give to ideas worthy of a far more thoughtful response.

The thoughts and ideas I had hoped would be discussed, were, to some extent, although like most of these things the debate seemed to entrench those whose views would most readily suggest themselves for moderation and empathy. My own thoughts were not entirely as I'd expected. I actually found the 'probably no God' campaign quite unsettling. I found myself looking at one of the buses and thinking it would be pretty bloody depressing to be run over by that bus, wouldn't it? I mean, it'd be fairly depressing to be run over by any bus. Particularly one of London's bendy buses. You'd lie there in the road thinking: Shit, I've been run over by a bendy bus. And then it would dawn on you – yep, it's going to happen again in a minute, and then the second half of the least popular form of public transport since the zeppelin would trundle over your prone and despairing body. A dreadful sequel to the first assault, almost as bad as *Weekend at Bernie's Two*. But believer, atheist, agnostic or other, it would be particularly depressing to be run over by the big secular bus, wouldn't it? As you're trapped under the wheel arch of a double-decker, realizing there's very little of your life left to worry about anyway, you look up and the last words you see are, 'There's probably no God.' That and a fat, sweaty driver looking down at you saying, 'Sorry, mate, I thought you were a cyclist and as such fair game. My mistake.'

'There's probably no God! But I'm dying! Crushed by a bus that claims there's no God! I want a refund. A rethink. Wait. Maybe there is a God. Sorry. I've led a good life, right? Not exactly Christian as such, but still, in principle, in line with many of the main ideas behind the central message of Christ or Mohammed or . . . Oh shit, who are the other prophets? I'm sending out an all-purpose prayer, any prophet, deity or supernatural power – HELP! I want to confess. I'm willing to repent. Oh crap. What happens now? Where am I going?'

'Let's get him to A&E.'

'Oh no! I made the wrong choice.' There is a Hell and its first level can be found at most A&E departments. I haven't had to use A&E much, but when I attended with my wretched sobbing daughter in one hand and her severed finger in the other I would swear to you that Satan himself had taken the human form of the drunken bastard with blood and sick on him in front of us in the queue. The doctors saved her finger and we were sent home and given all the care we could possibly have wished for thanks to the dedicated and brilliant staff. Gratitude to the NHS and its extraordinary doctors and nurses aside, if I never have to visit A&E again it will be a day too soon.

I don't want to be run over by the Humanist bus, and yes I do fear that my atheism would probably crumble in an instant if I was sufficiently scared. On the other hand, I wouldn't want to be run over by the Christian Party bus either. Bleeding in the road as the words 'There definitely is a God' loom over my head. A Christian Party-sponsored wheel squeezing the life from my limp body. I'd have no choice but to face up to the fact that the 'definite God' they're talking about doesn't care one scrap for me or my life as he's just allowed a bus to run me over. We're all children of God, they say . . . does that mean an adult's going to hit me? I'm not having that unless we get to play dress-up and there's a safe word. No, God doesn't care about me, even though I'm middle-class. Historically he's been immensely good to my kind of people. The poor and meek may be blessed but I'm not convinced He actually likes the working classes at all. I have a horrible feeling that if I was run over by the Christian Party bus I might be left there as a few people stood about rolling their eyes and muttering about 'the will of God' and deciding whether or not to commence some 'supervised hitting'.

Regardless of my own personal crises of faithlessness and what is fast becoming a pathological terror of death by bus, I still felt that Ariane's Humanist proclamation and the religious responses to it made for the most fascinating public discussion of the idea of God that I've seen in my lifetime. And all on the side of a bus.

Some Muslims used buses to advertise their faith too – in an altogether more horrifying and less intelligent promotion of religious ideas. Blowing a bus up will get people's attention but a well-thought-out promotional campaign will know what to do with that attention once it's been got. The terrible 7th July bombings represented a high-impact, low-concept act of religiously driven murder and all of us noticed it and talked about it. As an advertising campaign for Islam it didn't really win me over, to be honest. How about you? It was very eye-catching, I'll give them that. When I saw the images of the destroyed bus and understood that again an act of cowardice and stupidity had been used to promote some misguided notion of service to Allah, I didn't think to myself: Yes, that looks like the faith for me. In fact, I felt more certain than ever that the path towards the God of Abraham was one I could never walk down. Certainly these were proactive believers, but when a person is malevolent, hubristic or thick, being well motivated and willing to act is almost never a good thing.

A wanton act of murder for God's sake is no way to market your product. If I wanted to sell Cornish pasties and decided the best way to get you to try my folded pastry purse of meat and swede was to blow up the Eiffel Tower on a busy spring weekend, you'd think I was a very confused and vile person. You'd be right. Would you buy my pasties? No, you'd have a sausage roll and wonder how I'd ever convinced myself of such an astonishingly stupid notion. Did you want to try your hand at Islamic practice after the London, New York or Madrid attacks? No. Pasties, politics or piety – it's all the same to me. A religiously driven act of violence is nonsensical, and as worthy of consideration and compromise as one motivated by a Cornish snack, i.e., not at all. Destruction and brutality are not dignified by faith or religious observance.

I think it's important to be clear on this subject. The 7th July

Islamic marketing murder campaign was perpetrated by Muslims. Extremists? Certainly. Muddled? Undoubtedly. Devout and sincere Muslims? Yes, they were. Could they have done this if they were Jews or Christians? Yes, and they'd have been better funded, possibly with the backing of a democratic state. But these were Muslims. Some people like to claim 'they weren't true Muslims, because in Al Qur'an it says . . .' blah blah blah. Most religious books are open to so much interpretation you can claim the construction of a banana, tuna fish and gravel sandwich was inspired by the direct word of God. These killers were Muslim, killing in the name of Allah; that makes them distinct from a great many Muslims for whom violence is abhorrent and anathema to their faith. However, it was their faith and their determination that Islam is the right path for all mankind that galvanized their lust for this inglorious death and the destruction of the infidel. Other religious murderers have included Christians, Jews, Hindus, Sikhs and some seriously confused Buddhists. It's people who kill people, but some people kill people because their devotion to God makes it OK for them to do so and that motivation is alarmingly commonplace. Islamic terrorists and anyone else willing to kill someone for God are usually poor, badly educated and easily exploited. Religion, and most recently Islam, has proved the most excellent tool for encouraging deeds that most sane people would not consider under any circumstances. Politics can do it, but even the most extreme political views don't promise an eternity in heaven as a reward for stupidity.

If 7/7 or 9/11 turned anyone on to Islam I'd like to meet that person and talk with them for a very long time. I mean, what aspect of the Islamic promotional relaunch was it that turned you on to the product? Was there a snappy jingle I missed? Or was it just shards of metal and glass that stayed in people's heads? It made the power-brokers in religious conflict more powerful, each reacting precisely as the other had hoped. Recent terrorist atrocities have made plenty of people richer and allowed the perverse agenda of the very few to be forced upon the rest of us. This works when fear is rife and the powerful few convince us that in order to avoid extremism we must act in increasingly extreme ways. As an exercise in short-sighted stupidity it is similar to covering your body in wasps in order to avoid being stung by a bee. Islamic, jihadist terrorism has made the lives of ordinary believers much, much harder and I feel for many of them. I also wonder why their sincere disgust at atrocity doesn't convince more of them to abandon if not their faith then at least some of the structures of Islamic social and political life.

If you blow something up because you believe God wants you to, then you've been lied to, and arguably it's not your fault, but it takes a much deeper level of dishonesty and ignorance for anyone to convince themselves that the act will appeal to the wavering believer or convert the apostate back to the faith. My suffering is minor and trivial. I fly very rarely, thank goodness, but not once, as I've passed through the scanner for the third time with my shoes and trousers and belt and jacket and glasses and underpants on the *Generation Game* security conveyor belt, have I thought to myself – you know what, those criminal extremists really had a point, I think it's time to seriously consider becoming a Muslim. These days I undress entirely at the check-in desk and ride through the bag scanner on my back with my legs held apart singing 'Star-spangled Banner'. Sure it lacks dignity but in the long run that is offset by the time it saves answering security questions.

Perhaps I'm numb from having been marketed to since before I could speak, perhaps my tastes are too narrow, but I like more of a fun advertisement. Something memorable because it's funny or beautiful, less of the murder, martyrdom and mayhem stuff. I don't drink alcohol any more because I'm no good at it, but out of respect for the creative genius behind the Guinness commercials, if I ever do have a drink it's likely to be a pint of the black stuff. A cute little desert rat with an odd Hungarian accent, dressed in a smoking jacket and singing 'Compare the Meerkat dot com' has appealed to many of us more than we could ever reasonably have expected. It's annoying, of course, but it's oddly clever and it seems to have been massively effective. There are more adverts for sites comparing insurance companies than there are for insurance companies. I have a tragic image of a mournful, tweed-clad insurance broker, sitting by a dusty telephone wondering why it doesn't ring any more, no idea that a stuffed rodent and a tubby carefree opera singer have declared war on him and his kind. I don't get it, but I now look forward to seeing where they will take the taxidermy-based meerkat roadshow next. I don't work in advertising, for a million different reasons, but

GOD COLLAR

I'm certain that Alexander the Meerkat's antics would not have worked as well if his scratchy little head had been blown off as he screamed 'Allahu akbar!' and detonated a backpack full of hate and explosives in the name of cheaper car insurance. I don't know which controversy-courting agency put the 7/7 bus and tube campaign together for the Muslims, possibly Saatchi and Saatchi, but for me, not to realize that killing people will damage sales of your product or idea is clearly madness. That said, it doesn't seem to have harmed Nestlé.

There's probably no God ... That's the anti-faith pro-motional campaign slogan. It's been well received by those who already agreed with it. It tested mainly positive in the Marcus Brigstocke's belief system market research survey. Do you agree with this statement: 'There's probably no God'? Yes, I do. That's what I think. I think there's probably no God ...

But the truth is – I wish there was.

3

Are you there, God?
It's me, Marcus

I FIND MYSELF, A 38-YEAR-OLD MARRIED MAN WITH TWO children, loving my job, reasonably content most of the time, with periods of ecstasy and spells of gloom, and yet for reasons both explicable and inexplicable I wish I could find a God to believe in. It ought to be simple – decide to believe, stop being a smart-arse, find a church, temple, mosque, woodland ritual, statue of a thing, special book or ritualistic dance, and get stuck in. I know a great number of people far cleverer than me who believe in God without any trouble at all. So why can't I?

I wish there was a God. I'm sincere when I say that. I am not happy with atheism in and of itself. It doesn't provide any answers for me. It makes no claim to, it's not comparable with religion in that way, but all the same I wish it did. When you

49

get past the early flush of excitement about rejecting something as important as God, and then move through the defiance and righteous indignation of living as a non-believer ... what then? Well, in my case you start to see the value of faith and the comfort of communal worship. You start to envy the bonds provided by a shared belief in something positive. I wish there was a God and that He knew my address. I'd like to talk to him. When I feel sad or alone, when I'm afraid or anxious for someone I love, I'd like to feel there was some magic, positive force watching over me. Caring for all of us and seeing that it's all going to be OK. I'm embarrassed by this vulnerability, but not ashamed of it. I am no weaker or needier than most people, it's just that the intellectual rigour of what I've come to believe to be true is of very little comfort to me. I want God to make me believe that the feelings I have, and struggle with, will not last for ever.

I want a God. Just not the God who makes His home in the church, mosque or synagogue. I'd settle for that God perhaps if he could sweeten the believing and worshipping contract with a long and thorough letter of apology to mankind, a clear redraft and consolidation of all the major Abrahamic religious texts and the offer of a single public smiting of Dick Cheney – just by way of a send-off in honour of the violent Old Testament God and as a welcome to His new form as a freshly rehabilitated God of the People who not only likes gays and women but loves show-tunes and listens without trying to fix. I am given to understand that the inability to listen without trying to solve is the single biggest 'problem' that many women have with men. My wife told me this and I read it in a book. Luckily, me and some guy mates of mine have come up with a five-part solution to the girls' 'problem' which we think will fix it once and for all and cheer the ladies up no end. Bosh! Job done. Can we fix it? Yes, we can.

One of the pitfalls of being a comedian is that when I say something sincere it is often misunderstood as sarcasm. However, I do genuinely wish there was a God I could believe in. I've tried to tell people this.

'I wish there was a God.'

'Oh yeah, sure you do, Mr Funny Man.'

I've found that the more sincerely I wish for a thing to be understood and the more seriously I say something, the more people assume I'm taking the piss. When I occasionally give my mouth a rest and stop talking, I often notice an expectant look on the faces of people around me as a silence opens up between us. They are waiting for me to undermine what I've said with some snide quip or sardonic aside. I don't know what they're waiting for, the bloody idiots, that's SOOO not what I do!

Sometimes it is assumed that I will only mention a thing so that I can hold forth on the topic and bang on about it in a humorously overstated and wilfully pompous rant. OK, there is evidence for this. I do love to get my teeth into a subject I care about. From the safety of BBC Radio 4 I've sparred with a great number of adversaries on many topics, ducking and weaving with acerbic jabs, occasionally landing a knock-out punch. Though I seek to express myself through comedy a lot of the time, there are some things I'm deadly serious about, and the desire for a workable and available deity in my life is one of them.

I have built myself a fantastically enjoyable career sitting or standing behind a microphone or in front of a camera flinging brickbats at the world as I see it. I've employed sarcasm and overstatement to pleasing effect, I've pulled the heavily embroidered blanket of personal offence over my head and from beneath it have bellowed and sneered at those I have judged as guilty of sins as wide-ranging as theft, complacency, murder, hypocrisy, deceit and, perhaps worst of all, being a magician. All of which has been tremendously good fun and I'm immensely grateful for every moment of it. I don't even regret that it now means that my sincerity is called into question.

I wish there was a God. I wish for that God to exist now and for all time. I wish to be fully conscious of God and more importantly for Him to be fully conscious of me. I wish for God to be powerful, infinitely wise, kind, loving, fair and, when necessary, willing to carry out humiliating and painful corrections on my fellow human beings. Watch your back, Jeremy Kyle, for the judgement of the Lord shall be wrought upon you this day, and the might of the all-powerful Father and the terror of his heavenly host shall be unleashed upon thee, live on ITV at about midday. I think in the form of a DNA test where it is proved that Jeremy Kyle is actually his own father and then expresses massive disappointment at his son's behaviour and disowns himself.

I have occasionally let my mind wander on to the possibility of having a God who was so firmly in my corner that he wasn't fair, kind or gentle at all but vicious, vengeful and entirely in agreement with me on everything. I think a lot of people secretly wish for God to be like that. A God devoted totally to them, unabashed in expressing how much he favours them over all others. Plenty of religious Jews believe that is precisely the nature of their relationship with the Lord. If I were in possession of a God like that, it would then be a question of prioritizing the list of who would be divinely exploded into particles of dust first. Murder's so much more palatable if God does it for you. If you don't believe me, read the Bible, Qur'an or Torah. Divine homicide is positively celebrated in those books. People who had oh so recently stood blinking in astonishment as my God and I swaggered towards them with retribution glowing in our eyes would soon be nothing more than a vague memory of an old annoyance I had dispatched with impunity. Like a long-forgotten mosquito bite. Paul Dacre, the editor of the *Daily Mail*, might well be first on the list, then we would work our way through his poisonous legion of columnists. After that it would be on to the offices of the *Daily Express*. A free and independent press is immensely important and must be preserved at all costs ... provided all of its contributors concur with my increasingly fixed worldview. If not, all bets are off, and God and I are kicking arse. Richard Littlejohn, you tiny-minded xenophobe, my mate God wants a word with you.

What I'm describing is not so much a God as a sort of

psychopathic attack beast entirely devoted to me and my darkest inclinations. In truth, that's not the God I wish existed at all. It's one I imagine only from time to time and feel suitably horrified by. What I really want is the kind of God people describe when they choose to ignore the ugly history of whichever religion they're a part of. The God who seems to make people kind, generous and serene. I want a personal God who loves us all in a way that goes beyond words. A God who fills us with a sort of reassuring and magical light. A God who is the very expression of love so perfect that to feel all of it at once would be to lose yourself for ever in a place of sublime happiness. Even as I write this I'm aware of the limitations of my use of language in describing what I'd really like from God. I can feel the perimeters of my experience pressing in on my understanding of what might be possible from an infinitely powerful, benign and everlasting, organizing force in the universe. My imagination is limited by half-remembered descriptions of what God is. A bric-a-brac of a God borrowed from other people's experiences and assembled into something composite and less than satisfactory. It's all I have for now.

I'm also aware that many religious people claim to feel almost exactly what I have described. Perfect love, heavenly light, an all-consuming reassurance . . . good for them. I can't get there and I'm not really sure I believe them when they tell me they have. There are descriptions of God I've heard over the years that I find beautiful and inspiring. I marvel as I listen to those who are genuinely moved by their religious experience. It never takes long before I qualify what I've been told with the aspects of religion that enrage and frustrate me, but for a few shining moments I have thought of God existing in the very loveliest of places, expressed by people I trust, and I'd like to know Him.

When I talk to religious people, I'm not for the most part baffled or irritated by them. (I did once meet Stephen Green – alleged wife- and child-beater – from Christian Voice and was baffled, irritated, saddened, enraged, confused and livid and ended up feeling like the hand that shook his might never be clean again.) I am often quite envious of the devout. People with faith in their lives, who know that it's going to be OK. They know they are loved and that there's a plan. I don't think there's a plan – I feel like I'm teetering on the brink of chaos all the time. They are convinced there is a place for them and their loved ones to depart to after this life. I'm not. Every time I check into a hotel I'm pretty sure they will have forgotten my reservation, and if they have then what chance St Peter will have my name down? They believe in God and they believe He will see them safely to the good place and not the eternally burny one. I don't have any clue as to what will happen next, I don't even know where my keys are ... Or my wife, come to that, and that feeling scares me. It excites me too, as it suggests that anything is possible, some of which might turn out to be satisfactory or possibly even better than that. We all share a fear of the unknown, some harness it and enjoy the thrill of exploration, others are consumed by it and limit new experience and excitement to watching *Midsomer Murders* with the lights off. People with faith lead their lives in the knowledge that beneath them lies the safety net of a loving God. Even if He turns out not to be there at all it doesn't matter. They can walk the tightrope with a feeling that if they fall, they will be held. Whether that confidence turns out to be good for the rest of us is another question entirely. I would much prefer that a great many of the world's leaders were not emboldened by the feeling that they are doing 'God's work' and He'll catch us all if we fall. He might not.

If you believe in God, then there is a promise he will be there for you. He's eternal. Religious people know God is there for them and they trust in the kind magnificence of His love. They know they are right. I talk like I'm sure of myself a lot of the time but often I feel like I'm lost and, like most of the men I've met, the less I know the louder I talk. Believers know that the choice they have made to trust in God is the right one. I don't believe in God, but it wasn't really a choice, it just happened. I can't believe in God at present because none of the versions of God I've been presented with satisfies the questions that their existence poses. I can't seem to make up a God that I like or trust either. In any case a God created by me would be part of me, rather than me a part of it, and even in my most arrogant moments I don't wish to create God.

I know this is all based on illusion and that the faithful have doubts, worries and concerns too but all of my envy for their serenity in life exists in an imagined and perfect ideal. Never compare your insides with other people's outsides, it makes for unhappiness and there's no point making yourself unhappy with something based on a lie. I get the same thing with food envy. I can be enjoying a perfectly delicious meal and look over at someone else's plate and decide it's so much better than mine that I start to invoke the power of my psycho-killer God to strike them down and magically hoover the remains from their perfect meal through the air in the direction of my mouth. None of this is sensible or logical, I know that. Be it God, people or someone else's lunch, I can see that what I do is daft, but I can't seem to prevent myself from doing it. Hi, I'm Marcus, and I'm only just clever enough to realize what a pillock I am.

I never feel like it's all going to be OK. In fact, most of the time I'm pretty sure it's not. This feeling is not helped by the fact that I read most of the British newspapers every day. Take my advice – don't do this, unless you wish to become so deeply depressed that even a video of a bear cub sliding on some ice won't make you smile. Often I get up and have a good thumb through all of the newspapers and the *Daily Mail* as well. For those of you not familiar with the *Mail*, try to imagine a copy of the *Metro* with the nerve to charge. I read the papers so I know what's going on for work – not because I hate myself and can't be bothered to self-harm properly.

If you regularly read the British press you will know the world is broken. Very rarely do they tackle the ways in which it really is broken and could be fixed, but on any given day you can assemble a list of things that will give you cancer ranging between eating butter, watching films, breathing, having children, working, being unemployed, running, sleeping, picking your nose and not eating butter. You can read how the worst off bring it on themselves, especially those lazy, fly-soaked tykes lying about in dusty fields in Africa. It's the corruption, don't you know. You can read how often your children are exposed to paedophiles and how little is done about it. On the same day you can read how unfair it is that everyone working with children has to be checked in case they're a paedophile. You can read how women are being objectified by the media and then see a picture of an actress getting older and wince at the public decay of her horrid wrinkly body. Yuk! How could she grow older while people can see her? The ugly bitch! You can read how species and environments are dying out and then how the interfering nanny state wants us to reuse things we used to only use once. You can read about Princess Diana though there's nothing left to say and you can play the 'where's Madeleine McCann game'. It's a fun-filled game in which, with no new inform-ation, you are invited to imagine scenarios as to who's got her and what really happened. Why not take part in a phone poll exclusive to the *Daily Express*? 'Phone Polls are an un-representative rip-off. For YES they are, dial 08987221784. For NO I don't agree, dial 08987221784.' Yesterday's poll result – 89 per cent of *Daily Express* readers believe Madeleine McCann is living in Morocco with Princess Diana and recycling's for poofs.

Certainly the idea that God loves mankind is very hard to sustain if you read the newspapers or watch the news or go online or open the door and venture outside. The world's not OK, it hasn't been OK for a while and it doesn't look like it's going to be OK any time soon. To be honest, it's very often a bit shit. Not for me; my life is remarkable and relatively easy. I am comfortable and I live somewhere nice with very few earthquakes, wars, sudden floods or famine. But the world is a hard place to live in for a great number of people and I find that difficult to deal with. You can write it off as predictable, middle-class guilt, an overactive empathy gland fuelled by excessive liberalism perhaps, but knowing what it is doesn't make it go away and it bothers me. You can fairly easily convince yourself that it's all good out there in the world but you can only sustain that view if you choose to wear blinkers. My desire for God to be my friend may well be nothing more than an attempt to find a convincing pair of blinkers.

For every disaster, accidental or man-made, there is almost always someone declaring that it's a miracle God spared them from whatever nightmare unfolded around them. Always they seem happy to credit the Good Lord with the success of their miraculous salvation and never so happy to lay the blame at his door for wreaking such havoc on them in the first place. They crawl from the rubble, scraping dust and tears from their eyes with sobbing relatives draped over their exhausted body, all of them praising the same loving God who had just put them through a very real living hell. If as a witness to the many human tragedies that unfold on a daily basis you focus on one person and the fact that they survived, then perhaps you could conclude God is indeed a benevolent intervening force for good and is merciful and just. Of course he's a loving God – look, He saved (insert foreign-sounding name of poor person here – Raul, perhaps?) from the terrible (delete as appropriate: gunfire, volcano, earthquake, tsunami, roadside bomb, avalanche, plane crash, mysterious barnyard attack). But I'm always left with the same question. What about the hundreds of others who died in this Godforsaken event? What about the parent and child who were ripped apart by the force of whatever horror it was that gripped them? One surviving just long enough to see the other die, face twisted in fear and disbelief as their exhausted lungs manage to draw one last painful, gurgling breath and then give up. What happened there then? Did God decide they and their families were not worth His time? Are miracles limited to one or two per disaster? 'Sorry,' says a bashful and shifty God, 'I couldn't save that one. No reason, I just couldn't . . . erm . . . sorry . . . Hey, look over here at miracle boy Raul, who just walked unscathed from the chaos. Check me out and marvel at my love for mankind.'

I'd like to develop a faith in God so complete it would enable me to make sense of what I see around me. It would be a fantastic thing to have God in my life. But I can't seem to get there, and the harder I've tried to understand God the less I like what I see. I talk to religious people a lot, I seek re-assurance from them, and I'm always fascinated as to how someone sustains their faith. I am both jealous and resentful at the same time that they have that benevolent force at work in their lives. This life and its many exhilarating twists and turns often seem to exist at the very limits of what we can bear. Sometimes the pain of it is simply too much for some people, who choose to end it all or go mad. I'm not flirting with either of those states of being and non-being and don't wish to over-dramatize my emotional turmoil, but all too often life leaves me perplexed, anxious and disturbed.

When I read that many thousands of people have put their names to a petition asking that Jeremy Clarkson be made Prime Minister, I wish there was a God. When I see that *America's Next Top Model* attracts millions of viewers, I wish there was a God. When I see MPs so disconnected from the reality of modern living that the few tatty scraps of empathy and kindness they left Eton with are all but consumed by self-interest, hubris and greed, I wish there was a God. When I see an overweight woman tuck a copy of a 'women's magazine' under the pizzas in her shopping trolley, I wish there was a God. Anne Robinson, Silvio Berlusconi, Mahmoud Ahmadinejad, Louis Walsh and the Pope make me wish there was a God. George W. Bush – safely retired, in a rocking chair staring happily at a bit of wood while someone makes his lunch in Texas, Tony Blair appointed as peace envoy to the Middle East . . . I wish there was a God. The God I wish for would put at least some of these things right, starting with the rocking chair.

I like talking to and debating with religious people. That can be fun and you can often learn the most brilliant things from people who disagree with you. Occasionally they'll get angry or indignant and fire a nonsensical question at you:

'Yeah, well, if we're descended from monkeys, how come there are still monkeys?'

And then you have to try to remember to be polite and not shout:

'Well, there are still monkeys in order to make you feel better about how few books you've read.'

Then the conversation usually ends. It's best to avoid the evolution/creationism discussion until you've established that both parties are familiar with the theory suggested in Darwin's *On the Origin of Species* and that they have some understanding of the creation story as told in any of the major religious texts. Without understanding this stuff it's only zealotry, antagonism or arrogance that would make you wish to continue to debate. I wouldn't row across the English Channel without any oars, nor would I debate string theory with a quantum physicist; I don't even own any string. I wouldn't wish to discuss who was funnier between Ronnie Barker and John Cleese with someone who'd never seen *Porridge* or *Fawlty Towers*. Why try to explain the joyous yeasty mouth-gasm that is Marmite to a person who's only ever eaten honey on toast? Simply arrange a research period, and instead of beating your heads against each other there and then, go away, do the reading and agree to come back in a few days' time to continue the discussion. I don't believe it's possible to understand Darwin's theory of evolution and still be a creationist.

Often it is the religious interlocutor who brings down the curtain on the conversation. You're chatting away, there's a good bit of to and fro, some heated exchanges, some challenging of ideas and rhetoric, and suddenly they say something akin to:

'Jesus wants me for a sunbeam and you're going to Hell.'

This is the point in the conversation where they refuse to employ reason at all and instead explain that they believe because they have faith and they have faith because they believe and nothing you can say will change that. No proof, no logic, no reason. There is nothing you can say. Wow! Faith is amazing. I don't feel like that about anything, apart perhaps from the love of my family and my ongoing commitment to Stilton – what a cheese. When faith is faith and won't be questioned at all, you have to stop saying anything and I find that hard. It's frustrating because it's the end of something that should have no end. The theme park of ideas announces it's closing early and you have to get off the ride and leave.

That's what faith is, I suppose, an end to searching, a moment where you decide that you've asked enough questions and are ready to make that leap into a place of absolute trust without evidence. Despite so many aspects of it baffling and irritating me, it's also exactly what I'm envious of. When I run up against the immovable wall of a person's belief it sometimes brings out a sulky malevolence in me. I don't wish to destroy another person's truly held belief. That is mean and vindictive, and seems to be unnecessary. I do, however, wish to understand it, and in so doing I am willing to take it apart. I also value it less when it stands as an insuperable obstacle to political and social development (see Ann Widdecombe). Regardless of my gentle respect for another person's right to seek comfort in whatever beliefs they choose, I would stand in front of the solid brick wall of religious observance and without hesitation seek to deconstruct it into its component parts and examine each one under the spotlight of reason. If that breaks it for ever then it wasn't what any of us thought it was anyway. It was a lie. If it can be examined thoroughly and illuminated without fear or dishonesty, each piece rolled over in the bright light of enquiry and then reassembled into what it was before, I'll be satisfied that belief is belief, faith is faith and God is perfect.

That hasn't happened yet. Not even close. I've often been impressed and certainly been given pause for thought by many of the exchanges I've had with the faithful, but almost always there comes a point where a line is drawn and the shutters of faith are rolled down right in front of my eyes. I want to scream.

'You can't stop talking to me now. You can't be a creationist. It's not possible. You arrived here in a car, a car has oil in it. We know where oil comes from and we can tell with astonishing accuracy how long it took to get there.'

It's often the way that the people who make the most use of oil know the very least about where it came from and how it came to be (see Sarah Palin).

We know where oil came from and how old it is and that means we know for a fact that the earth is much more than three and a half thousand years old. And yet the faith that so many profess to believe in suggests that the earth's about three and a half, possibly four thousand years old. One is faith; the other is fact. So I've won the debate. Haven't I? Don't you have to say sorry, I'll have another think about this stuff? Didn't the debate and the exchange of ideas that we just had arrive at a point where you had to admit that at least part of what you were saying was rubbish? Hey! Where are you going? Don't walk away – I'll go mental if you leave this stuff in my head.

They walk away because they can and because I can be a persistent and pompous pain in the arse. Fair enough. Also I suspect that the conversation is brought to an unsatisfactory close because to indulge it further would be to invite an unhelpful and destructive doubt into their belief system. If I were a believer looking back at someone like me and the turmoil that constant enquiry and questioning have brought me, I wouldn't necessarily choose to switch sides either. Sometimes they look at me with a passive look on their face and a warm almost sympathetic smile. At that point I imagine they are singing a religious song in their head to drive my insistent babble out of their mind. There's a spelling song I once heard that has an unforgettably perky and annoying tune to it. It was sung by some shrill American children, filled to the very brim with good Christian cheer (either that or they were about to be hit by a supervised adult), at high volume over the sound of a cheap electric piano.

I am a C...
I am a C.H...
I am a C.H.R.I.S.T.I.A.N...

And I have C.H.R.I.S.T. in my H.E.A.R.T. and I will L.I.V.E.
E.T.E.R.N.A.L.L.Y.
I am a C . . .
I am a C.H.
I am a C.H.R.I.S.T.I.A.N . . .

And so it went on. It's a delightful, fast-paced Christian
spelling song that tells dyslexics, just like Jews and poofs, that
they are not welcome in Heaven either. Trust me, I am
dyslexic and, yes, it took me a very long time to learn that
song. Also I once went to a toga party dressed as a goat.

I will never forget the day this evil ditty wormed its way
into my ear. And now you won't either. Come on, clap your
hands and sing it with me.

I am a C . . .
I am a C.H . . .
I am a C.H.R.I.S.T.I.A.N . . .
And I have C.H.R.I.S.T. in my H.E.A.R.T. and I will L.I.V.E.
E.T.E.R.N.A.L.L.Y.

I hope you found it pleasing, curious, titillating perhaps, but
trust me, when you try to sleep tonight you will hate me with
a passion I cannot fully describe in the pages of a book.
As you lie there, eyes wide open, your head pressed into the
pillow, your second full hour, wide awake, mouthing
the words

'I am a C . . .

Well, I'm not a C . . . But that bastard Brigstocke is.'

It's perfectly reasonable to ask – given how resistant I am to religion, why on earth do I think I want to invite God into my life? The truth is I don't know exactly. It's just a feeling that if there's something up there, or out there, or in here that could reasonably improve the quality of my life and of those around me, then I'd be willing to try it. I have a nasty feeling this willingness to explore a state of 'other' could bring me to God or just as easily see me develop a massive heroin habit.

4

Nothing bad happened . . .

I SHOULD PROBABLY SAY AT THIS STAGE THAT NOTHING BAD happened to me. I don't have a personal axe to grind with religion. There is no shameful and unsettling secret hiding away in my past that means that deep down I'd like to destroy every church in the land and lay waste to the clergy. I didn't once pick up a Bible and burn my hands on it. I wasn't spooked by the image of Christ looking wistful on the cross, though I do find the obsession with his death both odd and unpleasant. I wasn't grabbed in the souk by a beard-faced Muslim cleric who bellowed at me aggressively in Farsi, and neither was I sent to one of those schools where a man in a brown dressing gown coaxed me into the vestry and whispered in a sinister Irish lilt, 'You will put this in your mouth or no amount of praying will ever make you feel OK about yourself again.'

I'm not a Catholic. I wasn't buggered by a priest or anything similar. I'm not out for personal revenge. I've never been tempted to have hypnotherapy to delve into the space that exists before my memories began (they start from about the age of 17 – that's normal, right?), but I'm pretty certain that no religious representative has ever done any direct harm to me, unless you include being boring, dishonest or obtuse. There was a religious education master at my junior school who had really awful coffee breath, dreadful at the time but at least we'd have remembered and been able to identify him if he'd ever tried to kiss us. I am not out to destroy anyone's individual faith. Quite the opposite. I'd like to swipe some of it, distil it to suit my personal tastes and drink it down with gusto. I do have serious reservations about the tacit consent that membership of any identified religious organization provides for the church as a whole but that doesn't mean that I'm coming after the believers to prove them wrong. For the most part I'm pleased for them. They've found something to believe in. Why can't I do that?

While I have no personal experience of being fiddled with, whacked, bullied or tweaked by men and women of the cloth, I am appalled by the capacity of religious organizations to use the rituals and secrecy of their structures to commit terrible crimes against their own flock. Sometimes the horrors committed by the holy are grand and take place on an international scale, but very often they are personal and can isolate their victims for the rest of their lives. The Catholic Church is by no means alone in its inability to heave its decrepit flailing body out of the quagmire of revolting sexual abuses that are revealed every few months, but Catholicism has had a shocking number of complaints from those brave enough to fight for truth, and it now looks as if child abuse is as integral to Catholicism as a private education is to frontbench politics. They're not all at it, but enough of them are for me to seriously wonder what standard of GCSE passes Catholic schools are promising for parents to take that sort of risk with their little darlings. What's a little underage fellatio for an A star? There are three-year courses at the top universities for people with the right qualifications, and places for life in counselling and self-hating shame for children who've been touched up by a frustrated pervert who chats to the Lord in the morning and whispers sweet nothings to ten-year-olds at night.

If you can't manage to be celibate then – here's a thought – don't be a monk! Do something else that doesn't involve building up a head and scrotum full of unsatisfied lust waiting to go off like an unexploded bit of sexual ordnance. If you can't resist your inclination towards little boys, then don't go into teaching at an all-boys boarding school. If you're a nun who finds never having been touched by a man with lust in his eyes and a penis as hard as Chinese maths makes you want to beat women who have enjoyed that experience with sticks, then maybe your marriage to Christ isn't working out so well. If you place some wrong-headed value on celibacy and then pretend to be better than everyone else because you're not getting your rocks off, you are wrong. If you find it's harder than you'd thought to leave your bits and pieces alone and then choose a child as your sexual outlet because they're the least likely to expose you for the ugly pious fake you are, then get honest with yourself, apologize to God and get out of the position where your failure to live up to the impossibly difficult abstinence you've set yourself represents a real and present danger to other people. If that's where you find yourself then it's time to stop pretending you're better than the rest of us and try to normalize your relationship with sex. Get laid with a consenting adult. Have a series of earth-shattering orgasms alone or with friends who make you think Belinda Carlisle really was right and 'Heaven is a place on earth'. Make sweet and passionate love to your own fist if you wish. You never know, you might like it; just knock it off with the kiddy-fiddling. Let the kids get to sex in their own time; they don't need to have it introduced to them by a trembly self-hating adult, nor do they need to be told that to want to do it will make them dirty for ever.

Choosing to get your loving on with God isn't going to get you off when the throbbing bone of Satan is threatening to rip the front out of your cassock. Prayer and fasting might beat back the forces of carnal desire for a few people, but the risks involved in attempting that are treacherously high. Priest, monk, nun, mother superior, bishop, choirmaster, verger, pope or whatever job you take in the service of the Lord won't stop you being a human. You're flawed and randy just like the rest of us. If you believe that we are all created by God, then ask yourself why He put our hands at exactly the same height as our fizzy bits. It's not a coincidence, it's not a test, it's so we can, when it's necessary, please ourselves and then get on with what's left of the day. For the love of God or humanity or yourself, I don't care which, break the seal, take the pressure off and have a bit of personal sticky time before you do yourself or someone else an injury. Wank, you wanker, just wank.

If you're a Catholic authority figure who hasn't yet abused a child, the organization you belong to is protecting many who have. Even for the ordinary Catholic believer, there is no escaping the fact that as a respecter of the papacy you are supporting an institution which chooses, deliberately, to expose children to sex criminals and then chooses, deliberately, to keep those sex criminals away from the forces of the law. The Catholic Church has shown itself to be corrupt, irresponsible and dangerous. As each day passes we understand with greater clarity how the Roman Catholic Church is an institution that uses the shame its victims feel as the means to keep them quiet. That is a disgrace of the worst kind. Broken lives of silent guilt, inflicted by the 'Universal Church' on the most vulnerable in its care. It amounts to no less than the theft of childhood by those who claim to protect it, hidden beneath the righteousness of the faithful. You wouldn't save your money at the Bank of Rape, so why pray at a church whose record on child abuse means I'd rather employ Gary Glitter as a nanny than send my kids to a Catholic school?

Muslims do it too, and the structures of devout Islamic practice make it easier for the perpetrators and more dangerous for the victims to speak out. C of E clergy do it. Atheists do it, agnostics do it, even educated Jews do it; anyone is technically capable of committing acts against humanity and disgracing themselves. It's not religion that makes perverts but it does give them a place to hide and to practise their sickness within the protection of their church. When you add to that the ludicrous scribblings of holy writers from a couple of thousand years ago, whose views on sex were so retarded they make Ian Paisley look like a progressive deviant, it's no wonder that the pressure cooker blows its lid off so often.

The present Pope has a bad record when it comes to sex offenders in his Church. He is a fascinating man. These days he's known as Your Eminence, or His Royal Almighty Popeness, but before the white smoke billowed out of the chimney showing that the cardinals had found a man who didn't look like he would change too much of anything, he was plain old Mr Ratzinger – it sounds like a foul, rodent-based children's snack. 'Enjoy a Rat-Zinger, kids! Now with delicious chewy rosary beads, phenomenal wealth and chunks of hard-to-swallow, sinister past.'

Soon after he was made Pope, Ratzinger made a visit to Poland – something he'd very much wanted to do as a younger man. I'm not sure why he didn't make it; perhaps the Hitler Youth ran out of brown shirts, either that or he didn't pass the 'you must be this tall to ride this invasion' test. In fairness to the man, I don't imagine that avoiding membership of the Hitler Youth was that easy to achieve when he was a young man in Germany. I only avoided becoming a scout because I was fat, lazy and dysfunctional. I'm also crap with knots and had an unhealthy obsession with my own woggle. In terms of forming an opinion of the Pope (I've never met him, but I looked him up on Wikipedia and I'm not sure I like him at all), I find the fact that he was hoodwinked into joining the junior wing of the Nazi Party not nearly as worrying as his rising to the most powerful position in the Catholic Church.

In September 2010 he came to the UK, which of course was very exciting for a great many Catholics. The Pope has the ear of God. I'm not sure where he keeps it but he has it somewhere. For a great many believers, a papal visit represents a tremendous spiritual event and serves to strengthen their feeling of connection to their faith. I expect Tony and Cherie Blair were positively vibrating with excitement at the very thought of it, the money in their pockets jangling as they worked each other into a frenzy of zealotry. Alastair Campbell might not 'do God' but the Blairs would 'do Him' in a heartbeat, then charge Him for the privilege of their company no doubt. I also enjoyed the Pope's visit, though not perhaps as much. It was very exciting for the secular community to have a man that powerful come to see us and like all visits from international criminals it seemed likely to kick off a row. There was a plan to arrest him, which sadly came to nothing. Certainly there seems to be a pretty good case against the Pope with regard to decisions he made when he was a cardinal and I would think that finding a severed ear on his person would be likely to damage his defence somewhat too. It'd be a Hell of a hearing if God were called as a witness for the defence. What would He swear to?

'I swear to Almighty Me to tell the truth, the whole truth and nothing but the truth.'

Then humanity could spend the next 2,000 years inter-preting and twisting whatever God had said on the witness stand to suit whichever view of the world we already held anyway. 'He mentioned a Tuesday in Berlin in 1936 and that means gays are still evil and women can't be priests.' If the Pope had been arrested in the UK, and then prosecuted and sentenced, I would think there'd be a good chance that Britain would have been at war with the Vatican. I don't like war as a general rule, even in films I tend to side with the conscientious objectors, but in this instance I reckon we could have 'em. It does seem possible that the Vatican are in possession of the Ark of the Covenant, which, as we know, when opened would melt our faces off, so we should prepare for that, but in principle I think we could take the Vatican pretty easily, then hand it back to Italy where it belongs. Give it two weeks and Silvio Berlusconi would have turned the whole place into a twenty-first-century Bunga Bunga party to make both Sodom and Gomorrah blush. Obviously if the Vatican organized all their millions of followers worldwide to rise up against us, then Britain would be stuffed. But they've succeeded in keep-ing so many of them in dire poverty for so long that I doubt that more than a handful would manage the bus fare to the fight.

Perhaps not surprisingly the plan to arrest the Pope when he came to the UK was co-ordinated by Christopher Hitchens and Richard Dawkins. Trouble-makers, those two with their pesky thinking and all that. With the help of barrister Geoffrey Robertson and solicitor Mark Stephens, they prepared a case that looked to me like it might well have legs. I'm no lawyer and of course I respect Corpus Christi (whoever he is), but this Pope guy is guilty as hell and should go down.

In 1985, when Ratzinger was in charge of the Congregation for the Doctrine of the Faith, which deals with sex abuse cases, his signature appeared on a letter that argued the 'good of the universal church' should be considered against the defrocking of an American priest who committed sexual offences against two boys. As I understand it, this concerns a priest who raped children. Two under-aged boys were exposed to the horror of a sexual assault by a man in a position of trust. A man of the cloth. A priest. To reiterate, because it seems important: the man, the one in the position of trust, the priest, the man of the cloth, raped two children. He took from them a thing he could never give back. He used his position, as a member of the church they as children had been forced to attend, to enact a vile deed he hoped would never be discovered. This is what he did. His superior, Cardinal Ratzinger, the man whose job it was to deal with these exact issues, felt that, when confronted with the rape of two children, it was important to consider the 'good of the universal church'. He could have defrocked the man and taken away the position he had abused in order to rape the children, but he sided with the priest's view that the fewer people who knew what had happened, the better. So he kept him safe in the bosom of Catholicism in order to maintain the 'good of the universal church'. Presumably the priest said something along the lines of, 'Hey, get this bosom off me, I don't like bosoms, I like fucking kids.' I don't know; I wasn't there. I'm guessing.

Christopher Hitchens, who does verbosity and bellicose like no other, put it rather well when he said of the Pope: 'This man is not above or outside the law. The institutionalized concealment of child rape is a crime under any law and demands not private ceremonies of repentance or church-funded payoffs, but justice and punishment.'

UK Justice Secretary Ken Clarke gave a statement saying, 'Our commitment to our international obligations and to ensuring that there is no impunity for those accused of crimes of universal jurisdiction is unwavering. It is important, how-ever, that universal jurisdiction cases should be proceeded with in this country only on the basis of solid evidence that is likely to lead to a successful prosecution – otherwise there is a risk of damaging our ability to help in conflict resolution or to pursue a coherent foreign policy.' Don't arrest the Pope, people will think we're assholes, and some of the countries where the Pope is still really popular trade oil and guns with us and blah blah bullshit.

So we didn't arrest him. He's not a real head of state because the Vatican is not a proper state, so the issue of immunity does not apply. We didn't arrest him because he's the Pope and he represents millions and millions of easily provoked worshippers. The Pope has questions to answer, and their impact on the 'good of the universal church' is not relevant. As far as I know, the Pope's not a paedophile, but he knows a few and he seems to care more for them than he does for their victims.

I was once a child and I'm glad no one raped me. I have children now and I hope no one rapes them. I know people who are Catholic and I hope no one rapes them. Generally speaking I am against the whole rape agenda. I find it extraordinary that there are some people who are now immensely powerful who apparently don't share this view.

It's been estimated that his visit here cost the UK a little over £250 million. When you add to that the cost of an Oyster card and the prices you pay in many of the good restaurants, we'd have been better off sponsoring the Pope to take an all-inclusive to Majorca for a fortnight and spending the rest on priest-proof under-crackers for choirboys. A lot of the £250 million was legitimately spent on keeping the Pope safe from anyone who might wish him physical ill. The rest of it, I suspect, was spent making sure the very significant number of people who protested his presence here and had legitimate questions for him to answer were kept so far away from the Pope-mobile that when he flew home in his private plane he'd have assumed that, just like everywhere else he goes, the UK is populated exclusively by teary-eyed supporters, each and every one delighted to see him.

It is also possible that some of the money was spent keeping us safe from him. I don't know what he had planned, but let's face it, that wobbly old German nonce-hider has form. For the amount of money we spent on his visit I think we should have been allowed to ride him up and down Pall Mall. I'm only really cross because I learned to swear in Latin just in case I got the chance to meet him. That's a bloodimus fucking waste now.

In his capacity as leader of the wealthiest church on earth, the Pope is able to make lots of interesting visits, particularly to places where there's grinding poverty. I'm not sure why he goes to these awful places when he could easily afford a couple of weeks in the Maldives, but he does. I presume he just enjoys being around the poor. Nothing makes you feel richer and more chipper than having a big pocket of folding cash and going somewhere really unrelentingly destitute. I'll often withdraw a couple of thousand pounds in cash and then go watch the broken and desperate pouring in and out of Primark.

In 2008, the Pope made a visit to the African continent. Across Africa there's a very large Catholic constituency all keen to hear what the Pope has to say. They'd better listen closely: he's a terrible mumbler and a lot of it's in German. He's not as bad a mumbler as the Pope before him, but to be fair to Pope John Paul II, he was 476 years old when he died. The Pope is said to be able to talk directly to God. I hope he doesn't mumble then. I can't see God liking that, especially with only the one ear. Maybe God's a mumbler too and that's why we hear from him so seldom these days. I like to picture God and the Pope as Waldorf and Stadler, the two old gentlemen in the box on *The Muppet Show*, both deaf and belligerent, shouting down heckles and derision at the freak show beneath them.

The papal plane flew down to Africa, he got out, kissed the tarmac, then had a good wash and got on with the business of looking at poor people. He spoke on a number of subjects, one of which was the ever-controversial topic of family planning. I suppose because he was on his holidays he'd given the subject some thought. Well, you have to when you travel, don't you? The Catholic plan for families is that they should be absolutely massive. The bigger the better. Hundreds of children please, the poorer the better, just keep 'em coming. If you can squeeze a baby out every time you think about the opposite sex, then God will be well pleased. Jesus loved children – blessed are the children; Jesus also loved the poor – blessed are the poor. So imagine how blessed you'd be if you had lots of poor children. Double blessed, right?

I'm not sure why exactly but huge families with next to nothing seem to uphold their Catholicism extremely well. This has been particularly effective where education has been a sparse commodity and, for those lucky enough to get any at all, the learning comes soaked through with Catholic dogma. I suppose if you're poor and struggling to feed your children, the promise of God's love and salvation would take on a very special appeal. Add to that a few good scare stories of a vengeful and jealous God watching your every move, limit reading material and access to health care, and bingo – your Catholic stew is ready to simmer. The Lord giveth and the Lord taketh away. In this case, the Lord giveth to the Vatican and the Lord taketh away from much of the rest of the Roman Catholic Church's empire.

In his helpful talk on family planning and the issue of contraception, the Pope explained to the African people how the use of condoms is making the spread of HIV worse. I'm going to type those words again because as I read them back I can't fucking believe that anyone in a position of responsibility and access to the facts would say something so dangerous, wicked and stupid. He went to Africa and explained how the use of condoms is making the spread of HIV worse. The Catholic Church doesn't like condoms or any other form of contraception. If a Catholic man wants to have sex but doesn't want to have a baby he has to put his penis in something that cannot conceive. This has proved most unfortunate for altar boys and their friends. I'm not clear as to why exactly the Catholic Church has hung on so very tight to their refusal to recommend contraception. I suppose it's hard to keep on putting people in a position where they are vulnerable and weak enough to accept Catholicism if they don't keep having children they can't afford to take care of. I find it impossible to imagine how his highness the Pope could travel across Africa, look at what's happened there over the years and still tell his many converted followers that condoms are what's making the spread of HIV worse.

How has he arrived at this twisted conclusion anyway? What games do they play at the Vatican on a weekend that might make him conclude that condoms are making HIV worse? Do all the cardinals pop on a blindfold and run about with their clothes off and mouths open, while the Pope fills a condom full of HIV-infected blood? He would then have to spin it round his head and after a count of three unleash it at an unsuspecting passer-by who might be unlucky enough to catch the virus. I suppose, in that way, the use of condoms really can make the spread of HIV much, much worse. If you're considering that as a way to spend an afternoon, I'd recommend you read the condom packet and follow the directions on there instead. It's much more fun, it's what they're for and it won't give you AIDS.

If they're not playing the spinning condom of death game at the Vatican, I don't see how they can conclude that condoms are the problem. Ready access to condoms and reliable information is the best way available of avoiding the spread of this disease, which continues to tear Africa apart and destroy families. If there is anyone reading this wondering why I am not advocating abstinence as the very best way of avoiding both the spread of HIV and unwanted children, it's because I like sex. I like it a lot. I wouldn't wish to ask anyone who is old enough to enjoy sex safely to do anything other than get plenty of it. It's fun, it's exciting and invigorating. In the right hands (and feet and mouths and fingers and armpits and bottoms . . .), it can be endlessly varied and creative. It's mucky and interesting and refreshing. If it's done carefully it can even be a delightful expression of affection between people who love each other. If you wish to go to Africa or anywhere else and tell people they've lost the right to enjoy sexual intercourse because they are unfortunate enough to have got ill, then go ahead. I hope you spot someone on the journey there who makes you tingle all over, enjoy an eye-wateringly brilliant shag and abandon your foolishness before you get quite justifiably punched in the chops.

The Catholic Church is not evil. It's too large and unwieldy to be described as either good or bad. Many of its members seek to do good, and succeed; others use the power of the Church for sins ranging between serious assault and sexual abuse all the way down to being a bit smug and judgemental. It has immense power and influence and I would argue that as an institution its inability to move with the times makes it increasingly unable to be helpful to its members. Certainly when the Church punishes a nine-year-old girl who had been raped and made pregnant with twins by her stepfather, I feel disgusted. The nine-year-old in question lived in Brazil and had been raised as a Catholic. When she became pregnant with twins in 2009, it was felt that this presented serious health risks for her, so her mother and two doctors aborted the pregnancy. She was nine. She had been raped and made pregnant by her stepfather and had to undergo the emotional trauma of a double abortion. The Catholic Church's response was to excommunicate her, her mother and the two doctors who performed the operation. Under different circumstances I'd say that excommunication from that church was a good thing and that the child should enjoy a life free from dogma and lies, but it was all she knew. Her life was that of a Catholic and when she needed the love of her community and the support of her church she was told that what she had done could never be forgiven by God. This decision was backed by the Vatican. Her stepfather was not excommunicated.

But I have no personal axe to grind with religion. There is much about it that upsets and confuses me, but that is based on decisions I have made with regard to what sort of person I wish to be and what sort of world I wish to inhabit. I realize, of course, that I am powerless over how the world behaves – often I can't even get my children to eat a pea, wipe their face or go to bed – but none of that discourages me in the slightest from attempting to reorganize the world as I see it. None of my resistance to religious practice is based on revenge. Certainly I was bored by my C and E upbringing. This is similar to C of E (Church of England) but in this instance stands for Christmas and Easter. It's an approach to faith that works on a quid pro quo basis. I went to church when I knew there was a loaded stocking or a chocolate egg in it for me.

I recall a feeling of having to endure what seemed like interminable services at school. Bits of something or other read out loud in Latin were especially odd. Only a maximum of 10 per cent of my school had even a fleeting understanding of Latin so if they were trying to make us feel anything other than excluded and bored then they failed. A few of us knew there was some rhyme about some ammunition and mass gathering of ants. This was supposedly something to do with conjugating the verb 'to love', I think, but Latin was not for me.

There were readings in English but they were from an old Bible and to a fat eight-year-old boy sitting on the gym floor with an increasingly numb bottom they sounded like this: 'And yay, hast thou within thine heart, with the glory of the lord, unto thee, something, blessed art the whojamaflips as they in the sight of Our Father who arty party, did verily praise the one Lord God giveth and taketh away again. And traveleth thee upon a donkey, but knowest thou that the lord doth . . . Here endeth the lesson.'

As a tubby pudding bowl whose small shorts were fighting a losing battle with the flesh spread beneath them on the bleached wooden floor, there were never words more sweet than 'here endeth the lesson'. Salvation at last! Relax, everyone, the lesson hath endeth. Why everybody'th thuddenly thpeaking like thith, I couldn't thay.

With those words the droning voice of whichever joyless, dead-eyed master was prattling on about thee, thou, thine, God, Jesus and some tribes from a couple of thousand years ago I couldn't care less about, was finished. Then just as you felt you might be excused to go and be a child for a while, some berk in a white robe would say, 'We shall now sing hymn number seven-six-three from the red hymn book.' Shit! His use of the word 'sing' was generous, to say the least. Three hundred disappointed children having faith rubbed up against them without a trace of passion or inspiration are inclined to make a sort of drone like the one you get if you accidentally buy a house too near to a motorway. It was the listless sound of passive lips gently flapping against each other, releasing a barely audible hum that carried despondent praise up towards the Lord, then, in the airless assembly hall, bumped hopelessly against the ceiling like a day-old helium balloon, realized it was never going to make it up to the Lord, gave up the fight and eased its way back towards the stupefied worshippers below.

Boredom doesn't tend to motivate people into great acts of rebellion or revenge. It drives you slowly towards inertia, with occasional outbreaks of rage, but that's not how I feel about religion. It was over for me as a subject once I'd been expelled for the last time, aged fourteen. After that even my parents didn't insist on Christmas Day church attendance. I often used to go because my much younger brother was made to and it seemed unfair that he should be the only one of us scuffing his feet mournfully towards the grinning vicar standing at the door of the church as earnest-looking families tried to remember the good reverend's name. Vicars must be stifling a veritable volcano of resentment on Christmas Day. The desire for the average vicar, seeing his church full for the first time since last Christmas, to turn to the assembled throng in the church and let them have it with both barrels must be stronger than the brandy-laced mulled wine that got him through the deserted evensong the night before.

'Where in the name of Mary Mother of Christ have you lazy, disrespectful bastards been for the past three hundred and sixty-four days? Eh? You think you can turn up here for one hour of carols and non-threatening stories about babies and stables, then go and eat yourselves into a turkey coma? Not today. Not this Christmas. I've had enough. Where were you six weeks ago when I opened the church for me, the verger and one bell-ringer, who it turned out had got squiffy on real ale and slept in here the night before anyway? Where were you then, eh? You bloody buggers? At home in the warm, drinking wine and eating cake. You think you can turn up once during the festive season, sing a bit, shove a fiver in the tray and piss off for the rest of the year to watch *Strictly Come Dancing* and YouTube? Well, not today. I've locked the door and we're staying here until the second coming or, failing that, until the police arrive. We shall now sing hymn number seven-six-three from the red hymn book.'

So I went to church on Christmas Day to keep my brother company and because my brother is one of the funniest people I know, particularly in places where being funny is not the done thing. He really comes into his own in a church, doctor's waiting room or theatre. My brother Henry makes me laugh a lot and there's no laugh more delicious than the stifled giggle of naughty brothers at the back of a church. I remember one Christmas service where all the children were invited to come to the front to sing 'Away In A Manger'. Henry was at the age where he had to sing it but was old enough to feel mortified by the experience. I got him with a trick I like to call the 'false start'. I've done it a few times when I've had to be in a church for weddings and funerals and so forth. It's a simple but pleasing trick and I recommend you try it. All you do is take in a deep breath as if you are just about to sing the first word of the hymn, but you do it much too soon. Usually there's about four bars of organ playing before the singing commences. So pick your hymn, then, at the right moment, you just catch the eye of the person next to you and go for the in-breath combined with the tell-tale raising of the songsheet and the wide open mouth. Nine times out of ten, they'll panic, think they've missed it and fire off with a loud but half-breathed note well before anyone else. In my brother's case he hit the 'Away' of 'Away In A Manger' with enough force that it still makes me chuckle to think of his livid reddening face and the genius way he tailed off the hymn when he realized I'd got him and his was the only voice filling the hushed church. 'Awaaaaaaay in a . . .' Good times.

I'm convinced that a lot of religious people experience similar subversive feelings during ceremonies. It's not because we don't care about the gravity of a church service. It's the opposite of that. It's precisely because it's important and earnest that we want to feel our way towards the outer limits of what's acceptable and test their elasticity. The thrill of shouting a rude word in a supermarket, of making stupid noises when someone is saying something important, of showing a mouthful of food in a smart restaurant – all these things provide the childish and silly thrill that I'm proud to say I've spent as much of my life as possible pursuing. Because I'm British, and pretty much devoted to the creation of laughter, being in a formal environment makes me want to misbehave. When I'm in church, the desire to fart is probably stronger than anywhere else on earth. It's not out of raging disrespect for God, His worshippers or the people running the service; it's just funny. To me. To my brother. I hope I'm not alone in this, though of course I accept that not everyone experiences the kind of puerile, helpless joy I find in being utterly, needlessly revolting. It's partly because you shouldn't break wind in a church, but let's not forget the role played by that very pleasing echo. It's like two farts for the price of one.

For a long time now I've wanted to sneak into a church at night and replace the little wafers they use to represent the body of Christ with Berocca. I think it would be lovely to see the body of Christ represented in the form of a highly effervescent, mineral- and vitamin-rich fizzy orange tablet, capable of administering 780 per cent of your recommended daily allowance of the Body of Christ. Sure, it's not bread as Jesus indicated would be appropriate, but I feel that Berocca better represents the lively and refreshing character of Jesus' life. With one delicious and very fizzy orange pill you could follow the teachings of the New Testament, get a health boost and make your pee glow like you'd successfully enriched uranium in your own kidneys. The receiving of the Berocca sacrament would make for a magnificent and spectacular communion. The kneeling congregation would lift their heads with tongues out in expectation, listening for the words 'The Body of Christ'. Then the cool, chalky sweetness of Berocca would meet their tongues. Odd, orangey, different but not unpleasant. Then time for 'The Blood of Christ', and the cup would be passed down and pressed to the lips of the faithful. A sip of red wine and within seconds a thick, vitamin-rich, dark purple foam would shoot out of your mouth. It's a miracle! But quite a confusing one that's fairly likely to make your eyes water and mess up your Christmas jumper.

I get the devil in me when I'm around religion and sometimes I just can't help myself. On a couple of occasions I've visited a mosque and jumbled up the shoes. A word to the wise – leg it, if you're doing that. Jumble, rearrange, hide a sandal if you wish, but when you're done, get out of there lickety-split. Barefoot or not, I have found that Muslims are quick when they're pissed off. I've never moved faster around Finsbury Park in my life.

I love a good mosque. A great many of them exist as part of modern dwellings or in a multifunctional space these days but some of them have truly awe-inspiring architecture. Not in Switzerland obviously, theirs are very dull, not a minaret in sight, but the others are beautiful. If you go to a predominantly Islamic country, you'll find they have a powerful PA system tucked away in the mosque too. They use it for their call to prayer, a very important wake-up for the sleepy Allah fan. It kicks off unpleasantly early if you happen to have gone to bed cuddled up with your rucksack only a few hours before, after a night dedicated to missing the point of visiting foreign climes amongst your fellow travellers. I think it was a little before 5 a.m. when the shrill, whining top notes of the adhan came wafting through my dorm window and saw me swear like a bleary git at the grapefruit pink of the rising sun. I've no idea what the chap was saying, I thought his voice was rather nasal and didn't hold out much hope for a singing career any time soon, but despite the grating drawl I noted that within minutes there were a goodly number of exhausted-looking men and women clearing their throats into the streets of

Penang on their way to morning prayers. They were drawn towards the noise like it was a magnet. To watch them trudge, jog, spit, walk, run and almost hack up a lung was inspiring and disheartening at the same time. It was so early and yet there they all were going to practise their faith. I wondered if I'd ever felt that much devotion to any one principle or idea in my life, and then felt slightly despondent. The mucoid flobbing all over the road and pavement isn't an official part of Islamic devotional practice but it's certainly done with religious regularity and a deep-reaching determination that both impressed and sickened me. Once you get used to it, the call to prayer is an oddly exciting sound. Nothing makes you feel like you're a long way from home more than the sound of something you don't understand at all but enjoy none the less.

I'd love to have a go on the mosque-top PA system. You can hear it for miles. I think cracking a few jokes would be a step too far, but perhaps breaking out a hard-hitting but respectful rooftop beatbox might be fun. Actually what I'd really like to do is get up in the topmost tower of the mosque, grab the microphone and perform an alternative Humanist call to prayer. Not as early, obviously. The Muslims do their first call at about five in the morning and I can't see atheists going for that. I'd do it at about 11 a.m., perhaps 11.30. After *Bargain Hunt*, but before *Cash in the Attic*. That's when most atheists are thinking about getting out of bed. I'd just pop up in the top of the mosque and in my best piercing nasal voice I'd half-sing the words: 'Good morning, everyone. Have you considered doing a decent thing for another human being today? Not for any eternal reward but just because people are fundamentally worthwhile. And remember, women's faces look nice.'

I have a bit of cheek around religion. I enjoy a bit of sauciness, some sass and perhaps just enough trivial stupidity to get myself killed. But this doesn't come from a personal desire for vengeance and retribution. It doesn't even come from a position of total disrespect for the faithful. It is just how I respond to things that confuse or exclude me. I mind very much what the faiths have done to people I know and to a great many I have read about, but my own experience with religion has been pleasingly simple. I think my desire to introduce elements of anarchy and rebellion to the sanctity of worship stems from finding the whole bloody thing so irritatingly stiff and unmovable. Come on, you pious, blink-ered sods, get cross with me about the Berocca, the sandals and the farting about, then perhaps once we're engaged in a proper dialogue we can talk about the stuff that really matters.

5

Believe in us . . .
Oh the humanity

I'D LOVE TO BE ABLE TO STAND ALONGSIDE MANY OF MY atheist friends and say I don't believe in God and it's fine. I'm fine. I'm Godless and content. I don't believe in unicorns, spaghetti monsters, giant mystical teapots orbiting the earth and I don't believe in God. Who cares? I don't need God. I'm not interested in meeting Him, impressing Him, bowing and scraping before Him or telling Him whether or not I've recently felt inclined to touch my own penis. I have the same level of interest in God as I have in Kerry Katona. Which is to say, very very little. In fairness, if God did the adverts for frozen prawn rings from Iceland in a state of hysterical inebriation, I'd probably buy one. I love a prawn. Just one of the many reasons I could never be a Jew.

But this isn't me. I am interested in God, to an almost

obsessional extent given how unlikely I think His existence. I've never stalked anyone before but if God had bins I'd definitely rifle through them.

Many people seem to be able to say with confidence they don't believe in God. Some say it with so much confidence I'm left suspecting that perhaps they do a little bit. They strike me as much the same as people who shriek 'bums against the wall' when they think there's a gay about. If you don't believe in God, what do you believe in? I'm not suggesting that while you're in the mood to make stuff up you simply replace your faith in God with something equally far-fetched. 'I don't believe in God but I've decided that worms – the pink slithery lords of the undergrowth – are now the focus of my devotion.' Worshipping the lowly earthworm is no more illogical than claiming the God of Abraham as the most important figure in your life. I'll grant you the earthworm lacks a certain mystical allure, though the continued wiggling of either end after dissection with a spade fascinated me as a youngster. Also, they reproduce asexually, so at the very least they have that in common with God.

So what should I put my faith in then? I have some faith to spare, I think, or at least a desire to invest emotionally in something comforting. Pillows, alcohol and large-breasted women can be paid for with cold hard cash and they will all comfort for a while – if you get all three in one night then I suspect comfort is pretty much guaranteed – but a truly comforting return on an honest emotional investment is harder to come by. The idea of believing in something has an irritatingly persistent appeal for me. But what? Not earthworms...

I could be Humanist, I suppose. But to what extent? Join the Humanist Association? I'm not hugely inclined to. I take membership of humanity as a given, with the possible exception of some bankers. I don't see dissenting from being human as an option. I could actively seek to generate a sense of belief in humanity as a force for good. A safe and constant place from which to gain strength, serenity and inspiration. I could try to make humanity, humanism or the human being itself my God.

No disrespect to humanity ... certainly no disrespect to anyone curious enough to have bought this book (I'll assume you're mostly human), but have you looked around? I find it immensely difficult to put my faith in humanity. I don't mean to be too disparaging but ... be honest, have you seen 'humanity'? Have you met many of them? Have a look now, peer out of a window ... Did you do it? Ghastly, aren't they? There's a lot of humanity out there. A good percentage of the people who make up the collective 'humanity' fall squarely under the heading of gits. I should know, I often am one. In the big Venn diagram of the human species with gits in area (a) and decent people in area (b), most of us live in the shaded middle area (c) of Fig 1. We try not to be gits but our innate selfishness, greed and fear prevent us from making the bold step into area (b) and away from githood. There are plenty who occupy area (a) pretty much all the time and who seem perfectly content to stay there ... You know who you are, and so do I. If you're wearing braces with matching socks – you're a git. If you moved billions of dollars from one place to another on a screen and thought it was hard enough work to justify a bonus of over a hundred thousand pounds – you're a git. If you wrote something where fear and selfishness were the main drivers for your thoughts – you're a git. If you steal stuff or waste stuff that others need – you're a git. If you watched your dog shit on a pavement and then walked away from the steaming offence – you're a git . . . If you've ever bought one of Jeremy Clarkson's books for yourself . . . you know who you are.

I'm above none of this. I'm every bit as capable of being a selfish tosser as most people. I try not to. Most people try not to, but most people fall short. I say this as a humanitarian. I am, in a very real sense, a fan of the species. As a comedian I stand on the touchline of life roaring support, screaming derision and trying to work out if there's a referee somewhere in the rabble with an exhausted, whistle-red face giving it all some direction. Fan or not – as any true supporter of a team event knows, it's important to be honest about weaknesses in the squad. For two seasons the 'top of the league' team who play in Stars and Stripes opted for an incurious, spoiled chimp to lead their dangerously violent and extraordinarily patriotic rabble in the big game of life. They chose an incurious and dangerous man to be their coach and lots of people got hurt. Stupidity is frustrating. Ignorance is pitiable and can usually be fixed with a little education. But incuriousness offends me and makes me angry. Incuriousness is steeped in immaturity, laziness and arrogance – a lethal combination for anyone unlucky enough to come into contact with the person who lives and breathes these qualities. Make someone incurious President of the USA and pretty much all of the world comes 'into contact' – particularly if they have facial hair and live above fuel. Folksy, Christian 'ya could have a beer with him' Bush Jr was incurious. I'm sure he still is. Say what you like about incuriosity, its practitioners are unlikely to care and it's self-sustaining by its very nature. Incurious George, the dull, pious, simian brother to the hairy star of the *Man in the Yellow Hat* books. A devout and narrow-focused Christian with a massive army. Jesus Christ, I despise that man.

If you care for humanity, as I do, it's likely that much of it will frustrate, confuse and anger you. I've been to an Argos. For those who haven't, Argos is like a shop only much more complicated and time-consuming. It's a way of purchasing things you are unlikely to need, which if you saw in reality (instead of in a glossy brochure) you'd scorn or scoff at. And all this in a shopping environment based on a total lack of trust. In many ways it represents the epitome of consumerist society's descent into nihilistic despair, but with betting slips and little pens instead of aisles and trolleys. You look into the Argos catalogue (comedian Bill Bailey brilliantly described it as 'the laminated book of dreams') and then fill out a scrap of paper to give to a person behind the counter. I've seen buttons sewn on to the face of a bear that had more life in them than the eyes of an Argos counter clerk. The clerk disappears into the back of the shop and, lo and behold, just three un-salvageable lifetimes later, returns to tell you there's been a stock error and you can't have the thing that you hadn't yet realized you didn't want anyway.

In a branch of Argos in Birmingham, I overheard two elderly Midlands women in headscarves talking in broad Brummie accents (warm, rhythmic and yet always under-scored with a strong hint of despair).

Headscarf 1 (blue & beige with nautical/anchor theme): 'This queuing system makes no sense at all.'

Headscarf 2 (polythene with bluish-rinse hair beneath): 'Hmmm, a bit like life really.'

Headscarf 1: 'Oh shit, I've lost my ticket.'

Headscarf 2: 'See.'

That about sums it up for me. The entire human condition explained in a few words by two mysterious, headscarfed philosophers out shopping for a foot-spa and some hair-rollers.

Humanity is exciting, but it can drive me into a funk so deep that even James Brown wouldn't wish to come down there with me. I've taken an international flight and passed through an airport. I have no faith in humanity. I've been in a Wetherspoon pub on a match day. I can't generate any faith in humanity. I've read a newspaper. I'm no longer certain humanity exists.

I appeared very briefly in a scene in Richard Curtis's film *Love Actually* (a pivotal moment set in a radio station). It was a sweet, uplifting movie that hilariously paid tribute to many aspects of humanity of which we should be justly proud. One of the central ideas revolved around the joy that can be taken from watching people meet in airport arrival halls. The flash of recognition, the smile, shriek, run and embrace. No bashfulness, no reserve in front of strangers – an open-armed place of joy, celebration and reunion. It's shot beautifully and even the hardest heart would struggle not to see that this idea of human connection and of Love ... Actually is a treasure and should brighten us all ...

However ...

I know, because I've witnessed it first hand, that just before that happy soul strides through the arrival hall doors with a trolley full of sombreros, suitcases and duty-free fags towards a hug and a face full of kisses, the same person has very recently had to deal with *baggage reclaim*! If you ever wanted proof that humans basically hate each other and don't care who knows it, go and watch them at baggage reclaim in an airport. That's why it's kept on the other side of the officials at customs, not because of smuggling, but because if we watched how we choose to behave at reclaim there would be mass suicides as the true horror of human nature reveals itself around a slow-moving carousel with bags on.

There is a yellow line around the reclaim belt. This yellow line is there for a good reason. If everyone stays behind it you can see the belt. You can see when your bag is coming, there is space then to step forward, grab the bag and move it away from the belt and on to a trolley. It's simple, it works and it's obvious. However, in real life the yellow line serves quite the opposite purpose. The yellow line is painted around the reclaim as a challenge to all travellers. Can you get you, your wife, your sunburnt children, Auntie Doris and three or four trolleys between the yellow line and the reclaim belt? Can you use shoulders, metal trolleys and swinging bags to knock the weak aside? Can you get needlessly aggressive and angry with people striving towards exactly the same aim as yourself and behaving in exactly the same way? Can you fail to see how easily we could work together if fear wasn't the driver of how we act? If you can do all of that, you win a prize. The prize is that within seconds of either arriving for a relaxing holiday or returning from one, you confirm to yourself and everyone else that the world is chock-full of gits and that it's every man for himself. 'Fuck you, Granny, I'm getting my bag. Come on, kids, squeeze in there and keep pushing, don't let anyone else in. Where's the other trolley? That's it, get that in as well. There, perfect, now no one can see, no one can move and no one can get a bag off the belt. Job done. Would someone either claim this concussed pensioner or put her back on the revolving belt, she's still in my way. Bitch!' I really enjoyed *Love Actually*, but it required a filtering of airport-based experience I couldn't quite relate to. Airports, and for that matter anywhere we are forced together with strangers, are for the most part monstrous, depressing and make me wish there was a God.

When you really get down to it, humanity does only one thing consistently well . . . it gets bigger, and that is all. We live lives coloured by pain, love, happiness, loss, confusion, grief, fear, satisfaction, foot-spas and hair-rollers, but the one and only thing we remain absolutely biologically and intellectually certain of is that the world needs more of us. As luck, God or evolution would have it the expansion of humanity happens to involve a process that's delightful and squishy and fun. So on we go, fucking ourselves out of air, food and space. More and more of us, rutting, bumping, breeding and whining. You'd think the evidence that the planet is getting overcrowded might make us pause to reconsider this idea, but the more people there are the greater your chance of getting laid and making still more of us. Statistically speaking, there are now enough people about that even John Merrick the Elephant Man could probably get a shag if he happened to be in Cardiff on a Saturday night.

I'm not a total cynic. I love people. Unless I haven't met them, in which case, like most of the rest of you, I suspect they are almost certainly hostile and will prevent me from doing what I want. I'd like to believe in humanity and remove my desire for a deity but I can't do it. Not yet. Not while semi-finalists on *X Factor* inspire more people to vote than the general election does.

I try to generate enthusiasm for humanity all the time, and there are of course many acts of love carried out by individuals and groups every day, which give encouragement. There is great art, music and culture, there is Pink Floyd, there is the Natural History Museum, there is snow-boarding, there are pasties. These are all great reasons to swell with pride at what a marvel the human being is. . . but I can't sustain that enthusiasm. The things that set me off can be as trivial and inevitable as war, cruelty and wilfully inflicted poverty all the way through to the really serious stuff like chewing gum on a seat, dog shit on a pram wheel or almost anything involving more than one person operating a motorized vehicle in the same place at the same time.

I think it's particularly hard to have a great deal of faith in humanity if you live in London. Which I do. London is a fascinating and exciting place, filled with a great many different people representing cultures, beliefs, languages, foods, clothing and vehicles of seemingly infinite variety. It's a pretty modern place and it has a Starbucks. For a city of its size and diversity, we Londoners get along pretty well. Multiculturalism is as near to a success story in London as it's likely to be anywhere in the world. The credit for that belongs more to lady luck than to the efforts of most people who live here. It's not as if Londoners are regularly inviting first-generation Bangladeshi families over to have dinner along with the delightful Polish couple who've moved in next door so that they can all learn each other's languages and discover exactly what takes place in the mysterious and fast-breeding 'Polski sklep'. People don't try to make it work, it just does. Perhaps white Anglo-Saxon Brits are aware on a deep level that there is very little of the world we didn't once visit, dominate and then improve or ruin (depending on which historians you read), and so we are now predisposed to expect 'them' to come and visit us. I can imagine the moment where decorum demanded that as the last plummy Englishman left India he turned to his hosts and with a stiff awkward handshake mumbled, 'Well, you simply must come and visit us in Blighty.

Any time you please. Just give us a tinkle and I'll see that Mrs Pierce puts the kettle on and irons the croquet lawn.'

You can tell that multiculturalism basically works because despite the best efforts of the right-wing press it almost never kicks off in London. Not along racial lines anyway. Obviously it can get a bit nasty at football games but that's because football's not very interesting so the fans have to keep themselves entertained. I believe they also get very cross if very expensive foreign player A turns out to be slightly better at football than eye-wateringly expensive foreign player B. Either way there's pleasingly little racial tension in London. It may boil or seethe underneath but the odds are that Mr Patel from Pakistan will sell butter from Holland to Mrs Chin from China who will bake a cake to serve to Mr Smith from Woking who will offer some to Mr Kovacs from Hungary after the meeting to discuss the Slovakian builders putting up Mrs Larson's conservatory. No one's sure where Mrs Larson's from but she has the most extraordinary way of pronouncing the word 'curtains'. Most people assume she's either Scandinavian or a very heavy drinker.

There are many journalists who would love to see us tear lumps out of each other but mostly we don't. Thus far, London and most of the rest of the UK refuses to oblige. That said, Londoners are very often within a step or two of leaping off the cliff of irrationality and going postal. It's no Marseille, which is permanently about half a degree below full boiling riot status. Even by French standards (les Français, ils adorent les riotes), Marseille is pretty bloody tense. I think it's fair to say that in London we do make an effort to make life as unpleasant for those of us who live here as we possibly can and for those who come to visit too.

We voted in Conservative clown and floppy right-wing Bullingdon waffler Boris Johnson as our mayor. We knew it would probably be crap, but we also knew it would screw it up for other people, so it seemed worthwhile at the time. As it happens, Boris has taken the coward's route and done surprisingly little that his predecessor hadn't already initiated. This is a good result for London, as many of us feared that British Bulldog, Wiff Waff and 'Are you there, Moriarty?' would be made city-wide compulsory weekend activities.

As someone who has chosen to live in a city as part of the battery human project, I have occasionally fantasized about moving out to the countryside. I have often heard tell of a sort of magical utopia that exists out there where strangers greet each other with a sunny if toothless hello, neighbours help one another with windblown fences and snowed-in vehicles. The jolly six-fingered landlord of the local pub knows everyone in the village. He does a lock-in on a Friday with flat beer and singing that lasts until the roast is served on Sunday. Everyone knows it's roadkill, but it's worth staying for the legendary Yorkshire pud – over a metre across of partly burned, partly raw batter mix. A place where babies are born on the living-room rug with the vet making do with a cleanish towel and a pair of nail scissors and everyone's fine. The countryside – honest folk, living simply where the only purpose a child will find for a PlayStation 3 games console is to use it to dam a stream as he fishes for sticklebacks...

However, first-hand experience has led me to believe that this vision of British country living is, in fact, bullshit. Come to think of it, on many trips to the countryside you can actually smell bullshit in the air. ''Tis the smell o' the country, moy dear,' claim the aggressively patronizing bigots who live there. 'No, it's definitely cow shit,' says the judgemental, impatient urbanite.

The countryside I've seen, and by that I mean the nice bits where restaurants don't 'shut for lunch', is usually manned by a few disgruntled, sour-faced 'locals' and the rest is made up of empty second homes for chinless city knobs looking for something to do with their bonus. A place where Giles and Fiona can spend the weekend with their ever-so-slightly-racist friends talking boorishly and without a whiff of self-awareness about what's to be done with benefit cheats and only a moment later how their marvellous accountant saved them a packet by putting their cash in a country where no one cares about anyone else.

Perhaps this view is framed by my time in London. Perhaps its impractically high density of people has made me hard, fearful and a cynic. If you think that, you can piss off. You don't know me ... There's a reason strangers are called strangers and it's because they're strange.

What is it about living stacked on top of each other that so appeals to us? Close-quartered city living is as irresistible to us as a greasy box of onion rings and every bit as disappointing. And yet most of us are afraid to stop doing it. It turns out that 'people' are 'the opium of the people'. Why jostle for position to be slotted into the vile human Jenga that is the London tube? Why queue with the sad, smelly and frustrated to join the queue who are waiting to be shown to the queue for . . . onion rings? Why? Who knows, but we do it in our millions and for this Londoner it has seriously eroded my ability to put my faith in people.

As a Londoner, you get home, bruised and frowning, at the end of the day and grudgingly conclude: Well, I've had a reasonable time of it, I suppose. I barged some people on the pavement unnecessarily. That was pleasing. I stopped very suddenly in that stairwell and made the woman with the suitcase fall all the way down into the underground system. I watched somebody struggle with a pushchair in an automatic door that looked a lot like it was actually chewing her Bugaboo. I drove like a selfish, petulant tosser and shouted at other people for doing very much the same thing. One guy was driving and talking on his mobile phone . . . I had to end my call to tell him what a twat he was being. I nearly crashed. Down came my window, mobile dropped into my lap, 'Look where you're going, dickhead, and get off your phone.' Then I had to mash the Nokia back into my sweaty ear and explain, 'Sorry about that, some pillock on his mobile, not looking where he was going . . . Ooh, hang on, a police car's just pulled alongside me . . . I'll send you a text . . . Wait, I'm trying to hold the wheel with my knees . . . Look out! Shit. You don't have a number for Injury Lawyers For You, do you?'

It's hard to put your faith in humanity. People can't be God.

They can't be my God anyway. To worship one of them individually would be creepy and I'd probably end up with a restraining order. Collectively humanity is too flawed to be worshipped or relied upon for much more than the odd cuddle or a cup of tea. Tea and cuddles are vital and excellent but the spiritual yearning I experience requires a little more than that. People have a horrible habit of dying. That's what my friend James did, and he was a really reliable mate. I need something rather more permanent than just people for reassurance. Statistically we're crap at living. Eventually we all fail at it and give up.

We present a very strong case against ourselves. None of which is to say that humans haven't been simply wonderful, imaginative and deserving of great praise. The pyramids in Egypt, *The Wire* on HBO, my daughter's giggle, the defeat of Nazism in World War Two and Stilton are all worthy of tremendous admiration and should be celebrated. Brilliant human achievements, but crucially human and not God-like. The few people who have bestowed upon themselves the status of deity have without fail turned out to be deeply unpleasant and more than a little bit rapey.

It's my firm belief that the greatest threat facing humanity today, perhaps the greatest threat we have ever faced, is the one posed by climate change. I realize this is a divisive issue. Not everyone's on the same page with climate science and the conclusions of its practitioners. Some people agree with me that it presents a clear danger to our continued existence and well-being – and the others are wrong. So, as I say, an immensely divisive issue. Fortunately, as divisive issues go – this one divides up along very simple lines between those who've read up on the subject and tried to understand it and some idiots with their heads shoved so far up their own arses that the only shift in temperature they're likely to perceive is when they fart. I'm being flippant (and vulgar, too, I hope). Of course, there are lots of different and worthwhile takes on this massively complex data and what to conclude from it. I read in the *Telegraph* only last week a fascinating new study that actually shows the ice at the Arctic isn't melting, it's merely hiding in liquid form. So, again, an interesting and different take on it, depending on . . . how retarded you are.

It's very difficult to get people in the UK to take climate change seriously. Not as difficult as it is to get the people who do take it seriously to see there might be a funny side to it. What a tedious, sanctimonious bunch of smug bastards we've become.

'Oooh, look at me, I'm better than you because I live in a yurt made of my wife's pubic hair and we knit our own hummus.'

Since I took a serious interest in environmental issues, these people have become my friends. Judgemental, tutting friends with thin vegan fingers ready to wag. It's a nightmare. Everyone's desperately trying to 'out-green' each other.

'How did you get here?'

'I cycled.'

'Oh really? On a bike, made of metal and oil?'

'Er, yes?'

'Well, I actually crawled here on my lips . . . so I win the big green prize and get to pull the patronizing, smug face I've spent all week working on in my mirror made from the recycled tears of a panda.'

Climate change at current speeds, according to over 95 per cent of climate scientists, is unprecedented and dangerous. Apocalyptic predictions range from the chillingly convincing all the way through to the hysterical and preposterous. In any case, I have become convinced that we need to act to mitigate now (yesterday would have been better but I'll settle for now if you're offering). It strikes me that to wait until we are 100 per cent certain as to what the endless streams of climate data will mean for humanity before we act would be as unbeliev-ably stupid as sitting in the fast lane of the M1 discussing whether or not the lorry hurtling towards you is red or blue. The available information suggests with very little ambiguity that this is something worth taking pretty seriously. But if it is taken as seriously and with as much finger-wagging as many 'environmentalists' currently do, then frankly I don't want to fix it and I'm not even sure our species deserves to survive. I don't want the future to be populated by the kind of people who spent their time enforcing the washing-up rota at college because 'it might have only been one cup, but it's the principle . . .' They weren't fun. Survival of the smuggest isn't what Darwin began to explain and isn't what I want to see.

I don't wish to see the survival of the shittest either. I'd hate for the environmental movement to get it so wrong in selling the idea of change that the future falls into the hands of panicky arch-capitalists like the Lawson clan insisting there's nothing wrong as the delta slowly swallows Bangladesh. Nigel, the ex-Tory MP; Dominic, the blinkered columnist and disappointing son; Lord Christopher Monckton, the pantomime evil uncle and oil man to the right of Sarah Palin – are all determined that over 95 per cent of climate scientists are liars. I don't wish to see the future of the planet influenced by the likes of the three witless boars who giggle and grunt a warehouse full of cretins through a *Top Gear* recording. 'Sure, the poor and least able to defend against it will die first but look at the torque on this . . . she's a beast!' I don't wish to see humanity, no matter what regard I hold it in, hoodwinked by lazy, deceitful writers like Melanie Phillips, Christopher Booker, James Delingpole, Ann Widdecombe and Simon Heffer. I am certain that the sum total of climate research these people have carried out before spewing forth on the topic is to read whatever it was they wrote in their own column last week. On a really good day, when they fancy being properly thorough, perhaps, at a push, they might read each other.

The case for change is being lost. It's not exactly a mystery, is it, that a bunch of refugee socialists, anti-capitalists and other such angry warriors in search of a fight are now camping out in the environmental cause and are failing to inspire a responsible and empathetic move towards sustainability. If only freshly wagged fingers turned out to be the green fuel of the future, we'd be all set for clean energy for ever.

It's difficult to get people to take climate change seriously in the UK because in this country it will probably mean two, maybe three degrees of warming. When you explain that to most British people, especially at the moment, they say:

'Two or three degrees warmer? Well, I think that sounds rather nice. I might grow a peach tree on my lawn. The whole wheeze sounds tremendous.'

So I try to bring them back to the reality of what we're looking at.

'No, no, hang on a minute, if we have two or three degrees of warming here, that would mean most of continental Europe would be an arid, uninhabitable desert.'

A bad ploy . . .

'Well, I like it even more now. I'm eating peaches and Frenchie is fucked, I couldn't be happier. Up yours, Pierre. Can't you swim, little froggie?'

I persist. 'No, please, we're talking about millions of people with nowhere to live.'

You see, it's hard to put your faith in a species that seems to choose to act against its own best interests and may very well have an inexorable urge to destroy itself. In years to come, lemmings may well warn their little lemming children about the mysterious suicidal folly of the human race. They could see the cliff, and they ran right off it . . . in Range Rovers.

For us in the UK, the European Union has intervened. They legislate for us or against us, depending on which way you choose to see it. In order to mitigate dangerous climate change, they say we have to get rid of all our old light bulbs and replace them with 'eco' bulbs. This was received with a similar welcome to the one Tiger Woods's wife gave him when he came home with lipstick on his club and bragging about sinking a hole in one. Perhaps you already had 'eco' bulbs in your home before the EU insisted upon it. If you did, then you'd be used to the fact that you will spend the first ten minutes in every room in complete darkness. You've no idea where you are, glaring through the gloom at the switch, thinking, hmm we should never have put a dimmer on that, should we? It's just making a horrible buzzing noise now. Then that pale flickery green light comes on and you realize you've peed all over the floor.

Oh, and on the duvet as well. 'Sorry, darling, did I wake you? Wasn't even in the right room. Who knew? My mistake.'

But it's all right, it's not a disaster. The new bulbs are just that – new, and as such are capable of terrifying a great many people if the spicy catalyst of hysterical journalism is allowed to do its bidding. Suddenly you have a fear vehicle capable of driving us straight into a pit of irrationality, wide-eyed, ill-informed and muttering something about Hell and handcarts. When we made the move to eco bulbs, the *Daily Mail* and the *Daily Telegraph* ran a nostalgia campaign for the old ones. Not a considered appraisal of the facts. Not an exploration of the pros and cons. Not even a lopsided weighing up of 'change because science says we must do something to mitigate' versus 'inaction because we don't like to be meddled with'. No, a nostalgia campaign – for light bulbs. They put their years of experience and journalistic knowhow into creating an emotional and patriotic response to a frosted 60-watt screw fit. There were beautiful pictures of bulbs on the front of the newspaper. The entire front page was filled with a close-up of a light bulb. It was as if the right-wing press had suddenly struck on an idea . . . 'too many foreign types', 'taxes too high', 'youth run wild', 'something about Diana' and PING the bulb appeared. As it turned out the 'light bulb moment' wasn't an idea at all, merely a pathetic bit of foot stamping because someone had asked someone else to try something new.

The right-wing press wouldn't refer to the old bulbs as tungsten bulbs, or filament bulbs, or shitty wasteful bulbs. No, instead they chose to call them 'traditional bulbs'. Traditional? Huh? The 'traditional' British bulb we've used in this country for well over a thousand years? As integral to the British way of life as cricket, bunting and grumbling about the weather (though never that it's getting dangerously warmer)? Long before electricity was created, the traditional British family would gather round the traditional British bulb and wonder what the fuck it was for.

'What is it, Mummy?'

'It's a traditional light bulb, son, a good, honest, British light bulb.'

'What's it for, Mummy?'

'It's traditional, son, that's all you need to know.'

'Does it work well, Mummy?'

'No. But it's traditional.'

'If it doesn't work, Mummy, why do we——?'

'Oh do shut up. Just stare at it and feel that senseless British pride swell within you.'

In one piece of exquisitely poor journalism in the *Telegraph*, the old bulbs were described as having Rubenesque curves. Now, I don't know about you, but that sounds to me as if whoever wrote it might well be having a closer relationship with the old filament bulb than most of us would care to imagine. Screw fix or bayonet, I wonder? Neither sounds terribly comfortable. Rubenesque curves? What on earth could the writer mean?

'Look, look at the lovely, pert, rounded, traditional bulb. Her Rubenesque plumpness so alluring and soft. Ooh, the sexy round bulb, with her bulging bottom and cheeky, almost see-through skin. Frosted . . . yes, and yet so invitingly warm and naughtily inefficient. I want her. I want that bulb, want to rub her curved, forgiving smoothness all over my body. She's my bulb, my sexy traditional bulb – not like these new "eco" ones that curl round and round like a black man's hair. No! A traditional bulb we can all be proud of and just occasionally back on to whilst singing "Rule Britannia" and wearing a pith helmet in the old tin bath.'

Going that dewy-eyed over a light bulb is insane. The new bulbs are flawed and imperfect but they seem to be better and more efficient, not to mention that the case for their use has been well put. Argue the case down if you have the knowledge to do so, but don't try to instruct people that light bulbs are 'traditional' or 'Rubenesque'. You degrade yourselves when you do that and it makes me think you haven't read enough.

'How many *Daily Mail* readers does it take to change a light bulb?'

'Why does everyone keep changing everything? I fear change.'

What I'd like to do is create an eco bulb in the shape of Princess Diana's head. That'll confuse them.

If we can't change a few light bulbs, we are screwed as a species. We're done for. And I'm not putting my faith in an entity as stupid, short-sighted and stubborn as that. If that's what I'm supposed to settle for, then I might as well believe in God.

6

Where to look for God . . .

IF YOU THINK YOU WANT GOD, AND I'M PRETTY CERTAIN that is what I'm after, it's very difficult to know where on earth (if that's the right place to start looking) you might find him. You're unlikely to run into God in Sainsbury's and even for lapsed believers I don't think there's been a single instance of him having popped up on Facebook with a 'Hey, remember me? Don't look at my profile pic . . . We've all aged sooooo much. Watcha up to? See any of the old gang? Had a text from St Peter but . . . Anyway, get in touch, we'll have a beer. Remember the song? Chuggalug Chuggalug . . .'

In the olden days God was about all the time. You barely had to sneeze and God would pop up in one form or another and give you instructions as to what you might do next. There was a time when one could barely move for burning bushes, visions, visitations and heavenly interventions. People popped to the market and as they struggled back with their reusable hessian bags of locally sourced fruit and veg, who should they run into? God, floating down to check in on his new creation. I can understand God's enthusiasm for the new project. I'm the same when I plant stuff in my garden. I'm a menace for it, nipping back every five minutes to have a look and see how the tomato seedlings are progressing. Any new shoots on the runner beans? Slugs been at it? Birds have probably eaten the lot by now . . . Come the autumn, half of it's gone to seed and most of the fruit hasn't made it past green and bullet-hard or it's been missed and become a pulpy dollop of snotty rot on the vine. After the first wave of enthusiastic fiddling and interference, I'm sorry to say I lose interest. There seems to be a better than average chance that God is the same gardener I am. I've a horrible feeling this may be autumn and the heavenly father's wellies are nowhere to be seen.

God hasn't visited Earth for a very long time. Sure, there are odious bigots like Stephen Green from Christian Voice who say the floods in New Orleans were God wiping away the sins of America's Sodom and Gomorrah and an alarming number of American Christians with similar theories about the 26 December 2006 tsunami in south-east Asia, but no one sane thinks that. Sometimes people claim some sort of visitation but it usually amounts to little more than a bit of bread with a faintly Jesus-shaped image on it or a sweet potato that looks like Mary as long as you ignore all but one bit of it, in a certain light, from the right angle, if you're pissed and lonely. Muslims tend not to find images of the Prophet Mohammed in slices of bread. Thank goodness, too – no one wants to see Hovis the subject of a mental jihad because they accidentally baked a forbidden image into a loaf of malted granary.

Perhaps with the advent of cheap travel God no longer chooses to spend His holidays here. I'd hate to think of Earth being like some sort of musty and neglected Butlins, which no longer holds any appeal for God because He's realized that for the same money He can have two weeks all-inclusive in some exotic Galaxy far far away. If our home is God's Butlins then I hope He remembers fondly the exceptional value and entertainment we provided with our hilarious knobbly knees and old-fashioned singalongs. It seems more likely that God viewed Earth as a business destination and now He's either done a merger and moved on or He thinks there's no future in the humans market. Whatever the case, He doesn't come and see us any more and that's a shame. I say it's a shame because if I were Him (and despite the boorish over-confidence afforded by a private education I make NO such claim), I would come down, just once should do it, and make it plain to everyone that I existed and that the correct path for those who wish to spend eternity with Me is to become (insert whichever religious viewpoint you find most appealing here). Druid?

Some people have suggested God no longer comes to see us because He's dead. Maybe He is, but if the God of Abraham ever existed then a large part of His appeal seems to be predicated around the idea that He is eternal. Evidence suggests otherwise, but the evidence for or against God's existence or the promise of his eternal presence doesn't concern me as much as the need for Him to have done so. That fascinates me, and the possibility of it and the recognition of my desire for that sort of heavenly reassurance resonates right through my atheism. You can't prove for sure that God does or doesn't exist. I concur with the theory that the burden of proof lies with the believer, not the sceptic, but it's very unlikely ever to be a provable thing one way or the other. That being the case, is there a more interesting question to ask? I hope so.

Where is God? I know how to get next to God – you do that through cleanliness. I know how to meet my maker – you do that by picking a fight with someone devoutly religious. God is everything or God is nothing. Well, if He's everything in the truest sense, He's also nothing, and then I'm confused. Even a narrower take on that notion still makes God a bogey and a virus and a parasite living in a child's eye and that, to me, diminishes Him. I can't buy into the notion that God is everything and everything is as it's meant to be. This is because I arrogantly believe the world to be an imperfect and improvable place in need of our effort. A lot of the time it's chaos down here and if there is a plan, it's a shitty one. Maybe I'm wrong, but whoever it was that planned dementia, childhood leukaemia, AIDS, cancer, malaria and for BAE Systems to be one of the UK's biggest exporters needs to take their plan back to their celestial drawing board and have a think.

It's been suggested to me that I judge God by too many of my own criteria. I wrongly assume that because I have created an idealized moral code for the world, it must be the right one.

119

I am told sometimes the presumption that God should meet with my approval is not the point of God. He sees all, does all, created all and knows all. He knows the dire suffering that is so commonplace in the poorest areas of the world is no more than they can cope with. It serves some higher purpose only He understands. Of course, empathy makes me imagine how I would feel if fortunes were reversed and I found myself living on the edge of starvation in a shanty town while a very confused Kenyan man tuts and paces up and down the corridor of a Wandsworth semi waiting for the bloody dishwasher man to come. When I imagine myself trying to manage in extreme and challenging conditions, I see terrible outcomes. I'm not used to it. I've been to Wolverhampton but apart from that I'm totally ill equipped. I'm 'Westernized', comfortable and weak. Leave me in sub-Saharan Africa without a mosquito net and water and (fat reserves aside) I'd be a hopeless wobbly wreck within minutes. I'd give it all of three days before I'd become little more than an additional burden on the people who live there. Perhaps they might put together some sort of telethon fronted by Lenny Henry to save my sobbing white ass. Who knows? But if my empathy gland is too swollen, if my assumptions about the world are too fixed or just plain wrong, if my morality is not supposed to apply to God and His divine higher plan . . . if all that's true, then why in God's name did God make me like this? If He's all-knowing and has a plan, then I'm right to think the way I do about Him. I'm part of God's natural order. My scepticism, my cynicism, the questions I have for God – they're all just as they're meant to be. God made me mind about what He does. God made me hate the versions of Him I've been offered so far. God knew I wouldn't believe in Him and that I'd find most of the routes to His house impassably thorny and distasteful. God is everything? God sees all? Knows all? Created all? Really? God, I need to talk to you, because this is a shitty and mean trick you're playing. Now, where are you? Hmm? Seriously now. Come out, come out, wherever you are ...

Nothing so far. I'm still searching. I have been told that God lives in Heaven and the only way there is through His son Jesus Christ ... That's not helpful because I've no more idea where Jesus is than I do his neglectful father. I don't think it's too much to say that as dads go, God was not a good one. Personally I'd put him up there with Josef Fritzl, but once you become a dad you do find yourself more judgemental about other parents. Granted there was no 'Fathers For Justice' movement back in Jesus' day, but even if there had been I doubt the heavenly father would have popped on a Batman costume and climbed up the side of that tower in Babel to get his boy back. My son once asked me why I worked away from home so often. I felt a sharp sting of regret and sadness as I tried to explain to him where I went and why. It was a painful moment, but it's not a patch on being asked, 'Father, why hast thou forsaken me?' I mean, ouch. What a question. 'Sorry, son ... erm, Daddy's been really busy with work. You got the Action Man I sent, right?'

God is in your heart. I've heard that a few times but He doesn't show up on a CAT scan, and open-heart surgery to see if He's in there seems dramatic and dangerous. Sure it might end up with my death and then I'd get to meet Him anyway, but that's not the point. I had a heart murmur once. If that was God then I wish He'd speak up. I can't bear mumblers. I want to know where to find God while I'm still alive, and I can't find Him anywhere. He'll probably be in the last place I look. That's where things usually are.

The point is, if God's here somewhere, my wife will know where He is. She knows where everything is. She does a number of things extremely well, but the location of missing items is her speciality. She's like a sort of domestic sat nav device. She doesn't like it when I call her TomTom. For a while she was excellent at remembering where I was supposed to be, and held in her head an astonishing number of addresses and contact details for our friends. All this, and I get to have sex with her. As nicknames go, Filofux went down even worse than TomTom. These elevated powers my wife possesses to locate missing stuff could be a form of voodoo bestowed upon her by a wild Haitian priestess. An exciting and exotic thought, though locating God through the powers of voodoo is almost certainly frowned upon by the sort of people who do frowning upon things so very very well. If God's anywhere nearby, He'll be in the second drawer down, I suspect. My wife seems to locate most stuff in the second drawer down, though, mysteriously, it's never there when I look. Voodoo . . . My wife has no more idea where God is than I do. If she can't find Him, then He's properly lost.

If you can't get to God through religion, then it's hard to

know where to look. I could go to a church, mosque or temple and see if God's really in there somewhere, but I don't think He is. I feel more conscious of the idea of God in a holy place, but this always leads quickly to my feeling more certain than ever there isn't a God and never has been. Often when I visit a church, or better still a cathedral, I am truly and profoundly awed by the grandeur of the place. The towering ornate ceilings, the whispering enclaves, the chapels inviting your exploration to touch the cold, exquisite stonework, the solemnity of quiet in a place capable of amplifying the still small voice of calm into a cry to the heavens. The soft flickery glow of a candle lit in remembrance of a lost friend. The beatific face of a sole worshipper in the tidal swell of empty pews tilted up towards the warmth of a stained-glass window, eyes misted as the journey into faithful meditation soothes the crumpled brow . . . It moves me and then I wonder to myself – isn't this massive, imposing, empty building missing the point? Is this really what God wants? Is this what Jesus was talking about? A great, big, expensive, pointy, inspiring but usually empty building? I hope not. I've enjoyed a lot of churches I've seen, though I've learned that, like laws and sausages, the less you know about how they were made and by whom the better. There's barely a decent cathedral in the land that didn't involve poor people giving their time and effort for nothing but the promise of eternal salvation. That's all very well, but the people making the promises were in no position to do so. They didn't know they could offer that. The descendants of these people are now bankers. Most big religious buildings involved exploitative building methods and dead construction workers. The Health and Safety officer was a priest telling people that to plummet from the roof to the floor below would constitute a great honour and the Lord would look down on them favourably. Then He'd post the video up on YouTube.

I don't think God's in the big cathedral, and even if He is, that's not where I want to meet Him. It's too quiet and too removed from the life I lead. If I met God I'd want to be excited by it and do some shouting. Wow! It wouldn't do at all to meet God, to stand face to face before the Lord and, before you could begin to express your excitement at this defining event, to be shushed into embarrassed silence by a lady with a cat's bottom where her mouth should be. That's not the God I'm looking for, and if that's the only place you can find Him then I'll go without. Thank you, and here's a quid for the new roof.

I'd like to visit New Zealand one day, but if I have to swim there I'll probably not bother with it. That journey seems dangerous and long and who knows if I'd even survive it. As it stands, the long flight, the time change and the over-representation of backpacks and extreme sports enthusiasts are enough to put me off making the voyage to Kiwi-land anyway. I'm not a lazy man but the route to God through conventional religious observation is a swim to New Zealand as far as I'm concerned. I want God, but if the only way to have a belief system is to hand my life over to people whose politics make me shudder with disgust, I'd rather stagger my way through this existence without Him, thanks.

There are, of course, many places of worship where devotional practice is not hushed and maudlin but rather a no-holds-barred celebration of the coming of the Lord. The gospel and revival church gatherings I've seen have been alive with excitement and praise. Even as a posh English white man it's hard not to leap headlong into the upcurrent of these powerful and sincere meetings of the faithful. Hands clapping awkwardly and always out of time, head swaying to the soul-shaking harmonies of a gospel choir in full voice, mouth open waiting for the Lord to enter me and have me speak in tongues and pass out on the floor. It's exciting and happy and I want in . . . until you talk to the individuals involved. Once the singing subsides and the red palms of hands clapped in reverence and celebration have turned back to pink, you will find these are places where bigotry most vile is as alive and vibrant as the services themselves. Great music thrives in many Christian churches, but so does illogical, unchallenge-able hate, fear and selected ignorance.

The way Muslims worship has a profound and moving devotion to it. The preparation, the washing and gathering together to face Mecca and literally prostrate oneself before Allah speaks to a passion I wish I could find in myself. It also speaks to a rebellious defiance that insists any God who took the time to create me would not be so vain as to require that five times a day I stop what I am doing to say thank you and lie about on the floor with my shoes off. I can do that at home with a box set of *The West Wing* and a beanbag. I've seldom been inside a mosque. The impressive ones do some of what cathedrals do for me. It's easy to be awed by them, and to admire elements of the commitment made by worshippers inside them, but none persuades me that Allah is alive and Al Qur'an is the answer to my questions. Men in one room, women in another … not for my God, thank you. Frankly there's not enough music either.

Jewish temple worship is based on a version of the Old Testament, so, to be blunt, even if they were giving away pie at the door and the ceremony included letting loose to the strains of a deep James Brown soul classic and God showed up every Friday to say, 'Yep, you're doing great, kids, I love you and here's a present' – it would still hold the same appeal for me as an appointment with a dental hygienist whose wife I'd been caught shtupping the day before. Jewish temple and their reverence for the Torah make me turn on my heels as quick as you can say, 'Hey, but Neil Diamond's a Jew.' I don't care, the God of the Old Testament wouldn't like me and I know I don't like Him. This is not where He lives.

So where do you find God if you can't go to church?

In my search for divine guidance, I've checked in all the most obvious places. They don't do God in John Lewis. I asked and was met with a very blank stare and the offer of a squirt of 'Something-or-other' for men. She blasted a mist of something sickly at my wrist, missed and soaked me in it. I don't mind people thinking I'm odd or even crazy. I have a view of the world framed by my experiences and I'm ashamed of very few of them. Crazy is fine, but smelly sort of bothered me. I only asked if they thought God would be down in household items or whether he'd been moved to the Christmas department, what with the family connection and all. Next thing I knew I'd been squirted and I smelled like Peter Stringfellow's neck. You cross the line from charmingly eccentric into dangerous and untrustworthy nutter if you're strange *and* smelly. It's a shame neither John Lewis nor Selfridges do God. There are plenty of people who would no doubt put Him on their wedding list. Anything to guarantee that church venue and a place in the local school. I decided that God was unlikely to be available in 'all good stores now'. That said, I was surprised to see how much religious insignia was available on the high street if you don't mind looking like you're a magnet who's just been dunked in a tub of cheap metallic tat. River Island and Topshop looked like they were expecting Mr T from *The A-Team* to pop in and stock up on crucifixes.

I checked on eBay to see if anyone was selling an old God they didn't need. Plenty of people have abandoned their faith and perhaps one of these desolate lost souls had considered its resale value. The seller would have to photograph their God for sale, so I didn't expect to see much from apostate Muslims, but surely, given the number of Gods once devoutly worshipped and fought over who've now been abandoned for the latest absolute, unerring truth, there had to be some unwanted deity on offer to the highest bidder. I was disappointed. There was someone who looked like they might be about to let God go, then at the last minute they pulled out.

I've no idea which faith that might have been ... Catholic perhaps?

I suppose you wouldn't want to get God off the internet anyway, would you? For a start, it would be so hard to know what state the God you were buying was in anyway. Of the people who shop online, I would guess all but a very few will have made internet purchases that, on arrival, turned out to bear closer relation to ambition than to the actual size you were after. I am primarily referring to clothes here, although I suspect the same rules apply to sex toys too. You almost certainly couldn't trust the seller in any case. How do you establish and then maintain your eBay trusted-seller rating if you've already sold one monotheistic deity to someone else?

If God were for sale on eBay, I'd have to bid against some of the large faith organizations and most of them have more money than they know what to do with. Instinct says they could spend it on the poor and needy, but as I said they literally have so much they don't know what to do with it. In any case, if the Catholic Church wanted to buy God, they could probably afford to buy Him direct from the seller with enough left over for a really lovely new pair of red shoes for the Pope.

Even if you did manage to find the right God at the right price from the right seller, you'd then have to get your deity delivered. 'Collection only' might be an answer, but if it's collection from a place of worship I probably don't want that God anyway. You couldn't very well turn up at a synagogue and tell them Barry said it was cool if I came and took God out the back way. If He's not to be collected from a place of worship, then where? And how did they get hold of God anyway? What qualifies it as a worthwhile deity? It might be knackered. I don't want to turn up at a warehouse and have a pair of ill-fitting overalls shuffle into a back room, only to return with a crumpled cardboard container, a clipboard and a mumbled 'Sign here, please', then watch him bump my parcel-taped packet through the hatch, the contents of which are to become the ordering principle for the rest of my existence. It's all too risky. I don't expect that would be a serviceable God as we would recognize Him anyway.

There's a good chance that any God bought off the internet would end up in the box with my video camera, electronic picture frame, MP3 player, mobile phone, leather coat and signed INXS record waiting to be put back on eBay. Return whence you came, minidisk player. I cast thee out, USB-powered desktop hoover device. Back, back, I say, thou slightly wonky Ra the Sun God. I haven't got round to selling these items back yet because I'm a bit scared of that sort of thing and I might not get what they are worth. Much better, then, to leave them lying in a plastic tub gathering dust and obsolescence. It turns out I have the same view of unused electrical items as the church has of reform. Who knew?

You couldn't get God delivered, because that would mean that at some stage He'd fall into the hands of the Post Office. I don't care if your atheism falls on the cynical side of Richard Dawkins. No one really wants to see God fall into the hands of the Post Office. Many have argued convincingly for the end of faith altogether, but not like that. Not for all human belief in the supernatural to cease in an instant because God got 'lost' in the bowels of a sorting office or conveniently dropped into the Postie's 'special' pile with cash-stuffed birthday cards and missing rent cheques. If God came to us care of the Post Office, they'd almost certainly bend Him. God doesn't like to be bent. God doesn't seem to want anyone to be bent. I've heard His followers be very specific on this point. It wouldn't matter how clear the bright red 'Do Not Bend' sticker was, if you weren't in when they tried to deliver God, they'd fold the bugger in two and drive Him through your letterbox with enough force to take the door off its hinges. You'd come home to find God lying whimpering and crumpled on your doormat with the pizza menus and the 'Polish Amelia – make good cleening howse' card.

You'd hope that most people might choose to send God by recorded delivery, but then you'd have to wait in between 5 a.m. and 11 p.m., not daring to move more than an inch from the brushes on the letter flap in case you missed it. After time, the demands of a full bladder would tear you away for those few critical seconds and sure enough, as you sprint back towards the pair of deep, buttock-shaped indentations in the coconut matting, you'd see it. That little red, grey and white papery bastard that spells hours of frustration and despair.

'We tried to deliver God but you were out.'

No!!!! I was having a wee! I was gone for less than a minute!

Tried? Really? You 'tried' to deliver my package, did you? How hard did you try exactly? You didn't ring the pissing bell, did you? That, to me, would seem to be the entry level of effort. The step one of '*tried* to deliver your package'. Extend the finger, lean in, locate button, advance and stiffen finger upon contact with bell/buzzer, then depress for between two and four seconds. There, trying, isn't it? Perhaps a knock too, or is that asking too much for grasping little mitts that can feel a gift voucher through four layers of envelope and card and have it away before the strains of 'Happy Birthday to you . . .' have subsided into embarrassment. Having made the heroic effort to ring the bell, how about, in the spirit of 'trying' to make the delivery, waiting more than the standard 0.0002 seconds before waddling off up the road in such a hurry. I can only presume that failing to accurately match up the number at the top of the address on the envelope with the one on the door takes more time than we've given it credit for, and this is the reason Postie can't wait for more than a few seconds to see if anyone answers. How dare you go on strike? Better pay and conditions? Fine, have them, have it all, deliver the post from a silk and gold sedan chair for all I care, but deliver the post. Twice, preferably, like you used to. And while we're at it . . . pick up those red rubber bands you've dropped. It looks like a sunburnt snake is shedding its elasticated skin in instalments on our pavement most mornings. My children believe that red rubber bands are a type of naturally occurring flora that only blooms after the shuffling feet of a daydreaming postal worker have germinated the rubber seed in London's streets. Never trust a man who can't whistle 'Whistle while you work' while he works.

God forbid the Tories get their wet dream fulfilled and knacker another public service by selling it to their mates. That way we would all have the right to have God not delivered by a deliverer of our choice and all for just £85 per letter.

I think it's fair to say I have had some issues with the Post Office. Issues I now realize I probably shouldn't keep mentioning on BBC Radio 4. All my letters smell of piss. Is that normal? No, I don't think it is. I refuse to believe that everybody who writes to me is individually pissing on my letters. Although, when I think about it, I suppose it is a possibility. But that's not the point. I don't want God, in whichever of His many forms he chooses, to come to us 'care of the Post Office', bent double, late, with a red rubber band round Him, in an envelope, pissy, ripped or otherwise.

Having pondered where else I might persuade the Lord to make Himself known to me and drawn yet another spiritual blank, I decided to put a personals ad in the *Daily Telegraph*.

PERSONALS . . . Would like to meet . . .

Boy seeks deity for walks, chats and possibly more. Non-smoker, GSOH essential.

One assumes God is a non-smoker. I mean, He knew how damaging tobacco was before He'd even decided to create cigarettes, marketing and Big Tobacco. His is a high-pressure job though, so perhaps, since the ban on smoking indoors, He can be seen awkwardly avoiding St Peter's gaze outside the pearly gates having a quick puff.

Usually in a personals ad the 'possibly more' means 'I'd like to have sex with you'. The 'possibly' is also an opt-out in case the person who answers is horrifically unattractive. To write 'I'd like to have sex with you' would certainly be more upfront, but I don't think the *Telegraph* would be comfortable with that and it spoils the charming allure of the coded personals ad flirt. Even the printed word 'bi-curious' is enough to get most men fizzy if the hotel room's lonely enough. I don't wish to have sex with God, He's screwed enough of humanity already and frankly I'd feel cheap. The 'possibly more' in this context refers to the notion that I could become quite dependent on the relationship over time and look to Him for more than just chats and strolls. If, after a respectful period of courtship, the friendship leads to some kissing and possibly even some light petting, then so be it.

I chose to place my ad in the *Telegraph* because I think if God reads any newspaper it's probably the *Daily Telegraph*, isn't it? He's the only entity large enough to be able to hold the bloody thing without needing to put an extension on his house. I mean, He made the *Sun*, but I don't think He reads it, do you? I don't think God reads the *Guardian* either. It would be very disappointing for religious people to get to Heaven and find wallcharts of interesting cheeses and charts of England's Kings and Queens hung up all over the place. So I chose the *Telegraph*. They were slightly baffled by my phone call, but given that they regularly have announcements in the births/deaths/weddings column like *Torquil Fartguard-Caffingham-Smear is delighted to announce his engagement to his thoroughbred hunter (16 hands) Lullabel-Blackshirt to be wed in his stables on January 4th 2011*, I didn't think they'd be too perplexed by my spiritual quest for an imaginary friend.

So up it went. *Boy seeks deity for walks, chats and possibly more.* I got no response at first, so I put it in again the next week and paid for an extra line. *Likes: taking metaphors too literally. Dislikes: gays.* I had one almost plausible response but it gave Croydon as the address ... I thought He's quite unlikely to have chosen to live in Croydon.

So it's hard to know where to find God. As soon as you step away from the conventional religious route, then you're very much on your own, with your best hope of finding Him being luck. This seemed very unlikely to deliver because I'm not usually a lucky person and God hasn't been seen wandering about on Earth since about the first third of the Old Testament.

At one stage on my search I was offered a religious sat-nav system at a car boot sale. It wasn't quite what I was after. When I turned it on it just kept on saying, 'I am the way, the truth and the light.' That's all very well but I was trying to get to Cricklewood. When I reprogrammed the destination to take me to Heaven, the soothing voice said repeatedly, 'At the end of your life ... say sorry.' I would, but who knows when the end of my life will be? I couldn't bear to be one of those people who spend their whole time apologizing. I'm sorry but I just couldn't. I don't think the spiritual sat nav really exists but it would be an excellent gimmick for any church seeking to make a few extra dollars from the gullible.

*

Plenty of people decide not to bother searching for God at all but instead indulge the desire to have something to believe in by worshipping stuff. Steve Jobs at Apple Mac doesn't exactly make false idols but he merely has to shove the letter 'i' on the front of a new thing and most of us are on our knees in wide-eyed adoration and worship. We are iSuckers. It's no coincidence that the iCon for this false idolatry is an apple with a bite taken out. Come on, Eve, take a nibble of this iPad and experience original sin at the stroke of a finger.

I was going to get an iPhone to see if there was an 'app' for God in there. For everything else 'there's an app for that' so I had an iThought, why not God? Good, I'll get an iPhone then and I'll download God straight off the apps page . . . Then I realized that if I got an iPhone I'd be the sort of person who has an iPhone, and frankly I'd rather be a fundamentalist Muslim. I realize there are almost certainly iPhone users reading this book. Hello, I hope you're very happy. Pop the book down and check your messages. Got any? No? Welcome back. Remember, I'm a book . . . Oh, what's the point, you'll have lost concentration again by now.

Here's a couple of pointers for iPhone users. 1: Grow up. 2: You just bought one, you didn't invent it. OK? I'll tell you what, here's an 'app' for you. Why don't you see if you can leave it in your pocket for more than a minute? Apply that application and see if your real-life friends start coming back to you. You know, human friends, real people, with meat and skin on rather than an avatar and a 140-character update beamed through space concerning their fascinating day shopping for toilet paper.

In case you're dismissing me as a Luddite, you're wrong. I'm not scared of iPhones. I like them. I think they're beautiful; I think the technology's absolutely breathtaking. It's exciting; who knows where it will go next? I don't communicate with my friends by telegram and carrier pigeon. I'm into innovation and I'm excited by the fact that we live now in the age of communication. Lucky us. If I didn't think I'd become one of you, I would get an iPhone. I know you've been enjoying yourselves with them and they're amazing, and look at this – it fires angry birds at pigs and they're beautiful and here's the stockmarket price and they're amazing and look my one's making a light-sabre noise and everything. But you must accept the fact that while you hunch over your little handheld device, thrilling at the marvel of being able to scroll through screen after screen of improving and enlightening information with just the swish of your finger, to everybody else you just look as if you're trying to wank off a gerbil. Trust me, once that image is in your head you'll never see iPhone users in the same way again. Every time I see some finger-wiggler gawping into his fist on the train and see the concentration on his face as his wrist gyrates softly to and fro, all I can see in my head is a little mouse, lying on its back, being pleasured by a numpty. That's the trouble with the iPhone. It's entirely wasted on the kind of people that want one.

Now there's the iPad too. The guinea-pig-sized pleasuring device. No, thank you. With the exception of Stephen Fry, who one assumes knows what he's doing, there really is no excuse for the iPad. If it didn't seem too ghastly and totalitarian I'd round up the first-generation iPad owners and make them stand on a rickety scaffold as I fired angry pigs at them from a huge trebuchet. People keep telling me, 'Yes, Marcus, but you can take a thousand books on holiday with you.' Good. 'You can have the entire online library right there in your hand on the beach.' Really? Well, I learned to swim and that's what I want from a beach, that and rock pools. So, have fun swishing through titles and trying not to go blind from the glare of the sun reflecting off the screen, I'll be in the sea having a laugh and looking for Neptune. In fairness, I'm more likely to go searching for Nemo. The new technology may be marvellous, but excuse me if I choose not to face iMecca every twenty minutes and touch my head to the floor in praise.

There is no app for God in the iPhone anyway. I've checked. There's an app with beer in it; I've been shown that too many times. Twice. It's because it's a free app, so everyone's got it. If you know an iPhone user, give it time and soon enough they will come up to you with their iPhone and show you the hilarious beer app. On the screen it looks like the phone's got beer inside it. It hasn't, it's a phone. But it looks like real golden sloshy beer that seems to move about in much the same way that real golden sloshy beer does. When the scintillator who's digitally pouring your time down the drain shows you this brilliant 'app', you're supposed to look delighted as they tip the phone and the digital liquid inside seems to disappear as if being poured out of the device. They will then place the corner of the phone against their smiling lips and tip it backwards to complete the illusion they are an utter twat. Then, as they pretend to drink, they give a mumbled commentary of what you can see isn't happening, but would be if they'd bought a pint. 'Ooh, ooh, look, it's like the beer's disappearing. Oh, there's a beer in my phone. Oh, where's it going? Mmmmm. Delicious . . .' They take the phone away from their mouth and without a trace of embarrassment make the 'I've just had a refreshingly large drink' noise – 'Aahhh.' They then look, smiling and expectant, straight at your face. What are they waiting for? Congratulations, perhaps? A round of applause? A real pint? A marriage proposal? Actual beer still exists, is available and does what it has always done. To me, digital beer would seem to be somehow 'less than' real beer. But, you know, go ahead and knock yourselves out, you lonely, lonely freaks.

I also don't believe that God invented man in the hope that eventually we would invent the iPhone and then finally He would be able to reveal Himself to us. Shining and full of love and pride at the marvel of His creation's ingenuity . . .

'Well done. You have passed my test. It is the iPhone. That is what humanity was for.'

And no one would notice. God would have to remount His cloud and sheepishly disappear back into the heavens alone, as every human being on Earth failed to spot He'd been to congratulate us. Stood as we were hunched and squinting at a tiny fistful of excitable rodent about to achieve yet another shudderingly good orgasm at the deft touch of a generation lost to the portable communications and gaming device. Gerbil wankers.

If you're reading this with a BlackBerry buzzing away in your pocket, you can grow up as well. You only chose the BlackBerry so it would look like a business call was really a text inviting you for a pint and a curry. At least the iPhone users had the courage to try full-strength phone crack. BlackBerry users are still getting their fix from the digital equivalent of laudanum. Certainly if the human fingertip was two millimetres wide then the BlackBerry would come into its own, but as it is, trying to use the keyboard to type a message on a BlackBerry is like trying to do keyhole surgery with a JCB.

That last tirade seems reasonably likely to have thinned my readership down to you elite few who are not afraid of a touch of light ribbing. The rest will have thrown the book down long before this chapter anyway, as it has too many words and not enough pics and URL links to YouTube clips of fat people falling over at weddings.

What I'm stabbing at, like a fat finger at a BlackBerry keypad, is that this is a question of what and how we worship. Even the most devout atheists continue to put their praise and reverence somewhere. It might be somewhere better than the church. Maybe. There's a fair chance it'll be reverence for Steve Jobs or Bill Gates or someone similar. There are many people who have lost the ability to distinguish between the things you own and the person you are. The portable communications device, brilliant though it is, is often at the heart of this mistake. Those people most affected by this syndrome will have put this book to one side to send a tweet asking if anyone anywhere in the world has ever done anything as crazy as making a cup of tea but forgetting the tea bag. I know because I am one of those people. If God came to see us, the first and last I'd know about it would be a tweet with #Godcame on it.

I like my phone; I spend too long gawping at it in the hope of validation from another lost soul like me. But I don't wish to worship my phone or have it define my existence. Anyway, I shan't dwell further on the deification of the false idols, even if they do have an app that can find a Michelin-starred restaurant in Preston. Amazing what they can do these days.

Back to the search for God.

I don't know if you've ever seen a documentary on the television, or perhaps heard one on the radio, about what it's like sharing your life with somebody who has Alzheimer's disease. It's so very hard. For the person who has it, it's a hellish, isolating and frightening condition, but for those who love and care for the poor soul who has Alzheimer's, I think it's probably worse. Because you can still physically see the person, they're still there with you. And yet mentally and emotionally they are completely removed from you. Lost in a different world where the stark sadness of a loved one trying to reach you and to revive that human connection is a concept with no traction in your reality. It seems to me that the visible presence of the Alzheimer's sufferer, the fact that you can still see them, that they are still there with you and they still look like they did before this disease took them to wherever it is they've gone – it's that which makes the mental and emotional absence so much harder to deal with . . .

That's what it's like having a mate with an iPhone. You can still physically see them, they're just not really there.

I can't find God . . . Not in the *Telegraph* or the sat nav. He's not in my heart and He's definitely not in my head. He's not available to download or to buy a pirated copy of and as far as I can tell He's not tucked into the pages of any special book, just as He's not loitering in a big imposing building waiting to be found. I really don't know where to look, so if you've seen Him please let him know I was asking after Him, and then tweet me to let me know what His plans are.

7

Who's who . . .
Who believes what?

WHEN I TOOK MY SEARCH FOR GOD ON A STAND-UP TOUR of the UK, I hoped the make-up of my audience would include a broad spread of beliefs. In order for the show to work well it was essential it didn't become some smug atheist love-in where we all sat about laughing at how ridiculous everyone else is for believing in silly ideas like God and such-like. I hoped for life-long worshippers and atheists through to recent converts to or from religious observance, holy men and women, pagans, Satanists, scientists, philosophers, goths, weirdos, extremists, stoned theatre staff and everything in between, all sitting together and laughing at my thoughts. When trying to sell a national tour, pretty much every comic I know will settle for anyone in their audience as long as they turn up and laugh. I was not disappointed by the spiritual demographic of comedy fans across the UK. Most groups were well represented and even the modest C of E ones were bold enough to identify themselves in a potentially hostile environment.

I didn't get a great many Muslims coming to see me. In all honesty, this was not a surprise. The UK's more strict Islamic community don't tend to come to comedy clubs. I can understand why, but it's a shame none the less. A cliché it might be, but laughter has the power to cross all language and cultural barriers; unless that laughter is generated by Jim Davidson, in which case it most specifically doesn't. The absence of a large veiled and bearded Muslim presence at my show was both a disappointment and a relief. A disappointment, as I like to be challenged and it would have been interesting. A relief because, despite striving to understand a wide variety of media, I know that, like most white middle-class people in Britain, I've accidentally bought into some of the ideas put about by the press and the truth is that some Muslims scare me. It's my responsibility to find constructive solutions to this fear, one of which is to own up to it. It's a prejudice in common with my fear of football fans, Christmas shoppers, large family gatherings and the studio audience of *X Factor*. It's based on the simple fear of the unknown. I don't understand why people would dress up in shiny cheap-looking shirts with paint company logos on and go bat-shit crazy over a football team, any more than I understand why a load of bearded men would kneel down in the road outside Finsbury Park mosque to listen to Abu Hamza. I feel very outside of these 'tribes' and

I experience some fear. Is this Islamophobia? I suppose to some degree it is. Is this prejudice the same as the views held by the English Defence League? I sincerely hope not, but perhaps I'm being squeamish. I just don't see myself marching alongside men who want to send Moroccans back to Iraqistan and think that a Hindu shopkeeper is going to try to convert them to Shi-ite belly dancing. A few Muslims came to see my shows; some wrote polite letters to me afterwards to set me straight on factual errors I had made. No one blew me up or threatened to sever my head. That is more than I can say for a late show in Battersea a few years ago when I accidentally made a joke about the sacred city of Manchester. There were some very devout Mancunians in the audience who took my blasphemy very personally and threatened to kill me.

On occasion, as I sat alone backstage on the *God Collar* tour trying to remember how I linked from Noah and the flood to the story of James and the grazed penis, I imagined what I would do if one night I walked out on stage to find a whole theatre full of cross-looking Islamists peering at me from the gloom. I think the eye-slits in the burka have the potential to look particularly frightening in the half-light of a theatre. Hundreds of pairs of eyes floating in the air, staring, judging . . . 'So a fella walks into a bar . . . is this thing on?'

The tour gave me a rare opportunity to talk with large groups of people about religion and to find out who really believes what. How alone am I really? I seem to share the quality of confusion with a great many people who find me funny. This isn't scientific enough to draw any real conclusion from other than to say that a great many people who find me funny are very very confused. When I previewed the show and was still working out what I thought I wanted to say, one of my promoters indicated that some sort of 'non-lethal' fatwa might be good for ticket sales. I said I'd settle for five stars from a national newspaper. Yes, I'll slag them off, criticize their critical faculties, unpick their writing, but give me a couple of stars and a 'funny', 'clever' or 'hilarious' and I'm all theirs. I accept the fact that I am essentially a needy approval whore. Now please love me.

Stand-up comedy errs heavily on the side of cynicism, scepticism and the rejection of any formal structures that are perceived to be imposed upon us ... that and knob gags. Stand-ups are for the most part a bunch of smart-arsed, Godless, mean-spirited, selfish, ego-driven spreaders of joy, light and laughter. Time spent in any green room will soon confirm that we are mostly competitive, back-stabbing, supportive, kind, well read, poorly researched, childish, filthy, vain, needy, loving, cruel and almost always a little bit late. I am convinced that the stand-up demographic contains a wholly disproportionate number of dyslexics. You should see most comedians' notebooks – they contain secret codes, the scribblings of inky-legged spiders, hotel addresses and some infantile sketches of penises.

Atheism is well represented amongst comedians, though it's important to recognize that atheist comics find they get more comedy mileage out of discussing their rejectionist position than the believer comic does from discussing theirs. There are some extremely funny and brilliant Christian comedians in the UK, which ought to go without saying but rarely has. Atheism includes so many varied schools of thought it can't really be compared to one faith or another and most Christian comics find plenty else to be funny about without having to bare their soul before a drunken rabble underground in the middle of the night. The comedy circuit is an environment where professing your love or enthusiasm for an idea without then undermining that with self-deprecation and insults is rare.

'Good evening, ladies and gentlemen. I believe in a loving and merciful God and I love my wife to whom I am faithful. The present system of taxation seems to work as well as you might expect from a functioning democracy and my journey here was pleasant and swift ... Hey, is this thing on? Who threw that? No, you piss off. Oh all right, I will. Damn this "turn the other cheek" nonsense. It might be the right thing to do but you hecklers are killing me.'

I often wish I didn't think man-made climate change was a genuine phenomenon, as I suspect undermining the efforts and earnest sincerity of 'people like me' who want to address it would be a doddle. If the dolts on *Top Gear* can pull it off by calling anything they don't agree with 'gay' or 'vegetarian' to the delight of the meat-faced petrolheads around them, then I'm sure I could. Religion has structure, faith is delicate and sincere and the churches of the big faiths contain ludicrous, old-fashioned ceremonies. These are the lowest-hanging fruit there is. None of which is to say that using comedy to challenge the orthodoxy of the church is not entirely worthwhile. A bishop's hat makes him look like a fish gasping at the sky; bashing a bishop is a euphemism for masturbation. Women in burkas look like Batman and Hasidic Jews have woolly dreadlocks dangling out of their funny hats. Boom, take that, orthodoxy.

When I subjected audiences up and down the country to my wholly unscientific demographic faith test (which was sufficiently imprecise and unrepresentative that it could easily have been written up as a conclusive and alarming survey in the *Daily Express*), I found that whilst non-believers usually made up the largest and certainly the loudest and most willing to be identified part of the crowd, there also were plenty of people with beliefs representing the three Abrahamic faiths and a few 'others' too. There were also a large number of people who declined to identify themselves in any of the three group options I offered: 1. Possessing a desire to believe in something beyond this existence, including anything from religion to spiritual curiosity. 2. Agnostic/not sure. 3. Atheist. I concluded that those who didn't identify with any of those groupings were either too thick to understand the choices or resented the imposition of being asked to identify the personal and private theological structure of their lives in public. It is also possible that they were none of the above because they were deities who'd come to see if anything I had to say was a threat. If they were, they must have decided I wasn't. There have been no lightning bolts or supernatural maimings so far. I'll let you know if the next time I go swimming, Neptune decides to poke his trident up me . . .

I asked the audience to trust me not to bully or expose them if they told me what they believed. I hope they were convinced of my sincerity when I tried to explain my search for God was genuine. I promised there would be no witch-hunt. When I told them that in Henley-on-Thames, there was an audible boo. They seemed to be quite up for the idea of hunting a few witches.

'Well, we've got the river so we might as well dunk a few elderly cat owners.'

When I asked first if there was anyone who would describe themselves as having some sort of faith, religion or perhaps even curiosity about the possibility of something beyond this existence, the hands went up very slowly indeed. Usually one hand would go up and then when that had been seen by another audience member they would feel safe enough to join in and before you knew it there were a good number shoving a believer's fist proudly in the direction of the Lord. They were waiting until they felt safe enough to join in, fair enough. Many of them seemed embarrassed, some even to the extent that they then pretended they had temporarily misunderstood the question.

'Oh faith? Faith, yeah sure. I thought you said face. Does anyone have a face? Sorry. Yes I have faith, and a face, so, yes, count me in.'

Of course, they had no obligation to tell me anything at all. They were there to be entertained and not to take part in a narrow and irresponsible census. On any given night there were probably many more sitting in the darkness with some sort of religious system at work in their lives but not comfortable enough to say so at a comedy gig. I did take great delight in reminding them that they only had to deny it twice more before they were in a whole heap of trouble. They couldn't be sure if I'd ask them twice more, but it's a tough call, isn't it? Slight awkwardness at a comedy show versus eternal damnation for thrice denying the Lord.

I tried to make that first question as inclusive as I could. 'Is anyone religious? Does anyone have some sort of faith or perhaps even a curiosity about something beyond this existence?' I wanted to invite in as many people as possible and dispel the fear that this might be a series of cheap shots flung at the inconsistencies in the Bible. Hilarious though books like Leviticus are, it's not why I don't believe in God so it didn't make the cut. This wasn't about mocking any one group. It was and is about trying to understand why anyone believes in anything and why I can't seem to. As a cry for help, I think making thousands of people laugh all over the country is better than a suicide attempt. The first few rows at Henley-on-Thames might not agree.

When I was previewing the show in a tiny club near Tower Bridge in London, trying it all out and seeing what worked, I asked if there was anyone with any religion, faith or belief system in the crowd. No one responded, not one person. It was very awkward. Up until then it had been going really well and people were laughing a lot and answering my questions. I was very disappointed when this bit drew a blank. Then as I tried to work out what to do with the next ten minutes of material, which really depended on at least one person identifying themselves as a child of God, a woman in the front row suddenly piped up. She pointed at the shocked gentleman beside her and announced, 'He's a Jew!' I'm sure it came out with more force than she'd intended but the impact on the room was massive and, I'm glad to say, hilarious. Everybody laughed, particularly our freshly identified 'Jew', as the tension of the silence was broken by a statement that made everyone instantly more tense. She didn't mean any harm, of course, and he seemed to find being grassed up very funny. It's just a good job she never lived next door to Anne Frank, I suppose.

Then I moved on to the next group. The undecideds. I asked: 'Is there anybody here who would describe themselves as an agnostic?'

Well, predictably enough some hands went up and then down again and then back up and then halfway down and it was like the Grand Old Duke of York was in charge of all the agnostics' arms, which then wavered for a bit before being dropped in exhaustion and replaced with a despondent shrug. They didn't seem sure of anything very much. Keen to make the religious amongst the audience feel all right about having been asked to go first, I set about teasing the agnostics for a while. Accusing them of sitting on the fence so hard they had corrugated bottoms. Hedging their bets so completely they had time to add topiary. So desperate to have it both ways, they looked like indecisive bisexuals. I imagined a row of agnostics on their knees at the pearly gates, looking contrite and self-piteous. Pleading for a place on the guest list to Heaven.

'Sorry, God, there wasn't enough evidence, but can we come in anyway? We'll be really good and sweep up and everything. Surely a "maybe" is as good as a prayer. I gave a quid to the Sally Army once . . . please let me in.'

Teasing aside, agnosticism is the system that makes the most sense to me. If you apply any degree of rationale to the question of God's existence, it is, at least for the time being, an unknowable thing. So you arrive at agnosticism. Open to the idea there might be a God but unconvinced by the available evidence. It seems the most scientific position to take. That said, I think for a great many agnostics the question of science, evidence and open-mindedness is not really the point. I am blown away by the number of agnostics for whom no further research seems to be necessary. It is possibly the biggest question mankind has ever addressed itself to. Is there a God? It affects this existence. It affects all past and all future existences. It defines who we are and what we believe in. Not to put too fine a point on it, it's the big one. And yet if you ask most agnostics, 'Is there a God?', they shrug, shuffle a bit, look at their shoes and mumble, 'Yeah, dunno . . . huh? No, not sure, you know . . . not easy is it? God, eh? Tsssk? Erm, I was going to look into it but there's a new season of *The Sopranos* out on DVD and er . . . well, I've got an iPhone . . . so . . . what was the question? I'll see if my slutty gerbil knows the answer.'

The nights the show went best were when there was a good number of believers and undecideds, but then I needed to establish if I held any appeal for the non-believers. I could feel them like a Jedi feels a disturbance in the force, waiting to be asked . . .

'So is there anybody here who would describe themselves as an atheist?'

Wooomph. The cheer was always the loudest and most confident. My 'demographic' are the vocal Godless. I'm sure it's connected to a piece I once wrote for *The Now Show* on BBC Radio 4 about my objection to the inherent hate and violence so prevalent in the three Abrahamic faiths. I was put up on YouTube and had an astonishing number of 'hits'. I'm often asked to speak at secular societies and atheist groups. I always decline because I'm not sure there isn't a God and it might not take that much to convince me there is. I just need to meet the right salesman. There were always plenty of atheists in my shows and they are, to whatever extent you wish to divide up into groups, 'my people', I suppose. So I sought to establish some friendly parameters for the excitable atheist. I thanked them for coming to see the show. I told them how lovely it was to see them and how much I appreciated their support. Then I pointed out that as a group it was time to realize they were not cleverer than everyone else in the room and could they please pipe the fuck down. Some were confused and possibly hurt. Surely the comedian whose six-minute diatribe on the Abrahamic religions on YouTube had so clearly nailed his colours to the mast as an anti-religious, atheist provocateur wasn't about to turn on them? No, I wasn't about to turn on anyone, but I don't wish to be defined by an absence of belief. There were a lot of atheists keen to see my show, and I thank them for coming, but amongst their number there will have been some gits. That fact seemed unavoidable. Being atheist doesn't make you clever or nice or logical or brave or moral or anything else. It's a choice and we could just as easily rally round the idea that none of us liked public swimming pools or Ugg boots, trivial though they are compared to the power of religious ideology.

I thanked the Godless again for coming and reassured them I hoped we could grow to be friends, but real friends are honest with each other and so I wanted them to know that I was as sure as I could be that announcing your atheist status was no more a guarantee of intelligence than saying you like custard. Some custard-eaters are clever, some are not; it is not the liking of the custard that defines the custard-eater as clever, though I suspect if you tested the theory you would find custard-eating atheists such as myself are amongst the brightest people in the world. Atheism is no more a badge of being clever than going to Oxford for a day trip and coming back with a special hat that says 'I went 2 Oxford' on it.

Atheists have made a different decision about God to the one made by believers. That is all. I think it can be convincingly argued that atheists have more often applied reason to the question than the faithful have, but this is not black and white, and the application of reason, whilst I admire it as a system, is not an indicator of IQ. In part, faith is the rejection of reason, but with rewards for the faithful that make the choice a reasonable one to make.

Some atheists are clever, some are not. You're not clever because you're an atheist, and you're not an atheist because you're clever. Trust me, I know some unbelievably thick atheists. The only reason these people don't believe in God is because they couldn't hold an idea that fantastic in their heads without going boss-eyed and getting a nosebleed.

I wasn't only trying to keep the whole audience on side by insulting each of them evenly, though I admit the idea of continuing with one third of them sulking was pretty un-appealing. The idea was to reflect my thinking on the subject back to a room full of people and make them laugh in the process. My thinking on the subject of God is at worst ill-informed (I'm quite certain there are enough books out there on God and belief and atheism for me to buy into one or more of them wholesale and give up my angst) and at best in line with a great many people who are just like me – confused. I'm an atheist but it doesn't work for me. I'd be something else if I could but I can't. I'm trying to make sense of it by reading, listening, talking, watching, waiting for something to make sense . . . I'm on hold.

'There are no available Gods at present, but your worship is important to us, please hold . . . There are no available Gods at present, but your worship is important to us, please hold . . . There are no available Gods at present, but your worship is important to us, please hold . . . There are no available Gods at present, but your worship is important to us, please hold . . . You are currently lost soul number . . . 6 billion in the queue. An operator will be with you as soon as possible. There are no available Gods at present, but your worship is important to us, please hold ... There are no available Gods at present, but your worship is important to us, please hold ... '

I have a horrible feeling that when I get through, it'll be to a call centre in Delhi, where a friendly yet aloof man named Unpronounceable will advise me to unplug my faith at the wall and then try switching it back on again.

8

God Delusion –
the modern atheist

I READ A WELL-KNOWN BOOK BY PROFESSOR RICHARD
Dawkins called *The God Delusion*. It's a fascinating book
regardless of what you believe and well worth a read. Richard
Dawkins says at the beginning of his book, 'I would like
everybody who reads this, by the time they put this book
down, to be an atheist.' Well, I was an atheist when I started
reading *The God Delusion*; by the time I'd finished it I was an
agnostic. I was going to read it again but I worried I might
turn into a fundamentalist Christian. I think the reason I
struggled with the book, despite the well-argued polemic and
reasoned discussion of the intellectual liberation atheism can
provide, was the unbearably smug, know-it-all tone of the
thing. Even if you agree with most of what is written in
The God Delusion, you find yourself having to rinse great

dollops of smugness off your hands when you put the book down.

It's hard to pin down exactly what it was I struggled with when I read it. I know that with only a few exceptions I found I shared Professor Dawkins's take on faith versus science. His position, in case you've not heard of Richard Dawkins, is that there is no God. He's as sure as you can be about that. If it turns out there is a God then I suspect there is a large 'Have you seen this man?' poster hanging off the pearly gates with a black and white photo of Professor Dawkins and a reward of 25,000 Eternities in Heaven for anyone who can point to his whereabouts. It's very difficult to pick out a clear example from the text of *The God Delusion* where he indulges this off-putting smugness in order to illustrate my point. *The God Delusion* has no sentences saying: 'Christians are ridiculous, Muslims absurd and Jews are just mental. All of them are beneath me and the lot of them should bow and scrape before science and its practitioners.' It's much better argued than that, but the tone is of a person who knows he has the right answer, and whether I agree with him or not, that insistence and certainty remind this reader of the unbudging and infuriating convictions of the religious zealot.

My problem with *The God Delusion* was enhanced by the fact that by the time I read it I had heard Professor Dawkins speaking on several occasions. Once you have that clipped, humourless and unrelentingly posh tone in your head, it's very hard not to read the book in the same voice. There may well be people reading this book who are struggling with the same problem right now. I'm sorry . . .

The God Delusion is just a book, an important and well-researched book, but just a book. Merely printed words on the page, ordered by a great mind seeking to persuade you that to believe in God is a delusion. You can't actually hear Professor Dawkins when you read his book, and yet every time I open a copy of *The God Delusion* I can clearly make out the curt, condescending clatter of the 'atheist in chief' filling my head with words. It's not his fault. He's clever and he sounds clever. I wouldn't want him to dumb down. He's posh and he sounds posh. I wouldn't want him to do a Tony Blair and plonk his accent in the mud of the Thames Estuary in order to convince me he's just like me. When I read, if I have reference for how the writer sounds, I hear them in my head. I can't help it. I've done it for as long as I can remember. It's very nice, if you're reading a Stephen Fry, to hear Stephen's languid, confident articulations rippling through your brain. It's absolutely ghastly if you're reading Janet Street Porter, and turned out to be inappropriately amusing when I read *A Brief History of Time*. I should also point out that my lips move when I read. They moved a lot when I read the biography of the Rolling Stones; I was in Accident and Emergency with lip strain by the time Mick and Keith had recorded 'Brown Sugar'.

I'm told that moving your lips and forming the words in your mouth as you read may be a sign that the reader lacks intelligence. I accept the charge and to be honest I don't mind particularly. I don't try to hide it or anything, I wouldn't chew gum to conceal my ignorance. I've seen people chew gum and it almost never makes you look brighter. The more I enjoy a book, the more my lips move. When I read *The God Delusion* they moved a lot to begin with – it was like singing along to a secular hymn book – then by the end they were more pursed and tense like I'd been kissed by a Dementor.

I found learning to read quite difficult and it took me a long time, which is one of the reasons why I know exactly what a Dementor is. I'm sure I'd have learned to read sooner but I bought a 'How To Read' guide book and by the time I'd got through that, the tale of 'Janet and John' and their fascinating relationship with 'John's ball' had passed me by. Shoelaces were similarly mysterious to me. I presume whoever it was who invented Velcro had the same trouble and paved the way for us dyslexic lace muddlers to run free in the playground without fear of losing a trainer. Thank you to him. And to Roald Dahl, who helped me not to be scared of books.

I found writing immensely difficult, time-consuming and dull. Thank goodness for the keyboard and the spellcheck. Without which that sentence would have read – thnak goondess for the keebord and spellcheque. When I did manage to write something it was usually sent back covered in red ink as the spelling mistakes and poor handwriting were picked apart by teachers not sufficiently interested in what I was trying to tell them. Only a sliver more precociousness on my part would have seen me send their marking back with a D minus for missing the point of children. I think if I took a sample of my handwriting to one of those people who claim they can tell you all about yourself from the way you hold a pen, their main conclusion would be that whoever's scribblings were gouged into the page before them must hate writing with a passion. That and I'm a Taurus with a mild fear of spiders. Give me a hostile audience, drunk and baying for a comedian's scalp, and I'm at home – offer me a landing card on a plane and I get palpitations and sweaty palms. I have, on occasion, been sufficiently tense at the thought of writing that I have cracked Bic biros between my fingers. I get through most books at the same speed as if I were reading them aloud. It's one thing to move your lips when you read, and another entirely to do it so fast that people think you're chewing a wasp.

If the truth be told, I also move my lips when I write. It's because I imagine telling you what I'm thinking. The point of mentioning any of this tragic dyslexic (very hard word to spell, by the way) tale of woe is that I find reading books like *The God Delusion* challenging and hard. I don't mind that, but it means my expectations are high. I want any book I read to reveal great ideas and open doors to new thoughts. It's pretty unfair on the writers but there it is.

I like clever people. I am drawn to them and find that the way they are able to inspire me usually outweighs the nagging fear that with their superior intelligence they are capable at any moment of turning on me and exposing my shameful lack of knowledge on any range of subjects. I like Professor Dawkins, though I would advise him to avoid appearing on television at all costs. He's one of those people for whom it does no favours – like Noel Edmonds. I enjoyed *The God Delusion* and felt excited by the forward motion it seemed to give to secular thinking. Also it pissed me off and I felt awkward about reading it on the train, so I hid it within the pages of a pornographic magazine.

It's not the good professor's fault. Dawkins seeks only to make himself clear in his book, and he succeeds. Coming across as smug doesn't necessarily matter if the argument is clear. It mattered to me, though. In terms of making a case that there isn't and never was a God, his *Greatest Show on Earth* is much better. It marvels in what there is to believe in, because we know these things to be true, rather than rummaging through reasons not to believe or seeking to dissuade those who do. *The God Delusion* is clear and straightforward. For some reason, though, when I try to recall what I actually read in the book, I hear Richard Dawkins's thin voice saying, 'When I woke up this morning, I realized I was cleverer and better than anyone else I'd ever met in my entire life. So there didn't seem any point being nice or polite to anybody. Just insist and insist and insist and insist that I was absolutely correct. Earlier I saw myself in the mirror and I thought, ooh, he looks clever, but not as clever as I am. Me me me me me . . .'

Every movement needs a leader. Please, imaginary friend up there in the sky, don't let it be Dawkins. That said, I have enjoyed pasting pages of *The God Delusion* into copies of the Gideon's Bible in hotel room drawers. Just to provide a bit of balance and to give lonely businessmen a chance to consider theology and its alternatives between weepy sessions of self-hating onanism and three 'final' visits to the mini bar.

In my quest for something to help shove the doubts in my mind into a neat and easily disposable heap, I read several books, including the Bible (Various), *God* (Alexander Waugh), *The End of Faith* and *A Letter to a Christian Nation* (Sam Harris), *The Persistence of Faith* (Jonathan Sacks), the Qur'an (the Prophet Mohammed and Allah), *His Dark Materials* (Philip Pullman), several A.C. Grayling books and most of the internet. One book that made a huge impact on me was *God is Not Great* by Christopher Hitchens. It's an angry, uncompromising book with not a single punch pulled. Even Gandhi gets a royal arse-kicking in *God is Not Great*. It's as bold and rigorous as you'd hope for from a writer like Hitchens. It's rare you pick up a book and find yourself pausing to look up from the page and tell a stranger on the train, 'Wow, Mother Teresa, eh? What a bitch!'

In many ways it's similar to *The God Delusion* only much, much drunker. Reading *God is Not Great* you get the image of Hitchens, a staggeringly intelligent man, pissed off his nut, challenging God to a fight. His blond, wine-soaked, think-all-you-can buffet of a head thrown backwards as he bellows up at the heavens, 'Come on, you belligerent swine, I'll fight you, you big barbarous fucker.' Which is insane, because if we know one thing about God it's that He moves in mysterious ways. Which I've always taken to mean He probably knows Kung Fu. If God turns out to be Vishnu, then Hitchens is in real trouble. Six arms will mean He can get Hitchens in a headlock and punch him, tweak him, flick him and ruffle him all at once whilst still reading to him from *The Book of Mormon* (a book that makes Bret Easton Ellis's *American Psycho* seem reasonable and sane).

I don't wish to undermine *God is Not Great* or *The God Delusion*. They're well worth the read regardless of what you believe (as are all the other titles I mentioned). For those of you who haven't read them, I'll very briefly attempt to summarize them. My perception of what they are seeking to do is to ask the reader to imagine the scales of good and bad standing before you. Can you see them? Yes? Good. Then they place religion into these scales and using science, history, evidence, philosophy and cultural reference points, they demonstrate how time and time again religion has tipped these scales into the bad. They show, for example, how mankind has turned to religion when we'd have been better off facing the issues directly in front of us. They show how religion has hindered advances in education and science. They show how religion has led us time and time again into appalling acts of violence. They even go so far as to suggest that religion may be holding us back from our next big evolutionary step. All of which is brilliantly well argued in both of these books ... until you realize that you can replace the word 'religion' with the word 'alcohol'. And unfortunately all the same arguments stack up in pretty much the same ways.

When you realize how many of the same needs, fears and desires are satisfied by alcohol as are by religion, your perspective on the relative shortcomings of each changes. Unless you're drunk when the realization hits you, then your perspective on the relative shortcomings of each is overtaken by rapidly alternating optimism and shouty paranoia underpinned by a mysterious and persistent desire for a kebab. Alcohol is a fruity poison we consume in order to escape from the realities, apprehensions, anxieties, mundanities and frustrations of our lives. Religion is a fruity poison we consume in order to escape from the same realities, apprehensions, anxieties, mundanities and frustrations, with the added bonus of eternal salvation and fewer hangovers. Poison may be too strong a word for alcohol; much of it is delicious. Either religion or alcohol are perfectly reasonable things to turn to in the face of trials like parenthood, having a job, not having a job, Friday, getting married, breaking up, Saturday, Christmas, death, Tuesday, passing or failing an exam, Wednesday, a parking ticket, an awkward dinner party, running the USSR . . . Almost anything apart from driving. Never pray and drive. Nominate a designated driver if you go out on the pray. Trust me, when you see flowers by the side of a road, you can be certain that, somewhere in that tragedy, someone was praying or drinking or both. They amount to the same thing really. They're both repetitive, mumbly and involve having conversations with people who aren't there. In the UK we have a very special relationship with drinking where even getting drunk will often be celebrated the next day by getting drunk again.

I'm not suggesting that alcohol can't facilitate tremendous fun, unless you drink in Wetherspoons, but the sense of community, friendship and the optimism associated with social drinking is remarkably similar to that provided by religion, and the associated feelings of guilt share more than a passing resemblance too. It's about finding temporary escape hatches from this reality. Booze, drugs, sex and religion slide back the bolt and for a while they throw open the door to somewhere else and we wriggle through to wander around in the space beyond because it feels like it might just be carefree or full of promise or something. It's different and that's what's important, a sense of something other. We drink and we pray and we imagine it all makes sense.

There's a film I saw online called *The Four Horsemen*. It's a two-hour discussion between four leading atheist thinkers, Christopher Hitchens, Daniel Dennett, Sam Harris and Richard Dawkins, in which they take religious ideology over an assault course of advanced secular thought, observing with glee as monotheistic superstition struggles to heave its elderly gut over even the smallest hurdles of reason and evidence. It's fascinating and provocative. It's exciting to watch and the clarity of expression and boldness of thought are stimulating. During the film, in which they dissect why in this day and age, given all that we now know, anyone would choose to escape from this reality into something so patently absurd as religious belief, they all appear to be drinking alcohol. One of them drinks quite a lot of it and smokes consistently; two of them seem to be drinking quite fruity-looking cocktails. None of them comments on it. Perhaps it isn't important at all. It struck me as a mildly disquieting irony. It's not that I wish they hadn't drunk alcohol during their meeting. I'm not judging it and it certainly doesn't invalidate what the four horsemen have to say about belief and atheism. I'm not a puritan teetotaller tutting my way through life with a puckered mouth like I'm sucking a lump of quicklime. You can be clever – the four of them are. You can be confident and certain of your atheism, but the realities of this life are easier and more fun to navigate if you open the escape hatch and get squiffy from time to time. To sit and talk about God with any three of these intimidatingly brilliant minds for a couple of hours would be a privilege but one best enjoyed with some lubrication and followed by a nice lie-down.

The similarities between religious observance and getting drunk are obvious if a little glib. Notice them and it's amazing how quickly you go from being a curious well-read atheist to a rather dull sober person standing in the corner of the pub asking, 'Have you read *The Beer Delusion*? It's very good. That's why I only drink digital beer from my iPhone. Wow, I'm lonely. Scotch and a Bible, please, barkeep.'

God and alcohol have a massive amount in common. Most drinkers and prayers choose to do their worshipping at weekends. You should be frightened of large groups of people worshipping all together, but not as frightened as you should be of individuals worshipping on their own, all the time. Amy Winehouse is the high priestess of one of these churches.

I should read more. There might be a book out there with the answers to all the concerns I have. Perhaps a little-known religious text that inspires without needing to fill its followers with fear. A version of the Bible or Qur'an where the role of God is played by someone really nice like Michael Palin or

Monty Don. Perhaps a secular text that speaks to the parts of me left cold by Dawkins, Hitchens and the rest. Maybe a children's book so simple in its ideas that the truth shines from it like the sun. I'll have another go at *The Very Hungry Caterpillar* . . .

But there isn't a book out there with *the* answer in it. There are a few with some of the answer, some with none of the answer and a vast number claiming to have all of the answer. The very best of any of these contains plenty of stuff that should be ignored or rejected because the answer is likely to be different for everyone. For religious people their special book contains the answer but only if they read very selectively and ignore great glaring chunks of nonsense. This is much easier to do if it happens to be the only book you ever read. Even the most fundamental nut jobs who believe the Bible, Qur'an or Torah represents the perfect word of God are left with no choice but to gloss over the hypocrisy and contradictions. They will, of course, insist that it's all true and all perfect until you point out these glaring errors and inconsistencies and then suddenly it's still all true but it's a metaphor.

Every time I've performed the touring show of *God Collar* or talked about these ideas with friends, a great many kindly people have recommended all manner of literary solutions to my quest for serenity, inspiration or whatever it is I think I'm after. 'Marcus, you must read . . . this' or 'I'll tell what convinced me is . . . that'. I've read some of the suggested texts and thanks for the reading list but I'm still neither wholly Holy nor the philosophically fulfilled atheist. I'm still confused and lost but now I have an urge to show off and the worrying feeling that books on faith are like literary crack. Just one more title then you'll quit. A.C. Grayling and one or two other philosophers have helped but I'm quite lazy and the idea of continuing to read books on theology, atheism, faith and philosophy fills me with a sense of dread and a yearning for a really good novel. At this stage I'd be willing to turn to Jilly Cooper to see if some randy jockeys and society hostesses hold the key to the satisfied existence.

I am an atheist by default. I am a moderately well-read atheist, but one without a sense of my secularism serving any real purpose. It's not proactive or positive. I don't feel any better about being an atheist than I do about wearing glasses. I don't find myself particularly keen to be identified with the new, rather dogmatic atheism I see around me. Raise a banner and march to the beat of the big atheist drum if you wish. Fill your days being busy not being a believer and correcting those who are, but I've got stuff I'd like to do.

The reason for this particular contemptuous malaise is that atheism is not a thing. It's an absence of a thing. Atheism can be wonderfully liberating, I suppose, but not on its own. It's as potentially exciting as the blank page, waiting to be filled with whatever the creator chooses. That is wonderful, unless you happen to be a crap artist with a sincere and well-founded fear of what your page might be filled with once you set about colouring it in. That's not a reason to hem in your potential by imposing God on to the scene and ceasing your questioning, but not all of us know what to put there and the blank page holds as much fear for many as it does excitement. For my wonderful daughter any blank surface is an invitation to draw Mummy, Daddy, some fairies, a unicorn and to practise writing her name in different colours. For me a blank page in the morning represents optimism and ambition. A blank page in the afternoon tells me I really need to look at my addiction to Twitter and porn and get some bloody work done. An absence of belief requires you to build a philosophy out of what you can believe in. Atheism is just identifying a sense of 'I'm not that', 'I'm not religious', 'I'm not one of them', 'I don't believe in the same as you'. That's fine as far as it goes, but I don't like fennel. I don't hang out with other anti-fennelists at weekends. I have no desire to get together and sing songs about how we hate the flavour of aniseed-based vegetables. Although I do. Sincerely. I'd be happy to start a Facebook group if I felt I had a constituency of support. I'd be happy to throw in chicory if anyone felt they might join the group if our aims were broader. Salad that tastes of earwax. What the hell is that anyway?

I have the Richard Dawkins website T-shirt – the one with the big red 'A' on it. I'm assured that the big red 'A' stands for Atheist, but whenever I see someone wearing one I'm always curious to see if it has the word 'hole' written on the back. The 'A' T-shirt is supposed to send a message out to passers-by that the wearer in question doesn't believe in God. Ask many church people to pick an atheist out of the crowd and they'll tell you not to look for the big red 'A' but for the pregnant ones with needles hanging out of their arms, smoking and calling

Winston Churchill a twat. Wearing the Atheist T-shirt is a bit like standing up on a train and announcing that you don't watch *EastEnders*. It's somewhat likely to provoke two thoughts amongst everyone else in the carriage. First, why did he need us to know that? Secondly, I wonder if Wellard is still in it. It's irrelevant to most people.

I don't wear my Atheist T-shirt. That said, I have three Pink Floyd T-shirts I wear often and with pride. (Even though I have 'technically' never been a member of Pink Floyd, wearing a fan T-shirt still invests me with the nonsensical feeling of belonging and is my diploma to prove I am a discerning music nerd.) I think it's about subtly advertising the things you might have in common with people you've yet to meet. The big 'A' T-shirt says, 'Hello, I'd like to meet other secularists who recognize the fact that I've read a clever book.' It's a non-believer's response to those people who have the Jesus Fish as a sticker on their car. They are telling other motorists, 'Jesus is my sat nav, please expect a courteous response if you cut me up. Jesus said – turn the other indicator.' The 'A' is supposed to say, 'I am an atheist and I don't need to hide it, thank you very much. I'm proud to let you know that I have made a different decision about life from the one my mother made.' I don't wear my one because I don't need strangers out of context to know that I'm an atheist, and it's a little too big.

For the secular community to come together and press for rationalism, knowledge, learning, science and reason to be held up as the holiest of holies is something I support whole-heartedly. I'll happily wave a flag for more thinking and less guesswork (I'm not totally convinced that waving flags will bring that about but it's a futile gesture and that's just what we need at this time). Even as I waft my flag to and fro I'll do so with the niggling fear that in reality I'm inviting a great many people to experience a truer but ultimately more unhappy life. 'Join us – we're clever and sad. Come on in, the water's really cold . . .' Perhaps we need some coming together in order to bring that about. For a start it would be helpful to know how many of 'us' there are. Counting atheists is what sheep do to fall asleep.

There was a move to convince people in 2011 to put on their census form 'no religion' so that instead of a hilarious acknowledgement that Jedis are here and must be respected ('These are not the statistics you were looking for'), the number of non-religious people becomes a respected group whose agenda, such as it is, must be considered. Every group claims to be under-represented; secularists really are, though . . . Honest, our lives are quite terrible. We have it far worse than everyone else. We're often hunted down by packs of the faithful and openly bullied in the press . . . probably. It would be delightful to see Jedi or Muggle or X-man made official religions by buggering about on the census form, but perhaps if it turned out that the largest group of people who expressed any preference were in fact non-believers then some of the political wind could be taken out of the sails of religious ideologues, leaving the faithful still free to practise as they please but with less collective power. It's not that I wish to see the faithful punished or neutered, but I don't wish for them to assume they speak for a majority they almost certainly don't represent. We wouldn't let Ronald McDonald speak for us in the House of Lords or anywhere else, so why a bishop?

Secularists have as much right to be heard as anyone else, even if as a group their opinions are disparate. I believe that a common goal amongst secularists is to push for humanity as we experience it here and now to be respected, before we consider how to please something that no one can prove is waiting for us when we've finished living. I'll never understand those people who refuse to take the plastic cover off the sofa in case someone important ever wants to sit on it. You sit on it. You bought it, get egg on it, fart into it, lounge on it, make love on it, sleep on it, lose money down the back of it and when it's knackered dump it on someone else's front lawn. Life's for living. You wouldn't spend your life dressed in black tie and remaining still and spotless in your living room just in case someone was preparing a formal dinner in the other room, would you? There simply isn't time. We wear what is practical and get sweaty and creased and covered in gravy as the occasion demands. We are busy living. Bugger pleasing God, let us learn how to please each other and live well. If there's a God to be found anywhere and He had anything to do with making us, then the aim of cherishing life, learning, loving and sucking the marrow out of experience surely would please Him somewhat. Wouldn't it?

Living well seems a good aim, but even with that humanist agenda settled and agreed upon, it's hard to make the case for atheism because in and of itself it's a vacuum. Atheism is an answer to a question which, with better information, we need never have asked in the first place. Atheism is nothing. It does nothing, says nothing and provides nothing. Those nothings are preferable to me, by some margin, to the somethings religion offers, and yet, be it because society tells me it is so or a meme or for some other unfathomable reason, I am searching for something else to believe in.

9

Why not, then?

THIS RELUCTANT ATHEIST WOULD LIKE TO BELIEVE IN God, if only I could, but I couldn't be religious. That is to say I couldn't join any of the major faith groups. I am most familiar with the Abrahamic faiths but I couldn't be a Jew or a Christian or a Muslim because I just don't hate women that much. I really don't hate women at all. If truth be told, I rather like them. Obviously, as a man, I'm often baffled by women. They are strange and exotic and clever and soft and multi tasky and alluring, and there have been at least three I can think of who have made me feel dizzy. They aren't from Venus and we men aren't from Mars. Martians are from Mars, Venetians are from Venus, men are from sheds and women are from shoe shops. The differences between the sexes are pronounced enough for generation after generation of comedians to build entire careers out of playing spot the difference between the two and keeping audiences in thrall to the variations. Sheds and shoes . . . As a comedian I have to pretend to be much more baffled by women than I actually am. Before I worked out what sort of comedian I wanted to be, I was almost contractually bound to say things like 'Oh, where's the clitoris?' The answer is that the clitoris is broadly where you'd expect it to be. The key is to keep poking until you hear a noise. Unless it's ouch, then you're probably in the wrong place. (Of course, in some places where religion is used to its most barbaric effect the clitoris is to be found beneath the scalpel of a maniac zealot, but it's harder to make people laugh with that observation.)

I deliberately used the word hate in my description of why I couldn't be a Jew, Christian or Muslim. It's a very strong word, and I don't use it thoughtlessly. I'm not suggesting that every individual Jew, Christian or Muslim actively hates all women but certainly none of them, man or woman, cares enough about the status of women in the world to address the leaders of their respective faiths to the problem. Perhaps complacency, contempt or ambivalence would have been better words but I think they might very well be worse. If not the people in these faiths, then the structure, culture and history of Judaism, Christianity and Islam seem to me to be deeply contemptuous of women and for that reason the followers of these faiths choose a path I cannot go down. I feel the same way when I see people shopping in Primark. They don't all hate the children and exploited poor people stitching wear-it-once-and-bin-it garments but they don't care enough about them to make a different choice. Amongst the Abrahamic faiths there is a level of misogyny that could make even John McCririck, the racing pundit, say, 'Steady now. The totties have some use!'

They all believe in the same God. Jews, Christians and Muslims all share one God on a sort of aggressive dysfunctional timeshare. Each grouping is convinced they know the only way to get into His affections. Some don't eat pork, some cover their heads, some drink wine and eat wafers or Berocca, some face east to pray, some celebrate Christmas, some dance, some ban dancing, most sing to the Lord, all are sincere and well-meaning and all are afraid of women to some degree or another. Many to a positively phobic and ludicrous extent. They all share the biblically misogynist God of Abraham. Lots of the followers of these faiths don't even know they are praying to the same God/Allah/Yahweh as the others. The linguistic differences between God's names are enough to convince many believers that their version of God is unique and exclusive. He's not. He's common to all of them, the big flirt, and His vanity and possessiveness make Him love the different ways each of them seek to butter Him up. 'Go on, girls, fight over me. Wrestle for Daddy's affection.'

They all believe in exactly the same God and yet these three faiths and their subdivisions have spent almost their entire history warring with each other in one form or another. You open any history book and it will show how war and religion are as intrinsically linked as Ant and Dec. You could have one without the other, but I'm not sure anyone would really see the point. If the main groups can't fight each other because they live too far apart or the match fixtures clash with some other fight they are having, then they just divide up and fight amongst themselves. The faiths are drunken men wandering through a town centre late at night looking for a scrap. If they can't find the much-hated tossers from the next town, they'll simply turn it in on each other. As long as the sincerity of their righteous rage is exorcised through hate and violence, then they seem to be satisfied.

Religious people will fight over almost anything. In a loving and forgiving way, of course. Take two people born in the same community, educated in the same school: they go to the same places, drink in the same pubs, they attend the same church, they read the same Holy Book. But crucially one of those books is printed in Arial font, the other in Times New Roman, and that's it. There's a schism. A fight over the font, which I'm certain must be blasphemous. There then follows a thousand years of bloodshed. 'Don't talk to them, they're Times New Roman Catholics.' This is war. They all say, 'Oh no, ours is a peaceful faith built on charity and forgiveness,' and they mean it too. Until they meet almost anyone who doesn't agree with them and then it's fighty, smashy, kicky punchy all the way. 'Did you come in the side door of the church and sit near the altar? Die, heretic.'

Violence isn't confined to the faithful. The Godless are all too often vile as well. History shows that secularism is no guarantee of sanity, kindness or harmony. But the faithful are more practised at it, and believe they are in the service of a General who can never be brought to justice for leading them. The chain of command between God and man is broken and there's been a dangerous military coup carried out by His self-selected pious lieutenants. In the absence of clear orders from the man upstairs, mankind has had to assume what God would have wanted. And it's war. Reluctantly, it is war. Apologetically, it is war. After long and careful reflection and against all the instincts of those who've had the burden of having to make this difficult decision, it is war. It is always war. In a just world, where the barbaric commander of these forces would make Himself known to us mere mortals dying in His name, He would be tried for war crimes in the court of human rights. It wouldn't work, of course. The rights of humans are of little concern to God. So for now, it's war.

It's important to understand some of the differences between the faith groups, because a lot of them are profound and serious. An obvious one, with special relevance if you live in Northern Ireland, would be Protestants versus Catholics. Protestants and Catholics believe very different things. Different entirely; their whole approach is worlds apart and diametrically opposed. Hence the 'troubles'. Protestants essentially believe that God sent His only son, our lord Jesus Christ, down to earth to die for our sins and that the only way to the Father is through the Son. Whereas Catholics believe something very different. They believe that God sent His only son, our lord Jesus Christ, down to earth to die for our sins. And the only way to the Father is through the Son *via a man in a hat* . . . You see, different entirely. There's no way these two groups could ever share an understanding and so even the most committed pacifist observers can see how it would become important for them to spend decades killing each other and destroying other people's lives in the interim. Stop me if I'm trivializing, won't you? Because some of this shit is important.

I know there are massive social divides between many similar faith groups. There are, of course, important historical differences between Catholics and Protestants in Ireland. Wealthy and callous English Protestants cut deep scars into the hearts and minds of Irish Catholics; they took land and exploited the poor ruthlessly. It's not that none of this is important. It is always worthwhile to understand the context of conflicts like this; however, for many it is the religious divide that matters now. It is the fuel of Catholic or Protestant dogma that keeps the fires of resentment burning and continues to ruin lives.

None of this is helped by the fact that many Catholics have had to stay in unhappy marriages while the Protestants have flitted from partner to partner as their foul lust and fickle hearts demand. That really pisses off the Catholics, many of whom are stuck in loveless marriages with more children than they know what to do with. Even the affairs of Protestants can be done from within the consequence-free debauchery of a condom. Sinners one and all. Henry VIII has much to answer for, the tubby, murdering shag-monster. Of course, there's the money too. One group is rich and powerful. Then history shifts a little and one group is rich and the other powerful. That never lasts because the powerful will usually strip the rich of their riches to make themselves both rich and powerful again, and so it goes on. Then political elites will emerge and the minority will rule the majority because they're propped up from elsewhere, then the majority think bugger that, there's only about ten of them and a million of us, why are they in charge? And somewhere underneath all of that is God. God stirring the pot and making it mean something that it doesn't. God giving people the idea that what they're doing is special. Add God to this mess and soon you have the idea that this perfectly normal, ugly human behaviour, the to-ing and fro-ing of everyday affairs, means something more than just a simple understanding that politics corrodes and people are flawed. We all are and it's OK, but as soon as you add God to the mix then before you know it children are walking to school while parents from the other faith spit on them, throw stuff at them and scream the most foul nonsense because their lot don't get to school via the man in Rome with the red shoes and fancy hat. I'm sorry if you're in it, if you've seen it, if you live it, or have lost a loved one to it, but it's all just bollocks.

If you want to know whose God is best – follow the money. If you want to know who will fight hardest for their God – follow the money. If you want to understand how religion has taken hold to such an extent and with such a merciless grip on so many of us – follow the money. If you want to know which religion does the most for the poor and needy – follow the money. Religion is big business. A lot is at stake. Ever so much more than the souls of the faithful, which are by comparison easy to account for. It's roughly one each and they divide into two sorting trays. Inbox for Heaven, outbox for Hell. Stick a few quid in the collection plate and you're in the inbox. Easy.

Rich, poor, bearded, hatted, remarried, childless or parent to a football team, they all believe in the same God. It doesn't matter how many times I say it, I still find it hard to get my head around that fact. When you look at what's happened culturally and historically, you'd think that all the faiths believed in different ones. To simplify the different approaches of the faiths, I like to imagine God as Birmingham. The large throbbing hub of the Midlands. I think of God as Birmingham and then Judaism and Christianity and Islam are the M40, the M5 and the M6 motorways. They're all going to Birmingham. They will all get you there in the end, they are just different routes. You will take whichever route you were nearest to when you began your journey. I'm sorry, but your belief system is no more profound than that. You may turn off, you may merge with another route, you may even break down on the way and give up on your quest for eternal oneness with the Holy Trinity of Birmingham, Dudley and Blackheath. Your faith and your journey to the one God recognized by Jews, Christians and Muslims is little more than a simple matter of geography. Born in the south-west of England? You're a Christian; to get to God you need the M5 northbound. Born in London? Muslim, take the M40 past Oxford. Jews, you're on the M6, and yes it's a special road made specially for you by God and he's dying to meet you. You are the Scarecrow to God's Dorothy and she's missed you most of all.

I'm not questioning the existence of Birmingham. I couldn't. I've been there. And very much like God, it seems to be where people go when they're dead. You often see people stopping Brummies in the street to enquire, 'Is this the afterlife?'

'No, mate, it's the Bullring shopping centre and over there's the Pallasades and New Street. Fancy a Mr Egg?'

'No, sorry, I thought I was dead. Well, on balance – I'm pleased.'

The Abrahamic faiths all share the same creation story too. It varies only slightly between the religions. It doesn't make any difference whether you think the creation story is fact, myth or metaphor. It makes no difference to the social and cultural impact it's had on mankind. Particularly on the differences between men and women. As we know, the creation story has it that God created Man. On the sixth day God created Man in his own image. In the image of God he created him. He placed Man upon the Earth in the Garden of Eden, which he'd done up all nice for him like a regular Alan Titchmarsh. It's my firm belief that the Garden of Eden had decking and a small pond. God said unto Man, 'You are the king of all you survey. I have created this for you, Man.' And so the Earth was given to Man as a gift, which was nice of God since he'd spent five entire days creating it all. Lucky old Man.

Sadly, as the story relates, it took all of about ten minutes in this tropical paradise with a lovely trellis and pergola before Man was bored. It's a shame, but that's what Man has always been like. A little bit listless, ungrateful and crap. Man had it all on a plate, but like the pillock he is, he was easily distracted and thought there might be something better going on somewhere else. Poor old Man was lonely because the Garden of Eden was really big and there were no flumes, quad bikes or bars. So Man stood there in the Garden of Eden, arms swinging floppily by his naked side, sifting sand through his bare and perfect toes, mumbling, 'This is rubbish. I'm so bored. I want to go windsurfing. How long till you invent windsurfing, God? I should have gone all-inclusive. I knew this would happen. It's like Gran Canaria all over again. I'm lonely.' Well, this put God in a very awkward position. God had bought Man the best toy ever and Man pointed out that it needed batteries . . . And God shuffled his feet and glanced around . . . there was a silence. Some coughing, a quick riffle through the heavenly cupboard and, lo and behold, God thought of just the thing to make His gift to Man more exciting . . . chicks.

So, as an afterthought, a secondary thing. Something that God had apparently not even planned. As little more than a gesture to cheer Man up because Man had become bored and listless, God created Woman. And he put women on the earth, and within about ten minutes women had ruined it for everyone for ever. Thanks, ladies, nice one. It's ruined now. For ever. You did that, girls. On day one! That's some speedy manoeuvring. It was only one tree you were asked not to eat from. Just the one! But oh no, you knew better, because women always do. What is wrong with you? You greedy apple-scrumping whores?

I hope you see what I'm getting at. Fact, myth, metaphor or whatever, that's a shitty starting point for any set of ideas. It was supposed to be a boys' club. God's a boy and that's how He planned it. But as any keen golfer will tell you – let women in and the whole thing turns to crap.

After Eve had disgraced herself with exactly the tools that God had given her to do so, God came down to see what was going on. Even though he had his divine CCTV on the Garden of Eden, he wanted to turn up and shame Woman in person. So God popped down and like a cruel, twatty, power-mad boss who's seen you swiping Pritt Stick from the stationery cupboard and knows it's in your bag and knows you're gonna get fired – he pretended he had no idea what had happened. He said to Woman, 'What have you done?' And Eve was honest and said, 'I've eaten from the one tree . . .' And He said to Man, 'What have you done?' And Adam looked at the floor, then at Woman, then back at the floor, then pointed at Woman and said, 'She made me do it.' And that's how it's remained for evermore. That's how it began. Women wrecked it and God knew they would and because of stupid bloody Woman, we live like this for ever. Cast out and suffering.

I know some women. I've met several over the years and some of them are quite nice. It just cannot be the case that all women are accountable for the downfall of mankind. I once paid a woman to show me her bottom on my stag do but even she didn't strike me as being singularly responsible for the burden of original sin. Come to think of it, she didn't strike me like that at all.

I have a mother, a wife and a daughter, each of whom I love. We don't always get on perfectly. My mother retired from her job as a headmistress some years ago but still likes to practise many of the day-to-day functions of a head teacher with whoever is available to be organized. It's been a long time since she left teaching but to this day, when she enters a room groups of adults and children alike arrange themselves in neat rows, sitting cross-legged on the floor, and as one slowly chant the words 'Good morning, Mrs Brigstocke.' I'm not very good at being told what to do and our agendas clash. My mother is, however, one of a very few head teachers I've met who has never expelled me. My wife falls asleep almost every time we go to the cinema or watch TV, leaving me to discuss what we'd seen with only myself or, worse still, fill in the missing forty minutes of the plot lost to a catnap. She's fascinated by medical horror stories and footage of operations that sicken me. She finds childbirth and all the details of how one passes large babies through small openings thrilling and never tires of discussing this 'miracle'. I'm as grateful to her as anyone could be for the safe arrival of our children but if I never hear about another vaginal tear or partially prolapsed bladder I'll be delighted. My daughter eats at roughly the same pace as an anorexic sloth with a sore tooth, she doesn't listen and she leaves piles of toys lying in places where you're guaranteed to fall over them or impale a bare foot on a bit of Lego. Despite all of these crimes against my person, I still love these women and at no point have I sought to saddle them with an eternal judgement of shame, nor have I cast them out of whatever garden we share. If they touch my CDs, mess with my laptop or interfere with the BBQ, then all bets are off. That's man's stuff, it's not for girls.

The creation story would have us believe that women come second and are to blame for all our ills. They don't and they're not. I can be ungracious and difficult as a son, exhausting and aloof as a husband and inadequate and controlling as a dad, but for my many faults I don't ever treat my daughter, wife or mother as second to me, my father or my son. I can be unbelievably selfish but I apply my disregard for the feelings and needs of others equally to any person I see as an obstacle to my getting what I want, regardless of whether or not they are male or female.

It's glib, of course, and shouldn't need pointing out, but women are equal to men. They are not the same as men and there are things that each is better equipped for but the basic rights of human beings apply equally to both sexes . . . unless you're religious.

In Catholicism, the universal church and largest of the Christian organizations, a woman cannot be Pope. She's not allowed to be Pope no matter how hard she prays and how much everyone is convinced of her goodness. In fact, they do a test. Many people will think I have made this test up for comedic effect, but I haven't. Trust me when I tell you this is true. When I say true, I don't just mean Wikipedia true, I mean 'weird-as-hell, only the Catholics could do it' true.

There is a period after the new Pope is selected and before he is crowned Pope in which a whole range of preparations must be made. Floaty white gowns must be stitched, the stereo in the Pope-mobile must be pimped, the red shoes must be polished and the Pope in waiting must be made ready. He takes a long bath, sound-checks the PA system in St Peter's Square and changes all the stationery so that his name and photo are on the top of all his letters. There is an immense amount of pomp and ceremony that presumably God thinks is important for his chief ambassador on Earth. Part of the preparation includes a few final checks before his Popeness commences waving, mumbling and ignoring sex crimes. One of the most important final checks is to make sure the new Pope isn't a horrid smelly girl. Because that wouldn't do at all. Before the new Pope is allowed to become Pope, he is required under Catholic law to sit naked on a chair with a hole cut out of the seat part of it. Like an old-fashioned commode. This is the part where you think to yourself, bollocks. Well, it has a lot to do with them but it happens to be true. The Pope sits naked on the special holy holey chair and is then carried aloft through the Vatican with his bits protruding beneath like a tiny turkey hanging in the butcher's window. The chair is carried to a special ceremonial place and then they stop. The new Pope must feel terribly exposed, nervous and a little excited. Stationed beneath the commode-style chair is a cardinal with an odd but essential job. He is the honker-in-chief. He must stand beneath the chair and, without looking up, because that would be weird and possibly hazardous, he must put his hand above his head and feel the Pope-to-be as his bits and pieces dangle just millimetres from the roof of the cardinal's hat. The cardinal must delicately probe with his fingertips to check that the inductee into the papal hall of fame has all the things you might expect a person to have when they are about to take on a job exclusively available to men. I presume the cardinal is allowed to make a honking noise upon contact. You're not really alive if you can resist the *honk* sound when giving someone's bits a tweak, are you? The temptation for the new Pope to play a practical joke at this stage must be overwhelming. He could dangle anything down there for his cardinal to squeeze, a selection of berries and a banana, some holly, perhaps even a balloon filled with custard. I think that hanging mistletoe would make for a particularly amusing and awkward scene, but I suppose overcoming the temptation to piss about like a teenager is one of the key differences between the Pope and me.

So Cardinal Honker reaches up above his head to check that the new Pope has balls and willy. It's an odd job for the cleric, of course, because usually if a Catholic priest is fondling genitals they have to bend down to reach them.

Once the test is completed and it has been confirmed that the new Pope has divine outsidey boy's bits rather than horrible, sin-filled, insidey girl's bits, they can carry on and the freshly honked Pope is allowed to lead the universal church in whichever direction he sees fit. That direction is always the same as the last Pope took it in. The Catholic Church is into many things and none of them is change. Catholicism has the clerical equivalent to a nut allergy – even a small exposure to change and the whole thing goes into anaphylactic shock, tongues swell up and people fall on the beautifully marbled floor gasping for air.

Why do they carry out this weird-as-hell, fetishistic test?

Well, they do this because they once accidentally had a female Pope and it nearly destroyed the Catholic Church. She was called Pope Joan and is thought to have done her Poping around AD850. She may never have existed, or at least never been Pope, but the idea of a girly Pope is enough to make the Vatican very nervous. Why? Because you couldn't possibly have a woman in charge of anything that important. Think what they might do . . . I mean, you know what women can be like . . . right, lads? Right? Who's with me? Sadly several billion people are 'with me' on this preposterous, outdated and monstrously bigoted view of the unfairer sex.

In the Church of England, a woman is not allowed to be a bishop. They argue about it constantly, which is a good sign, I suppose, but the pace of change is still slower than a goth on his way to a swimming gala. At present a woman is not allowed to be a bishop because that would be too upsetting. The idea of it is just too unsettling for most people, so for now a woman can't be a bishop. In the UK, regardless of what you are, man, woman or fascinating third category, if you are clever enough or work hard enough you can get pretty much any job. It's still much harder for women, but officially you cannot prevent someone from having a job on the basis that they are not a man. Broadly speaking, I suspect that's a good thing and for most people in the UK it's regarded as an important right. But not in the Church of England. In the Church of *England* if you're a woman you cannot be a bishop because God's OK with divorce, abortions and condoms but women are still pretty grim and not to be trusted. This sexist

GOD COLLAR

nonsense is the view currently held by the Church of England, of which the Queen is head . . . Well, as long as that all makes sense to everyone, then on we go. I'm not C of E. I am 'of E' though, even if I don't go to C, so perhaps none of this is my business, but that seems, if you'll pardon my language, fucking stupid and childish.

A woman can't be a bishop, that would be too weird, but, because women have been so very good, what with doing the flowers and playing the organ in church and stuff, they can now be the local vicar. In most places this is regarded with a great deal of suspicion and the female vicar starts her job from well behind the place a man might, despite having done nothing wrong other than to have been clumsy enough to have been born with a womb. This is the way with new things and women vicars are relatively new to most people, so you can understand an element of cautious appraisal before trust can be built. For many Anglicans it's a question of turning up to have a look and then deciding – nope, she's not Dawn French, this ain't Dibley and the whole thing is awful. If she's not a funny chocoholic with mythically large breasts, then it's never going to work. Women vicars, and perhaps soon women bishops, are finding ways into ministry because that's the way things are going. Any progress on this issue is good news and should be encouraged, but it is by no means with the backing of the overwhelming majority of Anglicans, and in much of the Commonwealth is regarded as a massive 'Up yours' to God and the Church. There've been a few high-profile defections to Catholicism from the Church of England over this issue; the Pope having furtively offered a special place in his gang for any C of E worshippers who felt that misogyny had been diluted by political correctness gone mad.

It says in the Bible somewhere that women shouldn't be allowed to preach, but it says a lot in the Bible, most of which is ignored by absolutely everyone. The Bible was written by powerful men, rewritten by more powerful men and then translated and rewritten by unbelievably powerful men. It is possible that keeping women in their 'place' might have suited these men better than it did the God they claimed to represent.

Sexism is hard-wired into all these faiths. Observant male Jews are required within their faith to wake up every morning and thank their God they are neither a gentile nor a woman. There's a nice way to begin your day. 'Morning, God, just me ... Thanks for not making me a woman, we'd all have hated that, what with them being not as good as men and everything. Nice gag with the periods by the way – they don't like them, do they?' What a horrible way to begin your day. It's one thing to enjoy who you are and be thankful for the experiences available to you, but to dedicate pre-breakfast gratitude to God for having dodged the girly bullet is foul. Then you don't even get to cheer yourself up with a bacon sandwich. Because of some outdated piggy-wig rules. I'd hate to have breakfast in a religious Jewish house. Imagine the tension over the porkless table.

'Did you remember to thank God for making you better than me, darling?'

'Yes, darling, I did. How long will you be away for the next time you are unclean?'

Some Jews are so confused by women and their place in the world that they make love with their partners through a hole in the sheet. The woman lies beneath a sheet with a hole cut out near her vagina and then the man pokes his penis through the hole and with a minimum of fuss gets the vile deed over and done with. No contact, that's the best way to show someone you love them. I've heard of public toilet partition 'glory holes' with more romance attached to them than that. I can see as a form of seductive foreplay there might be some appeal in the whole hiding-away thing and only genital contact, but it must make foreplay very tricky indeed. I'm not clear on what the rules are here. Are you allowed to put anything else through the hole? How can you be sure it's your partner on the other side of the sheet? She might pop out to the shops and leave a warm apple pie under there.

Muslim men put their women in bags when they go out in public! Like potatoes! They just pop a big cloth bag over their head and off they go. I'm not sure how all that works either. There's very little indication in the Qur'an that a woman should be treated like a racehorse being led into the stalls. Perhaps it all starts when you get married. The Islamic man stands facing his blushing bride (we'll leave out whether or not she wants to be there or how old she is for now), and as soon as they are married, the Imam says to the bloke, 'Would you like a bag with that, sir?'

'Oh, yes please.'

And bang – the burka goes straight over his wife's head like a massive degrading condom. Who knows if he ever even sees her again? If he really loves her he'll cut an eyehole out of the bit where her face is so she can make sure she stays ten metres behind him when they're walking down the road. Muslims, how dare you? Seriously, how dare you do that to a fellow human being? It may be none of my business as an infidel kafir, and that's fine, but it's why I'm not a Muslim. It's why when your fellow believers blow up a bus in the name of your shared God, I'm less shocked than I should be because I already know they hold over half of the world's population in such low esteem they can't even bear for their faces to be seen in public.

Both mothers and fathers encourage this ugly stupidity. I don't care if it's cultural, religious or an elaborate prank where in reality they are all pretending to be Batman. Is that really what God wants? Women in bags? Bags are for things, not for people. Grow up, Muslims. If you were out for a walk one day and I happened to see your wife's hair – the chances are I wouldn't have an orgasm. That only ever happened once and I don't take that bus route any more.

I've heard a few women sing the praises of the jilbab, nikab, burka and all the rest, claiming that the anonymity these garments provide is a relief from the ogling eyes of men. Proof that a person can both flatter and demean themselves in the same thought. How low a view of Allah's creation must these people have if they think making half the world shuffle about in a tent is the only way to defeat the urges of man? A member of the opposite sex might well find you attractive if he can see you. Does it insult Allah though? Does the behaviour it might lead to offend God? I don't think so. These coverings were a man's idea and it's men who keep the 'tradition' alive. It might well suit many women to hide themselves away from the world, there may even be good reasons to do so, but I've yet to hear one that explains why all women should be kept in bags. Certainly there are many ways to stop men from looking at you and finding you attractive, but eating disorders, self-harm, agoraphobia and head-to-toe cloth Dalek outfits are not, in this humble infidel's opinion, healthy or good ones. The covering up of Muslim women is justified by many people in many different ways, but the essential driving force behind it is this – a woman belongs to a man and should not be seen by other men. It's slavery.

If there are any veiled Muslim women reading this (if attendance by veiled Muslims at my touring comedy show is anything to go by, I doubt it), if this is one of the rare occasions you've been allowed by your husband or father to look at a book like this, and you choose to wear a veil, then go ahead, knock yourselves out. Possibly a poor choice of words, 'knock yourselves out', as I imagine that's one of the pitfalls of not being able to see where you're going half the time. You might well wear the veil because it's your choice. It's up to you. I've often been told that no one is forcing Islamic women to cover up like that but I think it's worth asking the question: what would dad, brother, hubby, uncle, Imam or the rest of the insular community say if your 'choice' was to go without? I wear trousers and shoes to collect my children from school. That's my choice, but let's not pretend there aren't social pressures at work here. They may be legitimate, but the notion of total freedom of choice is relative and to collect my kids in just a pair of pants or worse still in a 4×4 would be socially awkward for me.

On the rare occasions I've played live with Muslim women in the audience it's been affirming and pleasant. Usually it's just the ones wearing the hijab, but occasionally I've played venues where there were girls in a face veil, and at a comedy gig this is wonderful. It's a delight to see them there for a start, but the real bonus comes when they laugh. A little giggle and the veil seems to dance as the exhalation flutters and ripples the cloth. A hearty guffaw will see it lift off the face and float like a butterfly searching out the nectar of comedy in the air before coming to rest again on the face of the mysterious lady beneath. Sometimes from where I stand on stage you might even catch a cheeky glimpse of chin. I like it. Normally I would describe myself as being sexually underwhelmed by the female chin, but once it's taken away from you . . . well, it takes on a whole saucy significance of its own. It's like an ankle to the Victorians. You catch a glimpse, you're not sure, could it really have been a suggestion of chin? Did I just see what I thought I did? Ooh, I wanna get me some chin again. Just a flash. Then you start having bad thoughts. You start imagining things on that chin . . . like your balls. If you're very lucky you get a whole row of Muslim women one after the other and if you can get them to laugh in a coordinated way it's like a Parisian cancan of saucy chin action.

10
Rules

I'M NOT TRYING TO BE OBTUSE, OR NEEDLESSLY OFFENSIVE. I'm not interested in being dangerous or provoking the 'bestseller-list'-inducing fatwa or furore. I said all this on my tour whether there were Muslims in the crowd or not. Like all faiths, the vast majority are clever enough and reasonable enough to take what I say in context, be offended if they choose to be and move on. In any case, the veil issue has next to nothing to do with the Islamic faith. It's politics and it's prejudice and it's bullshit. All the faiths do it to one degree or another. Women always come out of it badly, but it could be any issue. The faithful grab hold of whichever piece of bigotry or hatred they wish to defend, staple it to a tenuous bit of 2,000-year-old scripture and then claim it as part of their belief system.

'This is holy for us now, so you can't touch it.'

None of it matters in the real world and everyone should be and could be free to criticize and analyse it. In any case, I'm not a Muslim, my wife wears what she pleases, including my Pink Floyd T-shirts in bed sometimes. That's not OK, and if you think it is you obviously don't understand how much Floyd mean to their followers . . .

'And so it was written on the fourth album, track three verses one to seven, that the wife of the man of the house of Floyd shall taketh not the garment of praise for the works of our fathers, Mason, Waters, Gilmour and Wright, lest she be scowled at from the Dark Side of the Moon and cast into the eternal bafflement of Ummagumma.'

See, it's in the scriptures and you can't ignore them because they're old and old stuff is always true and always best.

The rules of the faiths are not my rules. The law of the land, I am obliged as a citizen to obey. Some of these laws are derived from religious traditions and many should be challenged. We are fortunate enough to live in a functional democracy and the laws we live by can be changed if the majority choose to demand it. This is not so with religion. It is not democratic, so logic, reason or changed circumstances rarely gain the traction they need to make change acceptable to the institution in question.

There seems little sense in needlessly provoking or offend-ing people because they have or don't have a belief system. But provocation is rarely totally needless, although it may lead to terribly violent conclusions, which I personally would always choose to avoid. But the rules of the church, synagogue or mosque are not my rules and as a non-believer I'm not required to respect them or leave them unchallenged. Translations of the Qur'an tell me I mustn't make images of the Prophet Mohammed. There's been some fuss over precisely this issue with lives lost and blood drawn ... over cartoons. I'm not a Muslim. If you are one, then bully for you, but as a non-Muslim I can draw a picture of the Prophet Mohammed if I wish to. Not very well, I admit that. I'm not very good at drawing. But I could colour him in nicely. I'm good at colouring in, though my lips move when I do it ... I'm not sure what that means. If I had a decent sketch of the Prophet Mohammed, I think I could colour it in beautifully. I wouldn't go over the lines or anything. I have a horrible feeling that for many Islamists that is still a beheading offence, isn't it? I can see them now, gathered around my colouring-in book, shouting and looking cross with upsetting banners threatening to sever the head of the colourer-in. Perhaps they will have been sufficiently offended that they will bring babies in T-shirts and headbands emblazoned with messages supporting the righteous killing of the insulting infidel.

Here's a thought. If you're an offended Islamist, instead of leaping straight for the head-chopping sword, why not do what most of your fellow believers do and *fucking deal with it*! Put on a Cat Stevens record, have a cup of tea and sit down, you shouting, bearded tit. For a long time now, I've wanted to create one of those magic eye pictures of the Prophet Mohammed so that only really patient Muslims will want to kill me. It's the joyful image of a livid, trembling bundle of

Islamic fury squinting at the coloured dots and squiggles with half-crossed eyes. Waiting for the image to reveal itself. And then, as the bearded face of Mohammed appears in a shimmery three-dimensional image on the page, he screams:

'This is blasphemy . . . look!'

And passes the swirly dotted sheet to his Imam to show him what devilry has been perpetrated by the infidel scum. Ten to fifteen minutes later and the Imam still can't see anything but smudges.

'Try to look through the picture, not at it.'

'What?'

'Look beyond it.'

'We're not even supposed to look at it, let alone beyond it . . .'

'No, it's there, I swear to you. Clear as day, it is the Prophet Mohammed, praise be upon him. Try to half-close your eyes.'

'Now I can't see anything. No, wait. I have it. Are you sure it's the Prophet?'

'Yes, brother! Do you see it? Death to the infidel!'

'I think I can see a dolphin . . .'

'What do you mean, a dolphin? It's not a dolphin, it's Mohammed. He has a beard. What sort of dolphin has a beard? Give it back to me.'

These are not my rules.

There was a death sentence decreed upon a British teacher who allowed her class to name a teddy bear Mohammed. I don't think she believed the teddy was an accurate rendering of Allah's chosen messenger on earth. I think if the Prophet had looked like a stuffed children's toy, someone would have made a note of it at the time. I also doubt he would have been taken seriously if he sought to pass on the sacred and final word of the Lord in the form of Teddy Ruxpin. The most popular name in the class by a distance was Mohammed and so the children elected the staggeringly unimaginative moniker 'Mohammed' for the stuffed toy. The teacher agreed with their wishes and the next thing she knew she was in prison with a great many people discussing what to do with her bonce once they'd cleaved it off her body. It's a very good job they never found out the bear's full name was Mohammed the Pooh. It was a bear, get over it.

It's not that I think it's particularly clever or worthwhile to callously offend someone's deeply held beliefs, nor do I disregard the impact of riding roughshod over the rules and traditions of someone else's faith, but that's just it – it's their faith, not mine. Offence is fine, it's good and often useful, it's how we know we care about things, but to be offended does not entitle anyone to anything extra. You don't get to say, 'Well, I'm offended, so now you all have to stop what you're doing.' You're just offended, you'll be OK. Offence is the excellent barometer we use to gauge how much we mind about the things we believe in. Imagine what sort of dull uncaring dolt you'd have to be to never be offended by anything.

Personally I'm offended by blandness. While hundreds of sanctimonious people saw an opportunity to oust Jonathan Ross from the BBC after the Andrew Sachs phone-call disaster, I continued to be offended by the fact that a great many programmes are made with the express purpose of not offending anyone. What motivation for art is that? Imagine a life without any offence – awful. The trouble is blandness, like atheism, isn't cohesive. A lack of offence is very unlikely to bring together thousands of livid people all at once. Imagine if it did, though. I'd like to see tens of thousands of people all complain at once the next time Nicholas Lyndhurst is given his own sitcom . . .

Dear BBC,

I am writing to complain about how little I was affected by the programme I just saw. Not one moment of it offended me in any way at all. I didn't care about what happened, it challenged nothing I believe in, it affected me so little I ended up dribbling on to my own jumper as my body gave up some its functions. I would have been more stimulated if I'd injected morphine directly into my own spinal column. Please stop this sort of vapid, bland, inoffensive, watered-down, beige nonsense.

Yours sincerely

Unaffected of Wandsworth

Offence is yours to take. What you choose to do with it is up to you. How I choose to respond to your objection is up to me. If you're offended by me and I choose to acknowledge your position but decide not to change mine or to moderate my choice of expression, can we still be friends? Or is offence so very important that if I offend you once, then the relationship we had is over? Offence is taken easily by the faithful, on behalf of entities they've never met and people they'll never know. There seems to be an expectation that if a person's religious ideology is offended, this is somehow a greater crime than to offend someone's morals or politics or passions. It isn't, though, is it? There exists in all of the faiths hateful hysteria, ugly and punitive discrimination and lunacy, and some of this offends me. If you don't all stop it, I'll hold my breath. I will. I'll do it. Don't make me because I'll do it . . . I mean it.

I know lots of Christians. They're nice, they're fun, they're witty, they're clever, they wear jumpers and eat yoghurt. All the things you'd hope for from real people. I talk to Christians all the time and we get on well. But whenever I'm talking to a Christian I don't know well, I find myself wondering if they are one of those who have that monologue inside their head. They can chat away to you, a smile on their face and a song in their loving heart, but they're constantly plagued by that question worming its way through their brain . . . What are the gays up to? What are the gays doing now? Are they coming here? Do they want me to be gay? Is it going to be compulsory? Are they getting gayer? I saw Graham Norton on the television; I thought, that's as gay as you can be and then . . . gasp! Alan Carr!

Christians are obsessed with gay people. If you're not gay, it's probably nothing to do with you. If you think you're not gay but you're a man who really likes cock, then yes, there are some things to look at. If you're a Christian woman who thinks of kd lang's bottom and little else, well then, welcome to the sisterhood of lez. If you're none of the above, then shut up and stop worrying what the gays are up to. Most homosexuals are as interested in you as they are in soccer. Which is to say, not that much. Christians are more obsessed with gay people than gay people are, and that is saying something.

The most recent bit of political religious posturing revolves around gay weddings where a man and a man or a woman and a woman can be joined in a civil partnership. The religious argument has it that gay weddings undermine the institution of marriage. Two men getting married to each other because they are in love and wish to commit to that for ever or two women vowing to spend the rest of their lives in a union of love and respect undermines the Christian foundation of marriage. Does it?

Let's see now ... I've been married for nine years. I was with my wife for a long time before we got married. Of course, that was before her promotion to the lofty status of 'wife'. She took on the job as 'girlfriend' originally after seeing a body-language 'situations vacant' advertisement I displayed in a disco. She applied, was accepted and ultimately did so well that the firm put her on probation and she became a 'fiancée'. Eventually after an excellent appraisal and a large company do she was finally promoted to 'wife'.

Now, I would say that marriage has strengthened our relationship and moved us along together in a loving and occasionally equal partnership. We really value it ... but, come to think of it now ... when they brought in civil partnerships, it did undermine the foundations of our commitment to each other. I remember now, it was in the same week that they brought in civil partnerships for same-sex couples, I was in the kitchen listening to the radio telling me about the first two lesbians to marry each other and my wife walked in, and bless my soul if I didn't turn round to the woman who up until then I had been in love with and say:

'I hate you.'

I can only conclude that what had happened is that civil partnerships had undermined the foundations of what we thought we had together. I'm rather embarrassed to admit it now. On one occasion, when I'd recently been thinking about gay men celebrating a wedding anniversary, I inadvertently threw my wife out of an upper-storey window. The only way of explaining that barbaric act is that civil partnerships had somehow undermined the foundations of our married life together and that's what made me do it. It's terrible really. I got in the car and chased the limping, frightened figure of my wife up the road and in the end I ran her over. Thinking about it now, I can only conclude that what had happened was that civil partnerships had undermined the foundations of marriage to such an extent that I had no choice but to end our life together by killing my wife.

If you seriously think that two men getting married, or two women getting married, is a threat to your marriage – then get a divorce. You have nothing worth saving and you need some alone time in which to grow up. Of course, when gay couples divorce, it's proof that marriage and long-term commitment are not for them. When straight couples divorce it's because society (the poofs) has devalued the currency of marriage.

I'm not gay, but I stand shoulder to shoulder with the world's lesbians, gays and bisexuals. Shoulder to shoulder, mind – not behind! No one wants that! You see, that's the kind of harmless idiotic bigotry we want to keep alive. Straightforward bum phobia. Nothing deeper than that. It's odd that when homophobes talk about homosexuality, so much of their focus is on the insertion of penises into bottoms. It's like that's all they can imagine when they think of anyone being gay. There's so much more to gayness than bumming. Even the most cursory Google search will confirm that.

I went to a gay wedding. It was beautiful and fun. One of our closest friends from university married his long-term boyfriend and we were delighted to watch two adults who love each other declare a spoken and written commitment to each other because they see a future in which life without the other doesn't make sense. As far as I know, neither of them is ill and in need of a cure. They may wish to be prayed for, but not so that God steps in and rips out the gay 'cancer' that has made them fall in love with each other. They looked happy. They wore really excellently tailored suits and there was music. Sometimes, when I've heard people talk about same-sex civil partnerships, there is the question, 'Which one's the wife?' I can answer that for you, it's neither or it's both. It's not some deviant copy of a male-female union in which they sort of have to pretend to be like Mummy and Daddy, or none of it makes sense – it's a marriage and it has in common with all proper marriages the only property that is truly important and that is love.

Most of the Christian determination that gayness is wrong and evil comes from the story of Sodom and Gomorrah in Genesis. The story has it that God made man in His image and it then turned out that man was a colossal pervert and just wouldn't stop shagging things. The hotbed for this saucy action was Sodom and Gomorrah – try to picture Amsterdam crossed with Cardiff where the entire population are on a New-Year's-Eve, Viagra-fuelled stag and hen night that lasts for ever. Good times. The rules were if it moved, shag it, if it didn't move, shag it anyway and see if that gets it going. If it still didn't move, nick it, take it home and shag it. God took a rather dim view of Sodom and Gomorrah and decided to destroy it and everyone in it. A shame, as Tesco had just bought land on the outskirts and planned a 24-hour hyper-market to bring employment to the place. There was one man who stood alone against the tide of sexual debauchery and perversion. This man was Lot. He had a wife and he had two young daughters. God favoured Lot, because he wasn't bumming stuff like the rest of them. God sent angels of death down to Sodom and Gomorrah to destroy it utterly. This really pissed Tesco off as that's exactly what they'd planned too. The night before the mass killing, the angels took shelter in Lot's house. Lot let them in and refused to give them up to the men hammering down the door demanding to be allowed to have sex with the angels. Lot refused to let the men bugger the angels. Yay, Lot! Good for you! Nice one, Lot.

Then he offered his two virgin daughters to the men to be raped. He said, no, you cannot have the angels, but I have two daughters here, who are both young virgins. Would you like to have them to rape? Yay! Good for you, Lot! That's the spirit. Offer your children up to be raped. No wonder God favoured Lot. He sounds like an absolute brick. Then he offered up his wife too ... Perhaps there had recently been a spate of civil partnerships and that had undermined the foundations of Lot's marriage to Sarah. The men refused to have sex with Lot's wife. That's just rude, frankly. The man had offered them his wife, for goodness' sake! Surely decorum demands you at least try it. Then the men went away and the next day the angels killed everyone apart from Lot and his wife. Sadly, though, Lot's wife looked back over her shoulder at the genocide in her town and was killed instantly by being turned into a pillar of salt.

From this charming story we can conclude that being gay is wrong. Nothing else to conclude here. Nothing to see. Move along please. Don't be gay. Gayness is bad. God abhors it. Hellfire for the bad gay people. Lot was saved. Hooray for Lot. He wasn't gay and God spared him. Good old Lot went on to be a single parent in what I suspect was one of the most awkwardly dysfunctional families in pre-Christian history.

'Eat up your dinner now.'

'Or what, Dad? You'll offer me up to be raped again?'

'Look, I was under a lot of pressure. OK? I'm sorry. Could you pass the salt, please?'

'Oh, that's right, let's sprinkle some of Mum on our food and then all go out and see if we can't get raped.'

'Wow, you're hostile. Abraham tried to kill his little boy, you know, so think yourself lucky.'

'Piss off, Dad. God may like you, but I think you're an arsehole. And we had to move house. They were building a Tesco there you know. I was down for a Saturday job.'

There are so many strange rules one can take from religious books. Some are followed and thought important, many are not. I'm wearing mixed fabrics right now, which is expressly forbidden in Leviticus. I don't even care, they're comfy, and I haven't offered my children to anyone to be raped, I'm a maverick. Call me immoral if you wish, but I make my own rules. Jesus said, 'It is easier for a camel to pass through the eye of a needle than it is for a rich man to enter the kingdom of Heaven.' Now that may not be a hard and fast rule, but it seems that one of the main aims of being Christian is to enter the kingdom of Heaven. If you remind most wealthy Christians of the 'camel and eye of the needle' statement, they will most likely respond with:

'No, no, it's fine. We'll have the eye of the needle knocked through. I know a little Polish man who did our conservatory. He'll widen the whole eye of the needle up, and we'll get the camel through there no probs. By the time Marek's done with that needle's eye we'll have camels, donkeys and my huge 4×4 charging through in seconds. Now, what time does the kingdom of Heaven open? It'd be nice to get a good seat away from the plebs.'

*

There are some good rules that come from religion. Turning the other cheek seems like a decent idea, though there are only two cheeks to turn so it's still really two strikes and you're out. Unless you include the buttocks, but that can be more provocative than it is forgiving. Personally I quite like the Ten Commandments. As collections of rules go they're not bad and for me some of them are well worth following. That said, I'm sure that mankind had figured most of those out before Moses came back down off the hill with his stone tablets. I have my doubts about humanity, as I've said, but I certainly have that much faith in our species. I don't imagine that people were standing around in clusters, waiting for Moses, just indiscriminately having sex with each other, insulting their parents and murdering each other willy-nilly. Men and women stealing anything that wasn't bolted down, lying about each other's families, screwing each other and eyeing up the neighbour's spouse. The return of Moses with the word of God held in his mighty grip was not met by some biblical version of *The Jeremy Kyle Show*.

'He had sex with my wife!'

'Yes, I did, you whining little bitch. She loved it. By the way, your mum's a slag and a thief.'

'Yes, I know that, of course she is. My mum's always been a tart. Oi! That's my stuff you're nicking!'

'So what? Fwoarrrr, look at your ox! She's gorgeous. I'm having that ox. Look at her. Lovely. Covet covet covet.'

'Oi, look, Moses is back.'

'What's he got there then?'

'New rules apparently. Let's have a look at them, Moses . . .'

Then Moses would reveal the new top ten rules for better living and various looks of horror and disbelief would grip the faces of the assembled murderers, adulterers and thieves as, for the first time in their lives, they realized everything they'd been doing was now off-limits.

'What? We can't do any of it? You are kidding. Have you seen his ox? She's lush.'

'Let's kill Moses!'

'No, no, look at number six.'

'Thou shalt not murder? What? This'll never work.'

There are plenty who would have us believe that without the moral framework suggested by religion, we would be utterly lost to a selfish, violent and monstrous existence. These are usually the same people who give a knowing, self-congratulatory smile when they hear that someone has died of AIDS. 'As ye reap, so shall ye sow.' Yes, and as you dress your vindictive pious bullshit up as some closeness to a loving God, so shall you be alone. These people are wrong. Morality does not belong to the faithful and it never has. People are able to distinguish between what is good and bad because unless we are insane, drunk or a Conservative, we are able to empathize. Empathy is the privilege and the curse of mankind. We are ultimately selfish creatures out to create the best environment for ourselves and our offspring, and yet we are kind enough to know what that means for other people. Even arms dealers cry at funerals. They are oddly comfortable with mass burials, but a funeral for one will often make them shed a tear. If it looks like they can't coax one out, then a tiny sniff on the tear-gas handkerchief will coax the teardrops down their cheeks.

God chose ten rules to pass on to man. Just ten. He could have squeezed another one or two on the bottom of the tablets if He'd tried, but no. He could have used both sides if He'd chosen to. Perhaps He could have added a suggestion that people keeping other people as slaves was not OK, but He didn't. In fairness to God, that might have clashed with the values of the slave-owners whose job it was to get the Bible all written down exactly as it happened. In politics there must be compromise and God was in an awkward coalition government with Man by the time He thought up the commandments and He didn't want to push it. There was no mention of abstaining from child abuse in the ten – hence the current confusion in all of the Abrahamic faiths. Hardly their fault, is it, when God never specifically suggested that adults avoid touching bits with children? Maybe it was on His provisional list along with not driving a donkey on to an ox junction unless your exit is clear, and if you sprinkle when you tinkle please be sweet and wipe the seat. Personally I'd have liked to see some mention of what is an appropriate bonus to award a hard-working city banker. You have to remunerate them somehow or they'll go to the Channel Islands or Bahamas apparently. Off you pop then. A simple 'Thou shalt not give massive bonuses to people who do nothing more than move numbers about and hope they get bigger' would have done it nicely. Perhaps with an added 'Thou shalt pay thine share of the taxes in the country you got the money from, lest ye be known as a selfish greedy bastard and have the front of your shop smashed up by angry taxpayers'.

But He narrowed it down to the ten big, important ones. You'd think if you were choosing just ten you would choose carefully, wouldn't you? But no. He wasted the first four being prissy. He blew 40 per cent of the top ten rules for Man on His own vanity and paranoia. How needy are you, God? He spent the first four commandments essentially telling Man that we'd better bloody love Him or there'd be trouble.

'Thou shalt have no other gods before me, because I bloody hate that. I am your number one God, OK? Who's fabulous? I am! And don't you forget it! Thou shalt not make graven images, because I'm right fussy when it comes to art. I don't know much but I know what I like. Thou shalt not take my name in vain. I mean it, coz that really pisses me off, OK? Don't you dare talk about me like that, you bitch! Ooh, in all my eternity . . . Thou shalt keep one day a week that is special just for me, because, really . . . is that too much to ask? One day? Is that really too much? For me? Your creator? Come on, please. Just for a bit of "me time". I may be God but I have needs too, you know. Ooh, I'm filling up here. Look, the other six days you can do what you like. Except make graven images of me, I know what you're like, you'll give me a big fat arse. I am *never* that old. Oooh, stop it. Don't you talk about me behind my back. I can hear you, you know. Honouring other Gods!? I was here first! I am what I am! I am my own special creation!'

I don't know for sure whether God's that camp, to be honest. In my head, I think God might be Alan Carr. It seems pretty reasonable to conclude that God's a 'friend of Dorothy's', if you think about it. There is quite a lot of evidence to support the idea He's gay. He's highly creative. He only turns up if the music and lighting are exactly right. He wanted to father a child and He couldn't do it himself and He hates women. You tell me what's going on. I have an image of God on day one of the creation, draped in His best kimono, with ruby slippers on His moisturized feet and a very early recording of Judy Garland playing in the background ... resplendent in a throne of mother of pearl, nonchalantly fingering His firmament ... suddenly He leaps to His feet, claps once, throws His hands in the air and screeches, 'Let there be up-lighters!' And lo, there were up-lighters and it was good.

No one knows for sure if God is Arthur or Martha, or whether He has any preference one way or the other. The deliciousness of the irony of God turning out to be gay is too much for me to leave it alone as a thought. It's the moment one of the Westboro Baptist Church 'God Hates Fags' people goes to meet his maker and discovers that not only does God love fags, He is one. Bye bye, hater ... Then Hell turns out to be not so much the eternal burning fire it was made out to be, but a never-ending, compulsory karaoke bar playing songs from the shows.

Some people might find the idea of discussing God's sexual preferences upsetting or base, but to be frank – they started it.

Religious people have much to say about sex. Little of it helpful and almost none of it relevant to this time and density of population. If God prefers one sex to another or one way of doing it to another, then He's in the game and as such it seems perfectly reasonable to ask what, if anything, He prefers himself. There are no other Gods, we are told. We are made in God's image, we are told. God might well be a prodigious wanker.

Religion has involved itself in issues of sex with both theory and practical exams. It has failed and needs a re-sit. Show your workings, religion; most of this looks like plagiarism. A great many religious people claim exclusive insight into what God does and doesn't like in terms of sex. Mainly He hates gays and women, that much is clear. He frowns on masturbation, and though little is mentioned in the major religious texts, I suspect He holds a dim view of mechanical innovations such as the Rampant Rabbit and the Butt Plug. He likes procreation and in most branches of worship the conception of new followers is encouraged. Newly married couples are invited to 'go forth and multiply'. We have. It's not working. There's too many of us because the going forth was easier than we'd anticipated and didn't take long and the multiplying was fun and sexy. Got anything else? 'Go forth and role play'? 'Stay here and experiment'? 'Check into a Travelodge with consenting strangers and for goodness' sake wear a condom'?

Sex is often described as sinful. There's no way of knowing for sure if it actually is, but there seems to be a feeling that anything as enjoyable as that must be wrong somehow. If what

I've read is correct, it was only a few years ago that women discovered that sex might actually involve them too. Obviously for many generations women have 'taken part' in sexual encounters, but it seems they were thought of as little more than the garage in which the shiny boy's car was to be parked. Religion has scorned women's enjoyment of sex and the much-mentioned virgin status of Mary even suggests that if only women could find some way of not dirtying themselves with penises then they could pop out new followers and still be accepted in polite society. Why's it so damn important that Mary was a virgin? The creation of a new life through sex between a man and a woman is brilliant both scientifically speaking and in practice. It even makes for very enjoyable viewing if you're that way inclined. Mary was no better than any other mother for not having done it with Joseph. In fact, between a married couple, it's odd and a bit sinister that they had never managed it. A womb isn't magic and special and full of virtue before sex and then vile and ugly and full of sin afterwards. It's a womb and upon sexual and emotional maturity it is able to facilitate new life if its owner feels inclined to have sex with a man, or turkey baster if the circumstances are different.

Was it important to the story whether or not Joseph was also a virgin? If not, why not? Did it matter to Mary? Was he too experienced and known about Galilee as a bit of a playa? Was Joseph into some weird shit she just wasn't up for? Perhaps she was nervous because he had never done it before and might not know what was supposed to go where. Why is it only a virtue in a woman to have never got it on with a member of the opposite sex? Because the Bible tells us so. Written by intellectuals who found the idea of sexual competition with more virile men too much of a threat, so they rigged the game by loading the girly side of the dice with shame for all eternity. 'You can only be good and nice and virtuous if you come to me untouched by bigger boys who might make me feel inadequate.' Joseph the virgin would make just as good a role model as Mary. His blushing, spotty face would make just as fetching a statue, though I suspect graffiti might become an issue – male virgins aren't seen as innocent and demure and something to be admired; instead they are seen as somewhat desperate and pitiable with the possibility of losing control at the merest whiff of something sexual. Culturally speaking, the constant repetition of Mary's virgin status carries the potential for so much damage to the esteem of women and what their bodies are able to do. I'm not sure that the story would be more helpfully told if Mary was a right old slag who put it about like it was going out of fashion, blowing the inn keeper round the back of the stable in exchange for an extra blanket in the straw, but neither does her virgin status recommend her to me as anyone special.

God is not only fascinated with what we do with our bits and pieces, but with what they look like too. When you consider it, lopping the end off a boy's penis is a very odd thing to do indeed. We don't cut any other bits off; it's just the fore-skin. There is, as far as I know, no tradition in or out of religious practice where an arm, fingertip or eyelid is removed from young men. This excludes those removed by land mines and cluster bombs. Though many of these conflicts are inflamed by religion, it's not strictly a religious rite to have BAE Systems leave one of their goody bags lying about in a playground.

Circumcision is important to two branches of Abrahamic faith, Judaism and Islam. For Jews it is a commandment and for Muslims a religious tradition. If you love God, cut the end off your penis. Must I? I wasn't really thinking of loving God in that way. I had been hoping for more of a platonic arrangement, to be honest. But according to many religious texts, God is adamant that the foreskin must be dispatched as promptly as possible before it offends the almighty. It's not clear what God expects the foreskin might do. Rear up and pull funny faces at Him? It was a condition for Abraham that he must circumcise himself. Perhaps God wasn't satisfied with Abraham's reaction when He demanded that he spill his son Isaac's guts as a prank sacrifice. Even the most barbaric gang initiations don't go as far as Abraham's all-powerful gang leader. Having established that Abraham was like so many eager-to-please, easy-to-bully suck-ups, God thought: Hmmm, I wonder if I can get him to hack the end off his cock? Wow, I'm bored today, I should have taken longer over the creation, I've had nothing to do since, apart from a bit of tinkering and light murder. God explained to Abraham, 'You must take the chosen people into the promised land. I have chosen you, Abraham, to lead the Jews into the land of Israel, but before you do, I would like you to cut the end off your penis using a stone.'

A stone? Wow! Now, my first response to that would be to say, 'No, God, you're all right, the Jews are a smart bunch of lads and lasses, I'm sure they'll find their way into the promised land without having to hammer out my freshly severed foreskin and fashion it into a crude map, so let's just leave my old fella out of this and call it quits, eh?' But Abraham was keen to impress God and God was keen to be impressed, so the sensitive tip of Abraham's presumably sandy knob had to go. Resistance would have been futile anyway, when God sets His mind on something there's no stopping Him until He changes it back again. Most modern therapists would diagnose God as a bipolar, narcissistic, sexually deviant psychopath with violent irrational outbursts, and then written in the margin it would say: *Beyond conventional help – do not fuck with this patient!* So, Abraham's faith and his hand formed a conspiracy against the rest of his being and sought out his trembling and flaccid penis from beneath his robes and placed it against a large flat rock. From limited experience of nerve-racking situations, Abraham's willy would have been retreating up inside his pelvis as fast as it could manage, but to no avail, as Abraham was very clear that his polo-neck-clad member must now move into summer attire and become a Heaven-approved V-neck . . .

Down came the sharpened stone and the rest of what transpired, as some very confused and worried-looking Jews looked on in horror, needs no further description. Suffice to say that, many universes away, an alien making a deal with his own God about the green and purple hood on his spiral appendage looked up at the sky and asked, 'Did you hear that? That sounded a lot like a scream, didn't it? Did you hear a scream? No? Really? Now what was it you wanted me to do to my flangambulous glidnok?'

Abraham was an adult; it will have smarted a bit. Children mind terribly when their genitals are snipped, they cry out in pain, but a fully grown man . . . with no anaesthetic . . . with a stone . . . in the desert . . . Well, when you fully realize that's what the Jews had to go through, even the harshest anti-Semite would have to conclude, 'Israel does belong to them, and frankly if you're willing to do a testicle the same way, you can have a chunk of Syria too.'

When Jews are described as the 'chosen people', I hope for their sake that being chosen amounts to more than a bacon-free, half-cocked poke through a hole in the sheet. Anti-Semitism is a passionate hatred. Violent, ugly and irrational. Having known very few Jews growing up, it was only as an adult that I witnessed anti-Semitic abuse first-hand. I saw an email sent to a Jewish columnist whose writing and muddle-headed opinions I have no time for whatsoever, if truth be known most of what she writes sickens and confuses me, but seeing this email was a shock, doubly so when she explained that this type of threatening craziness was a regular occurrence for many Jews in the media. It made me ask questions about my own relationship with Jewish people. Do I have a view on the Jew? They're often funny, I know that, but what else? Being a Jew can mean many things. It's a faith group and a race (perhaps tribe is a better word, when it's clear it's not being used in a derogatory fashion); for some I know being a Jew is a way of behaving and a preference for certain types of food and little else; for others it's a life sentence. I suppose because I don't believe in God I struggle with the idea of a large group of people defining themselves (at least in part) as 'chosen'. It's not a full-blooded resentment I feel towards that notion but it has the makings of confusion, resistance and piss-taking. I asked a Jewish friend about the whole chosen-people thing and if he thought it was that idea that was fuelling much of the anti-Jewish feeling history has maintained. I said it could be perceived as arrogance. He told me I had it wrong and that it wasn't that the Jews were chosen by God, it was that God had been chosen by the Jews. I told him he wasn't helping and decided not to refer serious questions relating to death, hatred and fear to fellow comedians.

Jews are not special. There are plenty who think they are but they're not. At least no more special than anyone else. They're unique, and interesting, but despite what the Old Testament says, Jews are not special. Some Jews are nice, others are not. Some French people are nice, others are very French indeed. A tragic history, a much-disputed celestial promise and a good recipe for chicken soup are all to be recognized, discussed and respected, but these things do not make Jews special.

Frankly the idea that God called the Jews to one side and told them He was their God exclusively seems to have been profoundly unhelpful to everyone. It's so awkward, for one thing. What did God do? Whisper to the Jews so none of the other tribes could hear? 'I love you lot, you're my favourite ones. Sshh, don't tell the others, they'll be so cross. But really, who can blame me? Look at you lovely people. I ask you to wear little hats, you wear the little hats. I make you schlep across the desert, you schlep. I ask you to lop off your foreskin and, hey presto, you have it done within days of birth. Some of you even use your teeth. I can't help myself – you are some great Jews . . . Listen, for the Goyim, I'm just going to play jokes on them – it'll be our little secret. For these ones here, I'll send a beardy wonder boy to pop out of a virgin, they'll think he's my son, they'll nail him to a cross and never fully understand why. And they'll keep on moving the date of Easter, hilarious. Those ones over there, I'm going to give my final instructions for mankind, my last will and testament, to an illiterate paedophilic goat-herder in a cave. Don't draw him, they'll go bat-shit crazy. Good japes, huh? Only you Jews will be in on the joke. Because I love you so much. Because you're my favourite ones, what I've done is I've set you aside your own piece of land. It's over there amongst all those furious Arabs, good luck!'

God is the worst estate agent in the world ever. Not even Foxtons would take Him on. I know it's wrong to compare the plight of the Palestinian people to someone who's been gazumped, but I'm middle class so it's literally the worst thing I can imagine happening to anybody.

It's by no means only Jews who are circumcised. I think they went first but these days most American men are and almost all male Muslims. You see – the USA and the Islamic world have so much in common. Surely they could find some means of understanding each other . . . If only one American and one Muslim would each take out his penis and, looking into the eyes of the man they claim to have so much enmity towards, say, 'Look, look at my penis. It is the same as your penis, my brother. Ugly, maimed, wrinkly and flaccid. These are our penises. Let us be friends based on a decision that was made to slightly shorten our manhoods before we had any say in the matter.'

Because this story is a personal one I feel I must reveal (albeit only on the page) that I too am circumcised. I thought this was the only version of penis that existed in the world until I went to school aged seven and was puzzled by the number of deformed boys with frankly hideous growths hanging off their bits. Poor lads, I couldn't imagine how they went about their day, let alone managed to have a pee without spraying it all over the place like a broken hydrant. So if you have been reading this feeling uncomfortable about your circumcised penis, you are by no means alone. If you lost yours to some ancient or unsettling religious tradition, then count yourself lucky. I lost mine in a bet. That's the last time I drink in a Wetherspoon.

I don't miss it. I have never sought to track it down and reattach it to my body. I've grown since it was taken off so I doubt it would fit anyway. I believe it's somewhere in Guildford. For all I know the Post Office have it and are using it to bundle letters together before stealing them. I've never experienced phantom limb syndrome with my missing fore-skin. I applied for a grant as an amputee but it was turned down by the council, despite several letters, three pictures and a personal appearance at county hall leading to an arrest for indecent exposure. I said it's not indecent, it's circumcised; I didn't do it to myself. In the end they worried they might be seen as being religiously insensitive so they let me off and I got a special parking badge for partial amputees. So that's nice. It can be a little bit awkward if the warden asks you to show where the disability lies. Don't poke it through if you've got electric windows on your car. You could easily hit the button with your knee and no one wants a second one, do they?

It is claimed that circumcised men lose sensitivity when it comes to sex. I don't recall ever having got halfway through intercourse and losing interest because my broken penis just wasn't feeling it. I did once stop for a slice of pie but I think that has more to do with the eternal excellence of pie than a dull cock.

My circumcision had nothing to do with religion. Unless my parents have done a spectacular job of concealing our Judaism. I'm told the reason I was circumcised is simply that all the male Brigstockes have been 'done' for several genera-tions. We're just one of those families. We all also have the middle name Owen ... for anyone who wanted a moment's relief from the constant references to penises (penii?). The practicalities of it and the medical thinking for or against it seem not to have made much difference to those who elect to do it to their offspring or themselves, but the religious tradition fascinates me.

We're told that man is made in God's image. So is God circumcised? Is the foreskin the one mistake in God's design for man? Is it the flaw that fascinates and somehow enhances the work of the Lord? If women were asked to nominate one part of a man's body that looks like it may have been placed there in error, if you weren't nominating the entire penis, I'd like to think the foreskin would be quite a strong contender, perhaps along with the male nipple and the appendix. At one of the *God Collar* tour shows, in Norwich, I raised the idea that the only truly superfluous part of a man was probably his foreskin, and a very determined young lady shouted, 'What about the head?' I told her that historically men have had quite enough trouble thinking with our dicks without removing the head altogether. But she seemed adamant the head should go. Trouble at home. I only hope she had enough mercy in her to cut off her partner's head while he slept before doing anything similar to his penis. Turning up at the gym with your head missing might well rate a stare or two in the locker room, but a partially amputated cock will get you mocked.

Man is made in God's image and yet we're told we're supposed to remove one bit of ourselves. Why? Maybe man is made in God's image, but the original model for man came in the form of an Airfix modelling kit. Something I was very keen on as a child. The pieces arrived in a box with a Spitfire on the front and were all held together in a moulded plastic frame. You then had to gently prise the bits off the frame and assemble them in the right order. The trick was to identify the point where the plastic had been attached to the frame and file off the little sticky-out bit that spoiled the look of the finished model. Maybe when God made man we were attached to the frame by the penis and he forgot to file that bit off before putting all the pieces together.

Whichever way you look at them – through the prism of humour, in a court of law, as a drunken debate in the pub with friends, as a motivator for armed conflict in the pub with friends – many of the rules and traditions of the faiths are strange and impractical. So many of the ideas that once served a purpose are now out of date. Perhaps grains of desert sand blowing about under one's robes might once have made a pious man with itchy bits conclude that God was sending a firm message with regard to the foreskin, but that all changed with the invention of elasticated pants. The Qur'an, Bible and Torah should have a 'best before' date stamped on the back and the Old Testament stories a firm 'use by' date, with explicit instructions on how to dispose of it safely. If you think car batteries, paint and fridges make landfill sites unpleasant, wait until you see what pernicious toxins would seep out of a lump of discarded scripture. The question is how long could you leave a religious text before it was unfit for human consumption? With the pace of change in the modern world, I'd suggest that most religious books would have about the same shelf life as a yoghurt.

Any writing that seeks to answer the questions humans are driven to ask has to do it for all time. It must be conservative and speak to an eternal truth. If it doesn't, it will be hard for people to revere it, and the second bestselling book in the world (after *Harry Potter and the Philosopher's Stone*) must be revered or it is nothing. The Qur'an doesn't suggest that women be secondary to men until the rise of feminism, with a footnote suggesting the issue should probably be looked at again at that point. It would be better if it did. That's part of the trouble with insisting that it's the perfect word of God. No edits, redrafts or amendments. The Bible would be vastly improved in my view if it contained a gay love story or two. No pictures, nothing graphic, no ads for Aussie Bum fitted pants or Donna Summer CDs, just an affirmation that any God described as 'Love' is capable of loving any consenting adult couple without resorting to smiting and His tiresome eternal tut. How about a page or two in the Torah where someone's child turned out to be wiser than the parents, as is almost always the case in families where education is cherished?

Copies of 'self-help' books, which sell with such sufficient regularity that I predict the world should be fixed some time later this year, would never catch the eye of the needy and doubtful if their back sleeve promised to 'make you feel better ... for a bit'. 'Overcoming grief for ever' (except weekends when you have more time at home to think about the terrible chasm of sadness left in your life since the death of a loved one). Imagine a Paul McKenna book promising to make you thin ... until you pass your next buffet, then all bets are off unless you also buy Paul McKenna's *Overcoming Buffets*. Come to think of it, I suspect this is exactly how a great many self-help books work. Read this book so you know what's wrong, then buy these books so you understand how buying these books will give you the strength to buy these ones . . .

The promise of the faith books is that the truth they claim to speak is for ever, but as each day passes great chunks of them become less relevant and more often ignored by even the most observant of followers. Overpopulation, capitalism, environmental unsustainability, sexual liberation, education, equal rights, the internet, Cheestrings – while the faithful turn to their beliefs as a refuge from these realities, the truth is that each of these things and many more grind away with persistence and speed at the pillars of 2,000-year-old folk tales and superstitious myths. It's why the Church of England is so often in turmoil. It's more progressive than most of the others, which is to say they move at the same pace as a weary snail with a six-bedroom maisonette on its back, but still faster than the rest. The C of E acknowledgement that the world is not the same as it was this morning blows a big raspberry into the pages of the Bible, and the Bible says nothing in reply because all the people who wrote it are dead.

I know that for a lot of atheists the contradictions of the religious books are off-putting and undermine the case for the existence of God. I'm not interested in whether or not you can prove that God exists; that argument, along with evolution versus not reading enough, is a distraction from what matters to me personally. Is God any good? Are the books these faith groups cling to like driftwood in a raging sea of change worth the paper they're written on? If I signed up tomorrow and ignored the whole issue of proof, would I be electing to follow a way of life that is kinder and more serene than the one I have now? Can the Bible, Qur'an and Torah provide relevant examples of how to lead a better life without immediately undermining those stories with something any thinking person must conclude is steeped in illogical cruelty? The answer seems to be an emphatic no on all counts.

11

Jesus Christ!

I THINK I QUITE LIKE JESUS. HE SEEMS TO HAVE BEEN A NICE sort of fellow, and given the cards he was dealt and the awkwardness of an overbearing and ever-present Father, he did very well indeed. It can't have been easy for him. You only have to look at George Walker Bush to see how badly these things can go wrong. For Christians, Jesus and his teachings are supposed to make up the core of their belief system. They follow Christ and try to live by his suggestions. I think Jesus was a man of peace so obviously there are areas where modern Christians fall down, but a great many of them take the most positive aspects of New Testament teaching and succeed in applying those ideas to modern life. Jesus seems to have been very charismatic, a good speaker, something of a hippy, which I like, and almost certainly a socialist. Jesus managed to put an extraordinarily positive spin on the horrors of the Old

Testament and the excesses of his Father's wild mood swings and extreme behaviour. He was very much the Alastair Campbell of his day.

It's all very well for me to like much of what Christ taught, but I still can't be a Christian because I can't ignore the rest of it. It's a package deal, and to invest something as important as a belief system in it, and alter one's life accordingly, has implications I am not willing to bear. Maybe it's enough to do what any discerning adult with an education is able to do – take what you want and leave the rest. Cherry-pick the best of what Christ sought to do and draw a veil over the mad bits. I discriminate like this all the time. I enjoy my copy of *The Greatest Hits of the Osmonds* but I'm not sure I'd have the strength to listen to all of their albums. Or indeed any of their albums. The same is true of Tom Jones, although my research has shown that Tom Jones has only ever released Greatest Hits collections. Perhaps I should treat Christ like I would the starter section of a Chinese menu. Sure, the mixed starter platter sounds appealing – you get a bit of everything, it takes away the burden of choice and it does include sesame prawn toast, which I like – but when it comes it's always a disappointing collection of shiny, golden, deep-fried nonsense. Much better to do the research, ask the questions and order what you like. I'll have a number 7, a number 9, a love thy neighbour as thyself and the crispy seaweed, please.

The trouble with Christ is that he explicitly endorses the work of his dad (not carpentry, the work of his other dad: the dad Jesus saw for awkward weekend visits to McDonald's before being passed back to his mother). While the New Testament rethinks a lot of the ideas of the Old, it never goes as far as specifically condemning the worst bits. Nor does it seek to explain the extraordinary priorities of the Father. The New Testament doesn't have a line tucked neatly into the Gospels explaining that most of the stories from the Old are metaphorical and were written by men in the spirit of creating a sense of awe for a decrepit, malevolent God they had mistakenly assumed meant well.

The whole issue of metaphor is a very interesting one when it comes to debating scripture and its meaning. Some religious folks will insist that a piece of writing is fact until such time as it's proved to be nonsense and then without the blink of an eye they say, 'Oh well, obviously that bit there is a metaphor.' They play it like a trump card, but it's not. It's lazy and dishonest. At best it's a wild card in one of those irritatingly complicated games where a two means you change direction, queen is miss a turn, a five is pick up six cards and an ace means you have to get a round of drinks in and do the shit-head song. I understand why they do it. It's either that or admit the whole thing is based on a series of decreasingly well-intentioned lies. Switching your view to claim something is meant as a metaphor is no way to win an argument. Neither is war, so given the propensity of religious believers to perpetrate either or both of those two, I'd sooner the metaphor defence, but it's annoying none the less. It feels like arguing with a fish. I'd almost rather they didn't engage with the discussion at all, shove their fingers in their ears and start singing . . .

I am a C . . .

I am a C.H . . .

I am a C.H.R.I.S.T.I.A.N . . .

As science reveals more about our past and present, the position of the devoutly religious becomes more and more difficult to maintain. It's only a matter of time before religious communities are left with no choice but to shout, 'Ta da! Ha ha, joke's on you – the whole thing was a metaphor and we never meant any of it. You're right, we evolved. Sorry, metaphor got out of hand. Back to what you were doing, people.' They'd blush for a bit, see if anyone was buying the deception and move on.

Of course, there are some ridiculously naive people who claim everything in their particular holy book is fact, including the direct contradictions. Fact plus direct contradiction of fact equals fact squared. These people bring out a mean punitive side in me that wants to say, 'Fine, if you are willing to discard the brilliant work of dedicated and enquiring scientific minds, you don't get to use any of the stuff they've invented. Out of your SUV, American Christian dolt – it runs on oil, which we know was formed long before God made the Earth. There were dinosaurs. This we know because there are bits of them in the ground and it means your book begins with a massive lie. The universe is miraculous in its power to inspire but it did not come from a miracle. God did not create people 4,000 years ago because if He had, He'd have been done by the patent office as there were already people here. There had been people here for thousands of years. No more DVDs for you, Mr Creationist! No more toast, computers, aero-planes, rubber soles, cinema, mobile phones, Rampant Rabbits, Cheestrings, roller-skates, mojitos or MRI scans. Scientists either know what they're doing or they don't. Why the hell should you be allowed to ignore what they say on things that don't suit you, like climate change research and evolution, but embrace it wholeheartedly when it comes to cancer treatments and Nintendo Wii? The response, when faced with a life without scientific innovation, would be to fall down weeping and mumble something about it all being a metaphor anyway? Yeah? Well, now you get to play on your metaphorical computer because you sure as hell aren't getting a real one.'

Jesus was noted by historians as having had an impact on a tiny area of the world which, since he died, has spent most of its time at war with its neighbours. A shame, as one of his titles is 'the bringer of peace'. Tony Blair is peace envoy to the Middle East, an apparent parallel he no doubt enjoys as Jesus is his friend. It's one that I enjoy because the irony of it is too delicious not to. If Jesus was the Son of God, then he has succeeded in his Father's challenge to inspire humanity, up to a point. His message has glued communities together and doubt-less fuelled many great acts of kindness and charity. That's good, well done, Jesus, a success . . . apart from those millions of people born somewhere Christ's message has failed to take hold, through no fault of their own. They are condemned. Sorry, no Heaven for you, Mr Chang, you live outside the catchment area. If God was my dad I think I'd have addressed that obvious and glaring problem. I'd have tried my hardest on that one. If failure seemed certain after my best efforts, I would have eaten humble pie and gone up the management chain to the Father (all-knowing, all-seeing, all-powerful creator of all including Muslims, Jews, Buddhists, Atheists, Arsenal fans and Chinese people) and asked for help in rectifying this simple problem. How hard is it to admit that despite working your sockless sandals off, the job's only partially done? How hard is that admission of a problem, compared with say, oh, I don't know . . . being nailed by your hands and feet to a wooden cross? No, I'd have given a little knock on the big shiny door to God's office, shuffled past the 'You don't have to be mad to work here . . . but it helps' poster, smirked at the kitten on a washing line meowing 'Hang in there' and said, 'Dad, sorry to be a pest, but the thing is, I'm not really reaching them all. Don't get me wrong, it's going terribly well, I've already got twelve . . . well, eleven and one who's not sure, but because there aren't planes and conference calls yet I'm not really getting to enough of them. I can see you're busy, God, and the whole walking on water thing is brilliant. Really brilliant, as "convince them I'm from out of town" stunts go, it's a doozy and I'm not complaining. It's just that I can't seem to get that far with it, especially when the sea's choppy. Oh, and I could do with a wash. It's very tricky to get clean. I keep floating on the top of the bath. I mean, don't worry, God, the word is being spread . . . along with a fair whiff of BO . . . Anyway, I digress. I can't reach them all, Dad, can you help? Can we do this again or in duplicate with a brother or sister maybe? What about low-cost miracle travel? EasyPreach? I just think it would be good to somehow get beyond the tiny, parochial bit where I live? I mean, water into wine's great, really great . . . I love wine, who doesn't? John *really* likes wine . . . but the thing is the whole Son of God, messenger, one third of the Trinity, prophet, spread the love, preach the word thing is only getting to about one per cent of the population . . . at best. So . . . well, I can see you're busy. I'll just leave that thought with you . . . because . . . you know . . . a huge number of your people stand no chance of ever knowing that you made them, broke them, then sent me to fix them. Let me know . . . post a message on my wall. Tweet me. Whatever . . . Bye, Dad . . . Wow, you can be aloof . . .'

I'm not talking about making faith easy, or oversimplifying the challenges of a life devoted to God, but couldn't we give newborns an equal chance to compete in the spiritual running race that is this life? Why not do that? Blessed are the children, said Jesus. Blessed are the children, unless they're born over there, then fucked are the children.

Maybe it's no bad thing failing to qualify for the competition rounds to get into Heaven. I'm not sure it's for me anyway. The devil has the best tunes and I'm only going to Heaven if I can take my iPod. 'Only through me shall you enter the Kingdom of Heaven,' said Christ. Yes, and only through Windsor shall you enter Legoland, but I don't want to go there either. The idea of Heaven sounds good, I've described meals, women and holidays as heavenly, but the reality of Christian Heaven, as I understand it, is that there are no gays so the music will be crap, no Jews so the shows will be badly produced and very few Arabs, Asians and Chinese so the food will be bland. I don't want to sit with Jesus at the right hand of God. I suspect that God's right and left hands are both dripping with blood.

I've asked people to explain to me how Jesus' agonizing and humiliating death on the cross is helpful to mankind because I've never understood it. It served as pretty good PR. Maybe it was the last-ditch effort to get the word out beyond the Middle East. It gets people's attention when you tell them the details of how God stood by and watched his only Son die, bleeding and moaning in the sun, racked with pain. But why? I don't understand how Jesus dying like that is supposed to be help-ful. It's the kind of attention-seeking that martyr mothers do at Christmas. They cook everything, clean everything, make everything, wait on everyone hand and foot and then get all cross because they've done the lot. Put your feet up, have a Chocolate Orange and let's sit through the execrable Christmas special of a programme that's usually quite good. It's all very well, but what am I supposed to learn from Jesus dying for my sins? I'm still a sinner. Me and my friends still feel pain and live in turmoil. There was no shift in the fortunes of man when Jesus died. Is his pain greater than a woman drowned in a flood in Bangladesh? Or a child defeated by leukaemia on a hospital ward with pictures of Eeyore's sad place on the wall? Does Christ's death up there on the cross mean that a paedophile is absolved of blame for his or her crime? What? What's it for? It's the end to a good story and it gets my attention. I'm interested. Wait a minute. Please tell me it's not another cryptic metaphor I'm supposed to decode . . .

There's plenty about Christ to enjoy. I'd love to have seen him turn over the tables of the moneylenders in the temple. Direct action and part-time winemaking make for a heady combination and an exciting personality. If he ever did come back he'd have a field day on Wall Street. Sadly as a bearded Arab with a history of sedition and religious extremism, he'd stand no chance of getting past security at JFK, let alone coming anywhere near Wall Street. If he did come back, I fear all the new paintings of him would not be as a gentle melancholic-looking man clad in robes but in an orange boiler suit, crouched in a stress position with a black hood over his head at Gitmo.

Jesus was a friend to the meek and downtrodden, he promoted the redistribution of wealth, he came to heal the sick and to forgive the sinner. He'd make the front cover of the *Daily Mail* at least once a week as the evil face of 'Political Correctness gone mad!' Most of what Jesus stood for, I support, but the family firm is corrupt. There are young people with little choice but to work at McDonald's; some of them are nice, some clever. Most work hard and serve cheap McDonald's food to the best of their ability. In almost every small-town High Street devoid of personality and regional identity, somewhere amongst that desert of hope and ambition there will be the golden arches shining out a message of greedy, faceless corporate blandness. When I see the glowing window display promising happy meal plastic tat and salted fat for my children, I feel anger, then sadness, then hopeless resignation. When I'm hungry I don't want to be offered 'fries with that' because I don't like the company. When I feel needy I don't want to be offered an eternity at the right hand of God because I don't like the company.

It's not Christ's fault that God is such a consistently unpleasant swine. You can't choose your parents, right? But at some stage, given all that has been done in the name of God the Father and his prophets, you have to ask – was Jesus lazy? Careless? Was he inept? Perhaps Jesus was nothing more than unfortunate enough to be terribly naive. Jesus – the McDonald's restaurant drone. Innocently flogging spiritual burgers and fries to those who don't want to know where the sustenance came from in case they see how nasty much of the process and content is.

I can't be a Christian because I'm not willing to add my endorsement to what the church seeks to achieve politically. If you describe yourself as belonging to a faith group, you make it possible for the politically determined elements of that group to cite your membership as tacit approval of their agenda. Participating in a religion is not an aggressive act for most people, it's not cynical or mean-spirited; in fact, for the vast majority it's the opposite of that. Being religious is personal and benevolent. But would you drink in your local pub if you knew the landlord was a homophobe and a sexist? OK, bad example. A boycott on pubs like that in the UK might well mean that only two establishments stayed open and they'd both be on Canal Street in Manchester. Religion is political and the number of followers 'in' one faith or another gives power to those who would seek to exploit it.

It appears to me like a human pyramid. In Christianity, the impressive triangle of political power looks like this. On the bottom, with their feet on the ground, are the rank-and-file believers, churchgoers who occasionally arrange flowers and dabble in light charity work. They are not judgemental or mean or smug, and their faith is as honest as it can be under the circumstances. They enjoy *Thought for the Day* on Radio 4 but like it best when it's a Christian one. One row above them are the ones who are mildly disapproving of the somewhat occasional attendance of the bottom row. The second tier are religiously observant. They pray, sing, attend church, run weekend Bible studies and read the *Daily Mail* without laughing. They don't exactly hate gays but if they ran a Bed and Breakfast the poofs wouldn't get warm toast in the morning. Above them are the 'active' members of the church; they ruthlessly promote their passion for the Christian way of life and would not be in the slightest bit abashed to make it clear that Muslims have it wrong and will go to Hell, as will atheists, but not as fast as the Muslims. They oppose (for example) a woman's right to choose to terminate a pregnancy and think that being gay is a wilful, unhealthy and curable obsession. They are judgemental and cherry-pick from the scriptures to suit the politics they grew up with. Above them, very near the top, are the ones who say, as Stephen Green from Christian Voice did, that the floods in New Orleans were God's just punishment for homosexuality. They promote censorship and ignorance and think that bigotry is part of being a good Christian. They got a hard-on for the conflicts in Iraq and Afghanistan because the 'goodies' had better guns. On their shoulders are the violent few willing to kill for God. Christianity has already done most of its wholesale killing. It scratched that itch with the Crusades. Plenty of Christians still kill people of other faiths but it's more recreational now and they don't march so obviously under the loving Cross of Jesus.

The same system works in all the faiths. Bottom-rung ordinary Muslims, praying to Mecca and trying to be good, carry on their shoulders teetotal, wife-hiding, bearded zealots. Above them are the livid US-flag-burning, madrassa-educated, evolution-denying nutters, who in turn bear the weight of Islamists, who find an educated woman an insult to Allah and praise the idea of violent jihad, usually too scared to actually blow themselves up but if they know anyone with special needs or educationally subnormal they might have a bash at talking them into it. Teetering on the top are the likes of the Al Qaida murderers and their brothers around the world. Not Bin Laden, though. I suspect he wasn't a Muslim at all but a spoiled little rich kid with 'issues' he needed to look at. A lot like his warmongering nemesis George W. Bush.

If the bottom rung walked away and decided that with or without faith the religion they belong to was too corroded by power, then the whole ugly mess would begin to crumble. Where would Hezbollah recruit from if most Muslims decided that any connection to the violent political power of Islam was not for them? Where would Israeli Jews find the justification to treat Palestinians like so many of them do? Would Christians succeed in quietly persecuting women and gays? On the shoulders of the kindest, best-intentioned, gentle believers stand row upon row of increasingly nasty people with 'unquestionable' ethics, ancient books which they 'know' to be true and a very quiet God who likes to leave most of His ideas open to interpretation and metaphor.

These power structures are not unique to religion. Most democracies work in a similar way, but crucially in a functioning democracy change is always possible, freedom is generally cherished and old ideas sometimes pass away because the process is at least structurally able to consider new ideas. I sometimes imagine the most loony religious barbarians trying to foster support without the fear-filled power of the religious myths they exploit . . .

'Who here wants to fly a plane into the Twin Towers in New York?'

'Shut up, you wizened old bollock. No way. I'd die and I suspect loads of other people would too. You'd have to be insane to do that. Why would you suggest such a stupid and horrible idea? What's that bloody book you're reading? Eh? Here, have a look at this one, it's got a fella named Boo Radley in it.'

It's not that the atrocities of religious extremists are the fault of ordinary believers. But they do, to some extent, belong to the same group as the perpetrators of hate and fear. They do provide the platform upon which the nutters will stand until someone daft enough comes along and becomes willing to do something very unpleasant on the promise of a favourable audience with the big man after they've gone. It's all connected, and it all puts me off.

None of us is above these connected webs of corrupted thought. Religious or otherwise, you can't live a totally clean life. Not without opting out of the whole system of modern living and shuffling off to live as a carbon-neutral subsistence-farming hermit in a yurt. Even with that simple, turnip-heavy existence you'd be denying one of the core parts of the human experience – other humans and the negotiation of the social life. You can be moral and strive for the ethical existence but something you buy, eat, ride on or watch will be tainted by decisions you are not connected to. Morals vary and are usually dependent on budgets. A few rich people live 'well' and are generous or philanthropic. They are lucky; they have time and resources to be good. Some poor people are so lacking in the fundamental basics the rest of us take for granted that there simply isn't time for them to fall short of their own or anyone else's standards. They are lucky; they don't have time or resources to be bad. Most people fall between these extremes and do the best they can with what they have. Apart from arms, drug and debt-bond dealers – they're just arseholes.

I choose to bank with an 'ethical' bank, having discovered that my previous bank, Barclays, had made loans to senior figures in the Mugabe regime in Zimbabwe. I didn't like that, so I took the moral high ground, I acted on principle, I decided not to care how much work it took to change every payment, account, standing order, card and the rest, and I did the decent thing: I got my wife to move all our accounts to the Co-op. It was exhausting and complicated ... apparently. It's very tiring being good. The important thing is I did the right thing. Now Barclays sponsor bikes and cycle lanes all over London. I like that. The yin and yang of corporate responsibility.

Most people's money ends up being connected in one way or another to the arms, tobacco and oil industries. I wish it didn't, but the way we trade with the rest of the world means that even a simple transaction – for instance, £2 for a sandwich – is the end point of a number of strands that when unravelled will see all manner of evils spill out over the floor like puke on a night bus. The bread for the sandwich comes from wheat that has been contaminated by genetically modified crops, made by a company that engineers prices in the developing world and keeps people poor in order to make more profit. The baker has shares in BAE Systems and likes running over bunny rabbits in his tractor. The mayonnaise comes from battery chicken eggs from a farm whose accounts are in the Channel Islands providing finance for a bank that gives indirect loans to gunrunners who arm Somali pirates who murder people with them. The ham is from Denmark when there are pig farms in the UK struggling to get by. These Danish pigs are intensively farmed by a man so incensed by the Prophet Mohammed cartoon incident he has now joined a far-right organization planning to fire-bomb a mosque. The packaging will last so long on a landfill site that my great-great-great-great-grandson could still use it as a perfectly serviceable sandwich wrapper, and the guy selling the sandwich likes Justin Bieber.

One moment you were hungry, the next you have almost guaranteed the wholesale destruction of the world. There's no avoiding it.

I wish it were simpler but it's not, so you accept these facts and do the best you can with what you have. There are restaurant chains I choose not to eat in because of the impact of the way they farm and transport food, but I've eaten lamb from New Zealand whilst in Wales. I buy free-range chicken, but even the lightest push in the direction of Nando's sees me indulge that guilty pleasure with lashings of piri-piri sauce to hide the taste of shame in my mouth. I enjoy foie gras but I don't eat veal. I try to reuse the things I have but whenever Apple or Paul Smith make something new, I get excited and often buy it regardless of duplication, necessity or self-awareness. The point being, I like Christ and I'm no better than many Christians but I can't join their church because there's too much about their politics that makes me shudder. I can't be a Muslim because I like to see my wife's face when she tells me the amazing things she knows and the Jews don't want new members anyway. I won't be part of the pyramid. If I was in there I'd choose to hide somewhere near the middle row, then I'd wobble about like a circus clown with a bee in my oversized pants.

A person's individual faith is just that. It's personal and shouldn't be attacked. To identify with God as He is presented and to belong to a group that shares a similar reverence must feel good. Very few people, if any, choose to be Shi'ite or orthodox Jew or Lutheran in order to further the political aims of their church; but that is what it does. Many join a faith as a child, inheriting the beliefs of their parents, and without questioning it become a small piece of statistical evidence that 'most people' don't want evolution taught in schools, or that gay marriage shouldn't be allowed, or that women should be kept in their place, or that something violent should be done to youngsters who put empty Tango cans in hedges . . .

I think that for the vast majority of ordinary believers the act of faithfulness is largely apolitical. I am a UK taxpayer and as such I subsidize all manner of political acts I do not approve of. Perhaps if I had the courage of my convictions I would opt out and refuse to pay tax because I don't want to see my money spent making houses explode in the Middle East or secreting nuclear warheads on to Scottish submarines or paying for floating duck islands. I don't do that because I suspect that, just like the believer, I see the greater good served by what I choose to involve myself in. The charity and generosity of spirit embodied by most ordinary believers of any faith is what most are choosing to identify with. The hospitals and schools I pay for with my tax contributions are things I'm proud to support. To be religious in any of the Abrahamic faiths is not to be a homophobe, sexist, racist, intolerant bully or idiotic barrier to education, but on the shoulders of the faithful masses stand the ugly and corrupt. Jesus might have been a lovely chap but I don't see myself walking alongside many of his biggest fans because I don't think they like Jesus for the same reasons I do. I like the peaceful, loving, long-haired, bearded, socialist dude I see in Christ. I'm not totally sure but I think he may have pitched a tent next to mine at Glastonbury a few years ago. If it was him, then Jesus seriously likes Radiohead. The dude abides.

12

My God-shaped hole

THIS DESIRE TO BELIEVE IN SOMETHING AND TO HAVE A permanent, ever-present force at work in my life is hard to explain. If it wasn't, it would most likely be an easy thing to sort out and make for a pretty short book and a contented life. If it was as simple as my observing that everyone with faith in their life is better off than everyone without, then I suspect I could just find a way to believe, somehow. If the opposite were true, then I'd be more sure of my atheism and that would be that. But it's not simple and thus far it's not been easy for me to reconcile what I want and how I feel with what I believe and what I think I know. I suppose you could say I have a God-shaped hole. I am not suggesting that my anus is in the shape of God. We are told that God comes in many forms, so technically it is possible that my bottom looks exactly like God, but I doubt it. Of all the infinite forms God is able to choose, I suspect that my backside would be very low on His list. Possibly one or two places below a gullible person's toast or David Icke.

There are many atheists who react strongly against the notion of a God-shaped hole. They say the hole is not God-shaped, if indeed there is a hole at all. It is rather the case that having identified in humanity a propensity to believe there is a hole, and a desire to fill the hole with something comforting, religious salesmen have tinkered with the image of God and made him exactly the right shape to fit into the empty space. Well done them. Marketing men who identified a gap in the human soul market and sold hard with a bespoke product that made them rich and powerful. They found a way to create a need and followed that creation immediately with a product that satisfies. It's a man with the only train of camels in the desert convincing passers-by that in the middle of the desert lies the answer to all their dreams. This talent for ruthless salesmanship has developed and grown with each new generation and now has my daughter convinced that without a pair of Lelli Kelly beaded sparkle shoes, she will be judged from the feet up. Without a flowery pink overpriced pair of kiddy bling pumps over her five-year-old toes, she is somehow less than the other little girls who, until they saw the Lelli Kelly ad, used their feet mainly for running about, skipping and stomping in puddles. Marketing is done with great skill and precision and religion has led the way in brand awareness, brand loyalty and straightforward 'you can't live without this stuff' hard-selling.

If people have a hole that needs filling, then I would say that making God fit the hole isn't exactly difficult. You simply describe the hole as roughly round in shape and then create a roundish God that sort of fits if you give it a decent shove. Feeling alone? God is always with you ... even though you can't see Him or feel Him and He's silent and He gives no direct indication that He's there at all. Feeling sad? God loves you ... Even though the same number of shit things will happen to you as anyone else regardless of what you believe. Worried about a loved one? God will fix it ... In as much as: if the loved one is OK, God done it; if the loved one dies, or shit things happen to them, you either didn't believe hard enough or God moves in mysterious ways. The more you look at it, the more it feels like a con.

For any areas where He clearly doesn't quite fit, and there are so many, the faithful comfort one another with phrases such as, 'Ah well, that's the great mystery of the Almighty' or, 'If God had meant us to know everything, he would have made us Gods too'; see also, 'Ours is not to reason why', 'Go and ask your mother' and 'That'll be fifty Hail Marys, you impudent shit'. It's not exactly rocket science (note to self – find out how hard rocket science is ...) to dodge any of the really hard questions by saying slightly mystical things about eternity and everlasting love and the divine plan. It'll stop people asking too many questions if you make the answers cryptic and suggest that even the act of questioning is a betrayal. Add to that the notion that you don't even have to give voice to your questions, merely ask them in your own head and God can hear you and will be most displeased – and before you can say Stripy Joseph you have a perfect marketing campaign. It's fear-based but attractive too and the product lasts for ever. With that much going for it, the emperor is able to march about with no clothes on for as long as he likes and not a soul dares say, 'Hey, can anyone else see the emperor's cock? I think he might be a Jew . . .'

Much of the most effective marketing of Christianity avoided anyone asking questions about whether the God on offer was hole-shaped by explaining everything in a language the congregation didn't understand. Anyone who tried to speak Latin at school knows how important and clever it sounds and how only the brainiest and hardest-working kids pick up more than a few amo-amas-amats. The use of a secret code that keeps prying minds in awe is genius. It works a treat. I know I am susceptible to the romantic allure of a mysterious foreign tongue. I eavesdrop on people's apparent gobblede-gook waiting, hoping for hints and titbits that might chime with English or the smattering of French I understand. Ooh ooh, that bit definitely sounded like 'table walk talcum masala dong' – I wonder what they are talking about. It's probably poetry. I walk into foreign supermarkets and delight in products I recognize that have a label printed all in foreign. 'Les Nouilles Super' – delicious, gourmet treats and all you need is a kettle! Wow. 'Tasse-Zuppe' – ooh, exotic. I've even bought things I know for certain I don't like, because they looked better with the slight linguistic variation on the packaging. If it says 'Crème de Salade' on the bottle rather than 'Salad Cream', suddenly I want it. Imagine that same effect used to promise eternal life or threaten eternal damnation, all presented in the dead language of the 'educated'. If El Supermerkado Foreignio offered me Salad Cream in Latin and said I could live for ever if I bought enough of it, well, I doubt there are enough salad leaves in the world . . . Sold! To the man eating 'Flocon de Maïs' with a big dumb smile on his gullible face.

It doesn't much matter if the hole is God-shaped, hexagonal or roughly the same shape as the Channel Tunnel. If I tell you I have a hole, it's because I've identified something that feels like one. Some space within me that seems empty and yearns for direction and nourishment. It's not my tummy. Trust me. I've tried overeating to quite epic proportions and this hole can't be filled with crisps and cake. If I see some (albeit very few) people who seem not to be troubled by the notion of a hole because they've apparently filled it with God, then I'm curious. If they feel better and I don't, then I feel compelled to ask questions that my clever atheist friends disapprove of. Those who claim to feel better might be deluded. They probably are. My clever friends and I might be right. We usually are, unless it's a question about sport, then we're buggered. If they are serene and happier than I am, well then I have whatever the spiritual equivalent of food envy is. 'Please let me have a taste of your soul, it looks delicious.' It's not that I wish to stop trying to learn stuff or asking questions. I'm not envious of people in a coma just because they don't seem that bothered by who lied to whom in order to start a war in Iraq

or the cynical marketing of junk to children or the massive national debt. I like sleeping but I don't want to do it all the time. I enjoy thinking and asking questions and listening to the responses, but I might settle for some delusion if I felt better some of the time.

I wish I could explain succinctly what 'the hole' is. All I can say for sure is that I feel it and though some friends think it risible, I'm willing to ask if it's God-shaped. Richard Dawkins has a go at explaining the phenomenon of wishing to believe in something beyond ourselves in his *God Delusion*. There's a whole chapter in his book called 'The Gap' in which he attempts to describe the spiritual yearning that mankind seems to have felt since the very origins of our existence. I had hoped he might embrace the humour to be found in 'The Gap' also being a high-street clothing store but, alas, embracing humour doesn't seem to be the good professor's 'thing'. Imagine though for a moment if Professor Dawkins had applied his brilliant mind to proving, with the backing of his extensive scientific resources, that all of mankind's spiritual curiosity and ethereal musing through the ages was best defined as nothing more than the desire to spend eternity amongst a few shelves of navy blue hoodies and a baseball cap with 'since 1969' written on it. He didn't. It isn't. The Gap has been accused of using child labour; Richard Dawkins implies that describing one's child as Christian, Muslim, Jewish or whatever is a form of child abuse. There the similarities end.

Mankind has, for all of our recorded history, sought after something profound, magical, sublime and Goddish to believe in. We comfort ourselves with the idea that the incredible forces that brought us into being and gave us the power to ask questions, such as 'What are these incredible forces?', had a plan when they made us. We are not a mistake. There is a purpose to our being here and it's not just buying shoes, eating cake and bickering over how we got here and who gets to hold the remote control. So, when I reached the chapter called 'The Gap' in *The God Delusion*, I felt some excitement. This bit will speak to my experience, I thought. This should explain why I feel like I do . . . It didn't. This is my failing, not Dawkins's. He's written a few thousand well-researched words describing the desire for God and the mistake we make in seeing the hole as God-shaped and for many people I'm sure it was as satisfying and illuminating as the rest of *The God Delusion*. For me it was the point where I had to admit to myself that despite my desire to enjoy the book, I was struggling. I can summarize for you the essence of what I read in 'The Gap'. Essentially Professor Dawkins seems to be saying: 'Sometimes people have silly thoughts. Try not to.' And that, unfortunately, is pretty much it. He's a brilliant scientist, a diligent and eloquent evolutionary biologist, an engaging and talented writer, but that, to me, seemed to be the sum total of Professor Dawkins's understanding of the emotional complexities of the human condition. 'Occasionally, people have things called feelings. These are best avoided. They are slippery, non-scientific, cannot be proved and lead to confusion. If you wish to worship something, worship me.'

I don't know for sure what this 'gap' or 'hole' is any more

than Dawkins, Hitchens, the Pope, the Dalai Lama or David Blaine does. I know I have it in common with almost everyone I've ever come to know well enough to discuss such things, and I know that expecting scientists to explain what happens in those parts of my mind places an unfair burden on them which they are not briefed to deal with. Sometimes I'm sad, I need to get over it and read more. Or read less. Or read better books. Or not get over it, just feel it and be. It's not the aim of the great secular thinkers of our time to make me feel better about myself, nor should it be (even if feeling better is a key concern for most people). I wouldn't turn up to a science lecture, listen, enjoy, learn and then, during questions at the end, leap to my feet and ask, 'I understand in essence how the CERN Super Collider works as a means by which we might begin to understand "dark matter", but why am I unhappy? Eh? Riddle me that, Dr Brainiac! Why do I feel the tentacles of insanity wrapping their cold wet grip around my mind when I spend too much time alone? How's that for dark matter? Does the dark matter? Yeah? Thought so. Not so clever now, are you, eh? No wonder one of you dropped your sandwich in the collider. You big Swiss weirdos! Ha! I've learned nothing here today, I am still alone in the universe.' A waste of everyone's time.

The hole is all the stuff I have doubts about from the trivial to the magnificent. Why do other people listen to Lily Allen? What was funny about Bo Selecta? Is there life that we would recognize somewhere else in space? Is love the greatest of all human achievements? Which is better, Gorgonzola Dolce or

Stilton? Will my children ever forgive me? Amongst these and a million other questions, I have the creeping feeling that nothing matters. I don't like that feeling. I wonder sometimes if we are no more than a brilliant accident wandering about trying not to break too much stuff before we die and that is it. Life's like a narrow and fascinating antique shop. You pass through, you admire, reject, collect and inspect, and everywhere you look there are signs saying breakages must be paid for. All of what we touch is altered by our having been in contact with it, much of it gets broken and, if we're lucky, some new things are created. In the end, the hope seems to be that you have improved more of the things you have encountered than destroyed. It's no way to end your life, looking back over all you have done and seeing little more than a trail of destruction and feeling your face turn red as you mumble, 'Sorry, it just came away in my hand . . .'

I feel fear when I indulge this nihilistic view of existence. It feels like a void that sucks you in and might make you go mad. Like when you lie out on a clear night and look at the stars, marvelling in the beauty and magnificence of it all. Staring at burning balls of light sending their radiance in all directions, content to wonder and to observe . . . then suddenly you feel a terrible sense of aloneness and insignificance. There is a feeling of panic, almost like the Earth might release its gravitational hold and eject you into the nothing. It's best to do stargazing when you're drunk, stoned or newly in love. It's much safer then, you either black out, giggle or get it on. All much better feelings than a head full of 'Oh Christ, I'm so alone. What's the bloody point of anything? Why do people listen to Lily Allen?' Infinite thoughts are impossible to hold in the human mind. It's like trying to imagine a new colour. You can't do it. Dulux can do it by adding the word 'apple' to existing colours but we mortals cannot. We have the menu of colours provided within the light spectrum and that's all there is. You can't go a la carte and start creating colours with ingredients that don't exist. I sometimes think that if we saw a new colour we'd go mad. I think this may have happened to my wife when she encountered Straw Pebble by Farrow and Ball at just £90 a gallon! Maybe God is a new colour and that's why we never see him.

When we consider the infinite, we have to imagine an end point and something beyond that and another end to that and something beyond that and eventually a fence with some disappointing graffiti on it. 'Darrell sucks cocks . . . coz he's an ARSEnal fan' or some such poetic ribaldry. For me, allowing my mind to focus on the notion of the infinity of space and time feels like falling. I read *A Brief History of Time* and that felt like falling and failing. Inserting one paragraph into my head seemed to push the previous one out the other side. These thoughts of insignificance and fear and infinity and insecurity are what inform the notion that there is a hole. There are things the brilliant human mind cannot see, feel or understand and in those spaces there is a need to satisfy – with God, perhaps, if you don't mind his mood swings, with scientific enquiry if you're infinitely patient, with drugs and booze if you have really tolerant friends and plenty of money. I suppose the lesson I have learned is this – try not to think about things you're too thick to understand. That works about as well as deciding not to think of an elephant. See, now all you can see is an elephant. In space with an infinitely long trunk.

For me, though, questions of eternity and where we all came from and the point to life and all that are not really the core of the problem. I wonder about them and they sometimes disturb me but they don't make me envy the relative serenity of the devout. What I think about is something much closer to home and altogether more personal. Am I any good?

Even the simple act of typing those words makes my heart lurch a little in my chest. My brain floods with strands of enquiry that swirl, extend and congeal like blood in water. What is it to be good anyway? Sam Harris's excellent book *The Moral Landscape* helps the atheist reader to identify morality in the secular world and argues that it's not defined by religious observance or by messages from God but is innate in humanity and informed by scientific understanding. A.C. Grayling was kind enough to thrust copies of two of his best essays into my hands when I told him about my thoughts and struggles with faith and atheism. They helped me up to a point – as most books do, even if it's only to reveal their worthlessness – but these didn't seem to quell the voices of doubt within me. I think the good life is one that satisfies without excessive cost to others. For the idiot parked in the box junction, on the phone, smoking, with a child on the back seat, the cost to others doesn't enter into the equation, but for the rest of us we'd like to have the things we want but not if they come with the burden of too much guilt.

Basic analysis might suggest that my mundane middle-class angst is just that, ordinary and trivial in its inevitability. Perhaps then it's no more worthy of examination than the popularity of good wellington boots amongst the privately educated or the fact that a disproportionate number of my childhood friends have over-bites and have been in-patients at addiction rehabilitation centres. The view that someone's angst is inevitable because of their upbringing and therefore not worthy of examination gets right up my well-proportioned but not obviously aristocratic nose. If a person feels discomfort and there is a way to relieve some or all of that dis-ease, then why not do it? Even if it amounts to no more than piping up to say, 'Hey, me too, I feel like that.' Most of us ultimately want to feel we are not alone and identification of feelings and thoughts seems a good place to start. Unless you're on a train in rush hour, then it can be uncomfortable. Never again will I suggest a 'break-out' session and a group hug on the 08.19 to Victoria. It was not rewarding and no one felt comforted.

So am I any good? Well, I try to be, but I disappoint myself very often. I am a product of the things that have happened to me and the decisions I have made. I bought a copy of 'Lifted' by the Lighthouse Family and I must live with that choice for the rest of my days. Much of my life has been happy, some of it intensely sad, a fair bit of it very angry and a satisfying amount of it debauched and filthy. I've been frightened a few times. The most severe of these occasions was a visit to Dracula's House of Horror in Niagara in Canada. A wrong turning in the darkness saw me end up in the 'staff room' or, more accurately, Dracula's den of porn and half-smoked joints. That was frightening. Some of my life has been spent asleep and I make no apology for anything I've done in that state, including dreaming of naked vampires smoking spliffs. I am not a special case and make no claim to be. If you're not spending your time satisfying the basic human needs for food, water and shelter, then life is often filled with reflection, much of which is useless.

I had cheese with fig jam and salad for lunch with a few marinated anchovies in the salad in an attempt to make it exciting. It worked. It was as exciting as a salad is ever likely to get – slightly. I had an apple that has flown further than I ever have, some tea and a glass of water from the tap. This was consumed in south-west London in my kitchen looking at the rabbit hutch in the garden and the willow tree. My needs are satisfied, I didn't have to forage for the apple or stew the fig jam or milk something furious to get my cheese. I opened the fridge and there it all was with some organic yoghurts and the evil Cheestrings the children so enjoy. Lunch is pretty simple when you have a fridge and a few quid to spend on half-rotted milk – so I spent some time online seeking approval, distraction and amusement. I play music or have the radio on almost constantly; I don't enjoy silence. With these needs all met, and in the few moments I'm not suspending reality through social networking or consuming media at the all-you-can-eat internet buffet, I spend time considering my navel ... It's really deep because I've been overweight for a long time. It gathers fluff with alarming speed and rarely stints on the portion size. Mine ought to be a blissful carefree existence and yet I need as many of you as possible to understand that I find a fair bit of life uncomfortable and shit. I'm not carefree and I'm happy less often than I'd like.

There are many things I'm aware of that have framed and defined my existence and doubtless a great many others I am totally unaware of. I'm pretty sure I wasn't touched up as a child: my school wasn't that religious and I was fat anyway so they'd have gone for the other boys first. I'm also confident that I've never been abducted by aliens or belonged to a cult. I was too overweight and atheist for the Scouts and too mannish for the Brownies. I've either had too much or too little therapy, depending on who you talk to. Too much if you ask most of my friends; too little if you ask the ones who are in therapy. Not even close to enough if you ask my therapist. I am finding writing this book intensely lonely and I feel insecure about the result. I've realized that the career I've chosen in stand-up comedy and acting involves a great deal of approval seeking and it works a treat. I write a bit, I take the bit I've written to a stand-up club or to the radio or TV studio, I say it to some people, the people laugh, then they clap. I know I am loved and approved of. No one claps when you finish a chapter. Much to my embarrassment, I seem to have become quite dependent on applause ... Without it, how will I know if I'm any good?

If there's a St Peter I'd like to think he'd understand where

I was coming from before marking my paper a fail and pulling the lever. It seems to me I am more likely to be judged while I'm alive and the outcome will affect tangible things I know I believe in. You may have judged me by reading this far. You may have judged this book from just the dust jacket (a rookie reader's error). I'd love to say I make no apology for the things I am but I'm English so that's clearly not the case. The evidence for the defence looks like this.

I am a married father of two. I was born in Surrey in 1973. I have an older sister and a much younger brother who is probably my best mate. My parents are alive and still married. I was privately educated. I was expelled several times at ages seven, eleven and fourteen. The decision to expel me at age eleven was reversed after an appeal. With each expulsion I was moved further away from my family home (generally in a westerly direction) until we ran out of land. I think at this stage my parents would have been willing to look into educating me in the sea. I was sent to boarding school when I was seven years old and consequently spent two-thirds of every year away from my family. I saw my mother and father most Saturdays for the first few years, then less frequently after I was twelve and as little as possible after I was fifteen. I left home properly when I was sixteen, though I had spent very little time there after the age of fourteen, and what time there was could be classed as ranging between uncomfortable, disastrous and eventually criminal. This was punctuated by several very enjoyable holidays, some of which were spent together with my family and some alone.

My father worked in the City. My mother was a head teacher of a local private school (local to her, not to me). By the time I was seventeen I weighed a little over 24 stone and had problems finding trousers that would fit me. I had a 44-inch waist, sometimes 46. I was dangerously overweight because I couldn't stop myself from eating, despite loathing the results of every day of over-indulgence. I made a solemn promise to myself every night, alone in bed, wheezing and prodding with revolted fingers the wobbly shame that was wrapped around my body, that tomorrow would be a new beginning. It wasn't new; it was the same. I ate from bins if I couldn't find anything else and I stole a lot.

I started drinking when I was twelve, though limited availability meant that until I was fifteen, drunkenness was infrequent, though not perhaps by comparison with my peers. I started sniffing solvents when I was thirteen and progressed to a limited range of other recreational drugs with a preference for downers or opiate-style highs. Marijuana was a favourite and the associated 'munchies' were negligible in the context of a 17-year epic munch. At age seventeen I had a breakdown and was admitted to a residential treatment centre where I stopped drinking, using drugs and eating compulsively. Today, I am still sober and clean from drugs and deal with the negotiation between necessity and compulsion to eat reasonably well. This has been the case for over twenty years.

Needless to say these experiences have framed much of who I am. I don't wish to be evasive or to trivialize these important events, but neither do I want this to be a story about a poor little rich kid who missed his parents and then fell into a life of addiction, got saved by the do-gooders and blah blah blah. I didn't want to out myself as an addict at all, but it would be dishonest or at least duplicitous of me not to mention it in this context. It's too important to this story. I'm an addict. I'm not sure why. I doubt the reason for it, if there is one, is nearly as important as what I choose to do about it now. If you reached this section of my story and sagely nodded your head as if to say, 'Ah, yes, this all explains why the boy is so needy, angry and fucked up,' then you've missed at least 50 per cent of the point.

Part of the suggested recovery process for addiction is to turn your will and your life over to a 'higher power'. The literature explicitly avoids defining that higher power as anything other than a 'power greater than yourself' (Geoff Capes, for instance?), but after introducing the concept, refers to this power as 'God' for simplicity's sake. Most people are happy enough with this description. I worked with this 'God' very easily when I first started life without mood-altering substances and processes. He was a good worker, punctual and smartly turned out. I was tired and scared at that time so I didn't ask too many questions. Tired and scared seems a dangerous state to begin a new relationship in – I suspect that's what led Paul McCartney to marry Heather Mills and then look ... But that's what I was, tired, scared and willing to be helped by anyone who was able to. I think God was. Those with more recovery and less recently insane lives than mine said, Turn your will and your life over to a power greater than yourself, so I did as I was asked. I was not in a position to negotiate, haggle or skip things that might later prove to be important. 'I'll tell you what, I'll agree to believe in God, if you agree that I should be allowed to smoke the odd spliff from time to time and still eat Mars Bars. Deal or no deal?'

My life was in danger, I was drowning, so I swam to where the people seemed to be climbing out of the stormy water and drying off in the sunshine. Had I not had the help I did, I believe I would not be alive now. Could this assessment possibly be overly dramatic? The evidence for it is pretty strong. Even if my addiction hadn't killed me directly, I suspect that in a state of inebriated despair I might have tracked down the elusive courage I had sought on several previous occasions and taken my own life. I've known people whose addictions killed them. Close friends, some of them. Their stories were similar to mine. The drive in them to escape this reality took them to the grisly and undignified end point that most addicts reach. In any case, the 'God' I was asked to believe in bore no relation whatsoever to the one described in the Holy books, so I thought, well, what's the harm in it? It might do me good. It did do me good. I got sober, clean from drugs and more than halved my body weight in seven months. I fell over a lot after I did that. I think my legs got over-excited and didn't know how much blood they'd need to move me about so I kept blacking out at the top of staircases. In truth I quite liked it; it felt a bit like glue-sniffing does just before your brain shuts your functions down.

Then I lost God. Initially it was a slow breakdown in communication with Him. I stopped asking Him stuff and He didn't ever say anything anyway so when the feeling of 'being listened to' was replaced with a feeling of 'there's no one listening', I accepted that as my reality. I'm not sure God even noticed . . . When I tried to talk to God (it's been a while), He seemed very quiet, so I started to ask questions, and with each one unanswered God seemed further away. The route I'd had to Him before seemed unfamiliar and became less and less clear and then He just sort of disappeared, and the map I had that used to tell me where to find Him turned out to be a blank sheet of paper with a question mark on it.

He is supposed to be whatever you need Him to be. God's plan in God's time . . . accept powerlessness and hand it over to your higher power. Let go, Let God. All the clichéd phrases shared in the addicts' meetings work well. I was told, if you're struggling with it, let God stand for 'Good Orderly Direction'. Glib but effective. It's possible to be an atheist in recovery from addiction and to accept the process and the tools of recovery and even the word 'God' without believing in anything super-natural. When I did believe in God, it was a trust in nature that came closest to defining it. I began to see myself as part of a bigger picture and the scale of the natural world seemed inspiring enough to give a sort of reverential splendour to the idea. It's easy, I think, to feel a connection to something beyond yourself when you're standing on a deserted beach staring at the vast ocean before you. Less so if a condom washes up or a stag do arrive for skinny-dipping and drinking games. I gave a consciousness to the things that appeared in nature, grand scenes like a big tree, a mountain, the sea or rolling hills. It's not too hard with a bit of stillness and humility to take the natural and give it a little shove in the direction of the super. Talk to the wind and it's a cinch to convince yourself that each gust is trying to tell you something in reply: 'Go inside . . . get a coat . . . you should have worn a hat, look at the state of your hair.'

I have made groups of people seeking to recover from addiction represent a power greater than myself. That works quite well. Any two people seeking to achieve together what I am seeking to achieve alone are a power greater than myself, except maybe the Chuckle Brothers. As long as you are wary and keep questioning, then there is something moving and profound about the collective wisdom of individuals working towards a common goal, provided the conditions of assembly are right and there is no talk of raising a militia and invading Wales. If you use any two people as your higher power, I think it's important they are not the same two people all the time. That would get creepy and odd very quickly. I can picture frightened couples scampering into shop doorways as I trundle after them with a pile of theology books and tear-stained cheeks shouting, 'Wait, wait, I made you my God, you can't run into Starbucks and hide! I need you to shepherd me and stuff. Look, I made a list of questions . . .'

In recovery they say there are only two things you need to know about God. 1. There is one. 2. He's not you. I can accept the latter, I know I'm not God, because there are six people (four of them famous) who simply wouldn't ever have existed if I was the almighty. I've been told God is everything or God is nothing. I struggle with that one because if God is everything then he's as big a twat as I am and that's no good. I want a God who's obviously better than I am. You couldn't have a God who can never remember which side the Queen goes on when you're setting up a chessboard. It'd be ridiculous. So then God is nothing and I'm back at square one (I know the Queen doesn't go on square one).

Opinions vary hugely about what form God or your higher power might take. It's supposed to be personal: you believe in whatever version works best for you. Groups of recovering addicts are meticulous in upholding the total separation between what is discussed and suggested about God in meetings and any religious ideology or doctrine. It works. Lives are saved and enriched every day, mine amongst them. In America they have a constitutional separation between church and state and seem to have gone collectively, religiously, insane. It doesn't work everywhere.

The life I have chosen, in trying to avoid mood-altering processes and chemicals, is a 'good life'. It's important I think that, and that I believe it's one I've chosen, or else I'm inclined to derail the whole process and go for a long swim in a bottle of Southern Comfort. It's a good life, but it feels long. Very long, like a Soderbergh film ... Make of that what you will. There are worse things to be and worse places to be them, but I do wish I wasn't an addict. I'm tired of it. I'm tired of the constant vigilance against relapse. It's boring and frightening at the same time. Imagine being scared of a thing for so long that even fear becomes dull.

There is a high degree of accountability in the sober existence. I make mistakes like anyone else. My ego has plenty to say and he and I have been on some hair-raising excursions together with terrible and exciting results. I don't excuse 'bad' behaviour in myself. I accept that I disappoint myself and others up to a point, but I'm not comfortable with being an arsehole. I know a few people who are and beneath the resentment I feel towards them I'm also a little envious. The unabashed arsehole is a thing of some power and an odd nobility. I know when I make bad and unhelpful decisions; I do so awake and conscious of the consequences of my actions. I sometimes think that with the benefit of a 'day pass' into a bottle of something delicious I might enjoy a break from my usual sober thought patterns. Maybe with a big enough spliff, these many instances of my being to some degree or other 'an arsehole' might be acceptable to me. I could then rely on the often-repeated plea, 'I was drunk! We all were . . . Come on, we all do things we regret when we're off our tits! Sorry, baby, take me back,' or any other such catch-all basket of an excuse for being a bum. If I want to be loud or obnoxious or leap about like a git, I do it fully aware of my actions. I still do it, but I know I am doing it and I can see myself clearly at almost all times. In fact, I act like I am drunk much more often than you might expect for a spoddy teetotaller in spectacles and a cardigan. I live in a relatively constant state of self-awareness and seek to live a life that I can be honest about with almost anyone. This would be a lot easier if there were a God taking care of the whole thing for me. In the absence of alcohol, I wonder if I might get away with 'God made me do it' or even 'It's all part of His plan', but I don't really think so. He doesn't have a plan for me, and if He does, it's about as well thought through as the Iraq War exit strategy, only with fewer road-side bombs and a lot more Stilton.

I don't know if the hole's God-shaped. God seemed to fill it a few times along the way and I felt better but I couldn't sustain it and I can't seem to shove God back in there anyway because I don't know where He is. I don't think the hole is as simple as the space left behind when you stop eating, like a goose who's volunteered to blow its liver up in the name of good foie gras. I'm sure that being an addict has a bit to do with it, but I've done the recovery thing for a long time and I wasn't always this aware of a spiritual vacuum waiting to suck in a better set of ideas. The hole isn't food-shaped, alcohol would run through it and drugs seem just as likely to make new holes of their own. There's a hole in my being, dear Liza, dear Liza. There's a hole in my being, dear Liza, a hole ...

13

I believe that children
are the future

IF YOU EVER WANT TO FEEL LIKE A FAILURE, BECOME A
parent. I don't mean that I'm any worse at parenting than
most or that my children are particularly challenging or that I
don't enjoy being a dad. I simply mean that every day you fail
a little more in your effort to raise your children in the way
you thought you would when a black and white ultrasound
picture revealed the most beautiful half-formed, hunch-
backed, shrivelled, foetal maggot swelling in a sack of
amniotic fluid inside your partner's distended tummy. In that
moment you recognize every mistake your own parents made,
dismiss them and envision your own phenomenal success. You
acknowledge the ups and downs ahead but imagine balanced,
happy, communicative children who don't need to be nagged,
blackmailed or bribed into achieving the basics. A few

sleepless, blundering months later you find yourself begging for the fiftieth time for your precious little darling to eat just one bit of carrot. It's only the size of any one of the many peas now flung across the floor, table, chair, windowsill and ceiling. You then threaten the removal of the telly if they don't eat up, possibly swear a little, beg again, thump the table, then promise that if they eat up they can have an ice cream and some sweets and more telly and a present. Welcome to the fast-flowing central current of the river of failure, which will carry you, flailing and lurching for the bank, through almost all of your child's life.

I have two children. Alfie and Emily. They both like me. In fact, with some momentary exceptions they seem to think more of me than anyone else I know. As luck would have it, I adore them too and find them funny, sweet and beautiful beyond measure. It is an amazing thing becoming a dad. It's been done before, I'm told, but that doesn't lessen the sheer gobsmacking extraordinariness of it. The moment your first child is born your life is suddenly transformed, it's filled with light and colour and laughter and joy and inspiration and bafflement and love and adoration and exhaustion and fear and paranoia and regret and embarrassment and wipes. Wipes. The dominant theme of the first four to five years of parenthood is wipes.

My daughter Emily is the younger of the two; she's five. She finds my being away for work difficult to understand and the look on her face when I try to explain about where and why I go where I do has a very similar effect to how it might be if she reached in through my chest, tore my heart out from between my ribs and crushed it in her bare hands in front of my eyes. When I toured *God Collar* I tried to explain to her: 'Daddy's going away to tell jokes to strangers, that's how I get my needs met.' She was really very sweet and replied, 'Will you tell me a joke, Daddy?' So I said, 'Well, I don't really do jokes, it's more sort of concepts and ideas.' It's not easy being a parent . . . I think she understood a bit. She certainly seemed to get the idea that I was nervous about it. She was nervous when she was second angel on the left in her school Nativity play. A good production, slightly obvious scripting; some directorial tightening wouldn't have gone amiss. To be honest, I thought Mary overdid it somewhat, but she had to carry a lot of slack after Joseph pissed his trousers. Quentin Letts from the *Daily Mail* gave it five stars but he's pretty odd and very angry. I suspect he pissed his trousers too when Labour won a third term. Anyway, Emily seemed to understand about my pre-show jitters. As I left to start the tour she shouted, 'Happy Luck, Dad.' Isn't that adorable? 'Happy Luck!' That simple phrase touches me. It feels like it's not just emotional, it's certainly not physical. Her innocent kindness reaches me somewhere altogether deeper. Perhaps in the place that, if I had the language for it, I might describe to you as a soul. I think she took Happy Christmas and Happy Birthday, the best ideas in her five-year-old head, and smashed them together with Good Luck to send me away with the best and most positive message she could find for me. 'Happy Luck.' Lovely. Sure, 'Happy Luck' sounds a bit like a Chinese brothel, but you can't have it all, can you?

Emily loves spending time playing games. A lot of children's board games are unbelievably dull. I think we remember them fondly, but trust me, if you've managed to avoid Ludo, Snap and Guess Who, then you've missed very little. 'Is it a girl? Yes. Does she have a hat? Yes. Is it Maude? No. It must be. She's the only one with a hat . . .' It's not exactly knight to king four, is it? Here's a tip to minimize self-loathing – never save money by buying a cheap Snakes and Ladders board. Why? Well, because it has the same number of snakes as it does ladders. Technically, the game can last for ever. It's not a great game, Snakes and Ladders. There's very little to it. Roll the dice, move up the board and hope you reach a ladder that will whizz you closer to the end of the game. Pray to whatever you believe in you don't land on a snake, which will slide you back to where it all began. It's dismal, and because it's only a board game you can't even call Claims Direct and sue anyone for giving you the wrong sort of ladder or leaving a load of snakes lying about. So I sit as a dutiful loving father, opposite my wonderful daughter, with her smile and her dress and her hair and her endless patience for Snakes and Ladders, and we move together into hour three of game one. It's usually at this point that I land on yet another snake. Emily's delighted, but in truth all I really want to do in that moment is scream, 'Oh I wish I was dead. When will this interminable bloody game end. Please God have mercy on me and visit a plague on London. I wish I was on an actual ladder being attacked by real bastard snakes.' But in at least two of the books I've read, it says you absolutely mustn't do that. So instead I look across the table at her big excited eyes, and the joy in her little face, and all I can do is slide my plastic tiddly-wink down the snake's slippery bloody spine and say, 'Ooh, Daddy's on another snake, sssssssssssss.' And in that moment a bit of me dies. A bit of me dies because in that moment I'm thinking, 'I wish I was somewhere else.' I'm imagining I have somewhere better to be than playing a game with a five-year-old. There *is* no place better than that, that's the best place in the world, but I can't hold myself there because it's difficult. Difficult and relentlessly tedious.

I don't want to overstate my response to these instances of self-ishness and frustration on my part. This isn't why I need God. It's only guilt, it's nothing more profound than that. But it's cumulative, and because it's family, the feelings seem to run deep. Put them all together and add the constant worry that I am failing as a father and hey presto, you have the right emotional Stanley knife to cut yourself a nice little God-shaped hole.

I have the same feelings about my son Alfie. He's great, he's eight years old now and I think he's hilarious. Whatever it is, he's up for it. It's a good thing eight-year-old boys don't go on stag parties. The presence of eight-year-olds would escalate the simple pleasures of tying the stag to a lamppost, leaping in a canal and downing a litre of vodka Red Bull whilst standing on a table to something that many people would consider 'out of hand'. His enthusiasm and excitement for life show in every part of his being. He jiggles, dances, hops and lurches about with fascinating facial contortions to match and speaks of such wondrous things that I think he must be channelling the spirits of deceased fantasy novelists. Alfie is fun. Watching him realize the power of humour and begin to harness his ability to make people laugh has been one of the greatest joys of seeing him grow. I remember an occasion I was driving us home from somewhere or other. I had a friend with me in the front of the car who was telling us about a documentary he'd seen. My friend was explaining to us about a breed of monkey so small it could cling on to your thumb . . . From the back of the car a small but confident voice said, 'What, thumbkeys?' I was over the moon. Good lad, Alf! Of course, they're thumbkeys. I couldn't have been more proud if he'd accidentally discovered a new clean source of renewable energy. We all laughed, and repeated the word 'thumbkeys' until we fell back into silence. Alf let it be silent for a while. He rode it out, happy in the knowledge he'd made a zinger. Then out of nowhere, for seemingly no reason at all, he suddenly punched the air and shouted, 'Who's with me?' What a question. 'Who's with me?' Well, we all are now. He's in the back of the car; he's not even in charge of where we're going, but where he leads, so shall we follow. He is the thumbkey king and, yes, we are with him. That's probably similar to how Jesus ended up with so many fans. He had the courage to ask, 'Who's with me?', and know that simply by asking many would follow because it takes some guts to put that question out there. I love my son, but for the record I'd like to make it very clear that no part of me thinks he represents the second coming of the Lord. He made a funny, then he punched the air. He's brilliant, but I let Alfie down. All the time. I don't mean to but I do. I let him down because I'm not eight and sometimes I'm selfish and an arsehole.

I cycle him to school most days. It's a great chance to be father and son together doing something fun. Or if not specifically fun then at least blustery and dangerous, which is an excellent substitute for fun. I have a trailer bike for the boy. That means I have my bike and then a one-wheeled, low-seated, pedal-powered half-bike that attaches to the back of mine. We have three wheels but we still get to be twice as smug as a normal cyclist. It represents very good value. It's a lovely bit of time to spend with Alfie because it's just him and me after the chaos of the morning. And it is chaotic. You try for it not to be but it is. Most mornings the run-up to the departure for school is like the final stages of a siege. If you're diligent as a parent, then you prepare. The night before you get the school shoes ready, unroll the socks, put out the school uniform, help pack and prepare the school bag into which you slip the completed homework from the night before. If you're really on it you get the breakfast things lined up and ready to go (don't do this if your kids prefer toast, it doesn't do well overnight. If you like your toast like that, eat at Garfunkel's). So the morning is prepared and you retreat to bed, edging out of the room backwards, watching to see that all is still in a state of readiness. Then, during the night, the mummy-and-daddy fairy comes to visit, and takes all the possessions and clothes and bags and flings them randomly around the house. The parent fairy hides one key ingredient – usually a shoe – and then turns the two smiling, warm, huggy, beautiful children you kissed goodnight just a few hours before into a pair of screaming banshees. Your sworn enemies on earth with no concept of time. I'm quite an organized person really. Most mornings I come downstairs and it's like I've invited Amy Winehouse to spend a month living in my house.

So when Alf and I have pulled on our cycle helmets and high-vis jackets (we like to give the 4×4s a bright and easy target) and step outside to mount the bike, a lovely calm feeling descends on us. It's our moment . . .

But most mornings as we get on the bike, Alf looks up at me and says, 'What shall we play, Dad?' And I look back at him and I think, 'Why don't you just fuck off? It's eight o'clock in the morning. I'm a comedian; technically I don't have to be up for another thirteen hours. I'm already cycling you to school. What do you mean, what shall we play? I don't have a game in me yet. If at all.'

I'd hate for anyone to know this about me and think I'm trying to portray myself as some sort of cool, hard-hearted, uncaring thug. 'Yeah, look at me, I'm so cool I barely love my kids.' That's not it. Not at all. I'm trying to explain this stuff for exactly the opposite reason. This sort of stuff, these thoughts and fears, kill me. They make me feel alone and I wonder how much worse I am than anyone else. What sort of man am I? What sort of father? I want to be able to do everything my son wants of me but sometimes I'm not up to it. Even when I am it's not for long. I can't keep it going because it's hard and I'm sometimes an arsehole.

Alfie's imagination sparks the moment he wakes up. I'm

not like that; I'm not sure I ever was. Some time in the middle of the afternoon I may begin to have a thought, depending on the quality of the cheese board at lunchtime. Not so for Alf. The moment he opens his eyes in the morning, bang, his brain fires with a million disconnected thoughts. 'There's more clouds in the sky than there were yesterday, I know because even though the curtains are drawn I can see the light coming in. Why does Scooby Doo change shape when Scrappy's around? You're my father, you're hairier than me and yet we're still related. Can Bakugan fly? In Kasmania they have their own language. I am a Yenidushi. Where do duvets come from? Why is that bunk above me? What stops me from flying? If I eat that clock, will I tick? What is ham? Can I have Chocoflakes for breakfast even though it's not the weekend? If not, why not? What game shall we play?'

Where does it come from? I'm still asleep when this process begins for Alf. I wake up and there he is asking all of that and more. It's like opening your eyes and having the internet be sick on your head. I want to join in with him. I want to play the game, but he's too fast. It's like playing tag with Usain Bolt. I'm outplayed and I feel old.

Some days when we get on the bike, he says, 'Let's play Transformers, who do you want to be?' And I say, 'I'll be Optimus Prime.' And he says, 'You can't be Optimus Prime, you were Optimus Prime yesterday.' Then I have to conceal from my eight-year-old son that I don't know any other Transformers. At any time of day. Let alone at eight o'clock in the morning.

I was demoted a little while ago. We were playing Power

Rangers when we left the house on the bike. Alfie was in charge of casting, he always is, and I was given the role of Red Ranger. I am on the front of the bike so it felt right. Now Red Ranger is something of a leader amongst the Rangers, I am confidently informed. I liked my position. When we reached the top of the first hill, a little voice from behind me said, 'I'm sorry, Dad. I'm going to have to make you Blue Ranger. I don't think Red Ranger would sweat that much.'

That's how my day began. With a demotion on the basis that Red Ranger doesn't breathe as heavily as I do. That is tremendously disappointing before breakfast. And then, with my Ranger status only recently degraded, I was informed from the rear seat that we were being attacked by vulture droids. Again! It's happened twice this month. I've written to my MP about it. The vulture droids are out of control in Wandsworth. Alf's ability to immerse himself in the game and dream up enemies and solutions to their dire schemes is masterful. Vulture droids are nasty little sods too. With all the sincerity of Captain Kirk I heard from the bridge, 'We're being attacked by vulture droids, Blue Ranger, what shall we do?' Alf's stopped pedalling by now as he's far too involved in repelling various malevolent space beasties to also use his legs. So I heave the two of us up yet another incline, trying not to pant in case there's a Ranger rank below Blue, and wonder how I can match the intensity of the narrative. I don't want to let him down. 'I know,' I say with a determined and confident Blue Rangerish air, 'I'll sound the sonic ping.' I use my thumb to bend back the plastic clapper and release it the full four millimetres to ping the tiny metal bell on my handlebar. 'Ping.' It rings out with all the sonorous power of a mouse fart. I feel absolutely pathetic. It was all I had . . . the sonic ping.

It was a full five minutes before we reached a set of traffic lights I was willing to stop at. The game seemed to have lost some of its edge since the vulture droids incident. I turned around to see Alfie, perched on the bike behind me. With a blank, exasperated face he simply asked, 'The sonic ping? Really?' You've never seen a child look more deflated. It's like I'd bought him an ice cream, showed it to him, held it in front of his mouth and then flung it into the bushes.

I take advantage of the kids as well. I don't mean to, but I do, all the time. Most parents will know this already. It's a universal scientific truth that your children will do anything for you, and I mean anything. As long as you say, 'I'll time you.' It's not a good thing to know. With great power comes great responsibility and we have abused that power. It's dreadful and I do it all the time. It begins innocently enough. You say, 'Put your shoes on.' They say, 'No.' You say, 'I'll time you.' And they do it quickly, in silence and without distraction. In that instant you realize you don't have children any more. Not if you don't want to. No, you have house slaves. My kids will do anything if I time them. It's exploitation of the highest order. If I'm feeling particularly lazy or tired, that's when it comes into its own. For example, if the remote control for the telly is at the other end of the sofa from where I've flopped down, I'd think very little of bellowing through the rest of the house, 'Alf! Get the remote for your dad, would you?' If there's no reply or some resistance, I add the crucial catalytic converter, 'I'll time you!' and lo and behold my son is Dash from *The Incredibles*. Whooooosh! And the remote is in my hand. As if that wasn't exploitative enough, he then stands there, panting and with eyes wide open and asks, 'Well, how fast?' That's not a question I can answer as I don't wear a watch. Such is my betrayal. He will bring me a book from two storeys up if I time him. The situation is out of control. Last week the two of them reroofed the house. It's not good.

Children are so amazing; not just my children, all children. A new child is like a brand new Rubik's Cube just waiting to get fucked up. So briefly they are perfect and simple and then over time they are twisted and turned by the passing hands of each encounter into an unsolvable, messy puzzle. With enough time, therapy and money you might get one or two sides back to how they were, but with each piece you move, another seems to get further from where it should be – for the most part it's a gaudy jumble of colours with no memory or under-standing of how it all got there.

I heard two stories about children and greatly enjoyed them both. One concerns a theologian, a priest who had devoted his entire life to the study of his particular religious text. Each day he immersed himself in the Bible to become closer to God and to make sense of the world around him. Then one day he met a little girl and she asked him a question. She said, 'Why should I ask God to make me good when I want to be naughty?' And the priest said . . . nothing. Not a word. Because there was nothing to say. She'd understood the nature of free will. In a way that an entire life of biblical study had never revealed to him. So do you know what he did? He left the priesthood. I like that. She'd defeated him with her mind because she was a child and they're good at that stuff. When you think how many children have had their lives ruined, their childhoods taken away by someone in the church, it's delightful to consider that she got one of them back. Sure, it's only one priest right now, only one child with one question, but you wait until that information spreads. You wait until the power of that level of philosophical enquiry falls into the hands of other children. Wait until it falls into the hands of a child who out of nowhere and for seemingly no reason is willing to punch the air and demand, 'Who's with me?' Why, they could bring down the entire church. Probably quite quickly if I timed them.

The other story came from the wonderful Ken Robinson TED talk on education. It's the story of a little girl doodling in a maths lesson. Her teacher was annoyed because she wasn't getting on with the subject in question. She went over and asked, 'What are you drawing there?' The little girl looked up and said, 'I'm drawing God.' The teacher replied, 'You can't draw God. No one knows what God looks like.' So the little girl paused for only the briefest of moments and as if the answer were the most obvious thing in the world she nodded and said, 'Well, I haven't finished it yet.' Isn't that perfect? The pure beautiful wisdom of the child's mind. Because before we mess with it, a child can have God any way she wants. Any size, any colour, any shape. No politics, no bigotry, no rules, laws or judgements. No bullshit imposed upon it. God any way you like Him. Ha! Brilliant.

Atheist or not, I think that's inspiring. I'm Godfather to several children. I'm Godfather rather than 'secular sponsor', because I never want to be the biggest cock in the room. My friend's Christian and she said, 'Will you be Godfather to our daughter?' I said, 'I'd be absolutely delighted, of course. I'd be over the moon.' Obviously I can't offer a great deal in religious or theological guidance as such, but as a comedian I do know some cracking good knob gags so I hope that might balance it out a bit. I suppose I'm offering myself up as Oddfather rather than Godfather really. I explained that it is very important to me not to lie in church. I don't think people should lie in church. I'll debate theology endlessly with anyone who wishes to discuss it and many who don't. I'll argue and sometimes become quite indignant in defence of reason but I don't think you should lie in church. The atheist would argue that 'they' do it all the time, but 'they' are free to. It's 'their' church. It's 'their' place. To be honest, I wish 'they'd' stay in there more often. I believe the principle is important – you shouldn't lie in church. Unless you're getting married, in which case do anything to secure that dream venue.

So I explained that as a friend and Godfather I would come to the church to watch my Goddaughter have tap water dribbled on her head and become a child of Christ, but I was clear that I wouldn't make any commitment to shove her in the direction of a God who doesn't much like little girls anyway. Unfortunately, the message didn't get through to the beardy sandally man running the christening. I'm not using a lazy Christian stereotype when I say beardy sandally man. Honestly, he was both beardy and sandally. As was his wife. In fact, I'm doing him a favour by not mentioning the beige socks he wore inside the sandals. This was in a church that offers the Alpha Course. The Alpha Course is like circuit-training for Christians. You go in deep and come out the other side with your love of God and Jesus just as sure and strong as your certainty that there are no questions to answer with regard to homophobia, misogyny or morality. Trust me when I tell you that a fair few of the congregation at this christening were somewhat 'out there'. One of them was either speaking in tongues or had the worst speech impediment since George VI shut his lips in a door on a particularly stressful day of speech-making. The Alpha Course did a huge advertising campaign a little while ago. It was all over the UK. It was a colossal and well-funded poster campaign asking, 'Is there a God?', then there were tick boxes beneath offering A. Yes. B. No or C. Probably. Someone at Wandsworth station had put a big tick in the 'No' box. I can't imagine who it was ... (I timed him – he did it in under 4 seconds. He's a good lad).

The Godparents were taken to the front of the church and expected to answer questions. A microphone was put in front of my face and I was asked, 'Do you renounce the devil?' I replied that I tend not to renounce people I've never met. With the exception of Jeremy Clarkson, obviously. I think from the bit of paper we were handed that the answer was supposed to be, 'Yes, I renounce the devil, I turn to Christ.' And as we said it we were supposed to rotate through 180 degrees. Something any actor will tell you is best avoided. Speak, then move, or move, then speak; rarely should you attempt both at once, that's how people get hurt. Laurence Olivier once moved and spoke at the same time and had to be carried off the stage at the RSC by a stagehand and Dame Sybil Thorndike. But our instructions were clear: face the back of the church and proclaim, 'I renounce the devil, I turn to Christ,' and lunge forward. From the diagram I think it's safe to assume that Christ was in the front part of the church and the devil was skulking at the back. Why they let him in at all I don't know. You'd think of all places that the devil might be on the not-welcome list at the door of most churches. There should be a verger or usher asking the question, 'Are you with devil or with Christ? Devils on the left, agnostics by the font.' It was all very awkward, I wasn't sure what to say. Fortunately no one was looking at me because my wife's head was spinning around and vomit was flying out of her mouth. It happens every time we go in a church. We must get it looked at.

My children had been whisked off upstairs to play with little Christian toys. Little Jesuses, or Jesi, I don't know how you pluralize Jesus or indeed if you should at all. I was very uncomfortable with the whole situation. I didn't want to let my friend down. She's Christian, she's delightful and I love her. I panicked and we left in an awkward and embarrassed hurry. Not what I'd wanted at all. I wanted to be there to support my friend but not to lie in church. Perhaps I was expecting too much. In any case it's not my place of worship and I don't get to demand what happens in there.

A while later Alfie and I were cycling past the same church and rather pleasingly he spotted it and said, 'Oh, there's that church with those funny people in.' I thought about it. He was six at the time and I thought, well, now's as good a time as any, he goes to a secular school. So I started the conversation. I said, 'Yeah, that was a strange day, wasn't it?' He said, 'Why strange?' I said, 'Well, it was strange for Daddy because I don't believe in God.' And Alf, who was just six and goes to a secular school, said, 'You have to believe in God, Dad, or he'll send another flood like he did to Noah.' Wow! That conversation did not go as I'd planned. 'Who's with me?' Hopefully no one.

Who was it, I wonder, who put that idea into my beautiful six-year-old boy's head? The thumbkey kid. Who the hell was it who thought it was OK to tell a child that if his daddy didn't believe then God would punish everyone on Earth with death by drowning? And God so loved His creation that if one man with serious reservations in Wandsworth dared not to sign up for wholesale bullying and intolerance, then every single one of us must be killed. Murdered in a flood. Perhaps not the people in Scotland – it really is very hilly and they're used to heavy rain but all the rest of us – killed by a vengeful and jealous God. Well, I say all the rest of us, I wouldn't drown, I've got an ark. They've been giving them away with the *Daily Mail*; you get a cubit a week and collect the set to give 'right thinking' people a chance to survive when the 'big rain' comes to wash the streets clean.

I was appalled when Alfie said that to me. I wouldn't let him watch the film of the great flood. It's much too violent and horrific for a child. And yet there are toy arks for kids to play with and countless Christian nursery schools called 'Noah's Ark' and the story is celebrated. Of course, we make the flood story OK for our kids by getting them to sing the 'Hurrah Hurrah' song. 'Oh! The animals went in two by two. Hurrah! Hurrah!' In what respect is 'hurrah' the right choice of word here, for this indiscriminate act of homicidal brutality? It isn't. You wouldn't stand on a beach in Thailand on Boxing Day asking who wants to commemorate the devastating tsunami with a couple of rounds of the 'Hurrah Hurrah' song. No, because it's not fucking appropriate, is it?

It happens six pages in. The flood. *Six pages* into the Bible. God had barely even begun and in one fell swoop, one petulant, jealous strop, he killed everything. I had mis-remembered the flood story. I'd thought it came about halfway through the Old Testament. God made man and then man made focus groups and then quangos, and then Injury Lawyers For You, and God just lost it. Fair enough. Who wouldn't go ape-shit in the face of that disaster and bellow, 'No, this is not what I intended. Today I will murder every-thing. Today I play Old Testament Grand Theft Auto and I'm on a spree, bitches!' He killed everything apart from Noah, his wife, their children and two each of all the animals. All the people killed. All the animals killed. All the bugs, the plants, everything. Not the fish, though, they'd done nothing wrong. Though I think we're getting our revenge on the fish now, aren't we? If God doesn't get 'em, we will. Jesus was an occasional fisherman and he could make a couple of fish and a few bread rolls go a very long way (he was a regular Jamie Oliver), he even walked on water, but we have satellite tracking and nets over a mile long and think nothing of throwing two-thirds of dead catch back into the sea. Booya! Take that, creator/devastator God.

The flood story focuses very firmly on those who survived in Noah's ark. But picture for a moment the scene for everyone else. Children ripped from their mother's arms by the force of the water. Black fetid water rising with the bodies of the judged bobbing, bloated, on the tide. Waves of horrific, 'biblical' proportions crashing through communities, ripping lovers apart and dashing the helpless limbs of terrified people and animals against rocks, trees and whatever still stood of the humble dwellings of the faithless. God killed everything. Monkey, buffalo, rhino, stoat, badger, lion, giraffe, the lot. All things bright and beautiful, all creatures great and small. Dead. Especially the bloody bastard giraffe. God hates giraffes, He always has. He did the plans for them in imperial and then built them in metric. They were never supposed to be that tall. It's always pissed Him off. That's why He chose a flood. So that the giraffe would be last to go. The creature could watch with its big teary-looking eyes as all around the water creeps its way up his long, spotty, lolloping neck. Aware from the pleading bleats and mewls of those around him of the full horror of what awaits when the great flood closes over his head. 'Take that, giraffe, you smug, gangly twat,' sayeth the Lord. I'm paraphrasing from the original text obviously. Most of the really nasty stuff God muttered as he watched the carnival of kill is in the Dead Sea Scrolls; we're not allowed to see it.

But then, just when you thought God might be an irredeemably unpleasant character, He sent His rainbow. His promise to man that He would never flood the Earth again. Which is why so few religious people take the threat to climate change seriously. Unless they happen to live in Cumbria or Bangladesh. God put a rainbow in the sky. This was his promise to man that the flood thing was a once only. As I type these words the radio is telling me about a massive tsunami that has just hit Japan ... hmm. The rainbow wasn't a manifesto pledge then, I assume. If you read in the Bible about the rainbow and the end of the flood, it says, 'I place my bow in the cloud, and this shall be my covenant, my promise to man. And when I see it I will remember never to flood the Earth again.' I will *remember*? It's an aide memoire? The rainbow is God's Post-it note. A little sticker saying, 'Note to self – try not to murder everything.' Good for you, God. Go on, stick that message on a cloud and hope you don't forget ...

For me, the worst kind of genocidal deity is the scatter-brained genocidal deity. My research suggests that God kills 2,038,334 people in the Bible; 2,038,334 killed by God. It seems a lot, doesn't it? So I wondered just how many Satan kills. Is it higher or lower? What do we think? Quick game of 'Play Your Cards Right'. God just over two million, good game, good game. What about Satan? The prince of darkness, what do we think? Is it higher or lower?

Lower?

Maybe . . .

It's ten. There are ten people killed by Satan in the Bible. Ten people killed. In a bet with God. God bet Satan that Job would not renounce his faith. And he said to Satan, 'Kill Job's wife. Kill Job's family, kill Job's children and I bet you Job doesn't give up on his love for me because Job's my kind of guy.' Satan lost. But not as much as Job did.

Even if I knew for a fact that God existed, the God of Abraham, if I was absolutely certain He was real, if there were some way to know, perhaps if I had proof . . . I still couldn't worship that. That God is a pitiless, bigoted, paranoid, violent, inconsistent, jealous, genocidal, scatter-brained, murdering fuck. I couldn't hang out with Him. Not with the liberal company I keep. The dinner parties would be so awkward. 'Hey, this is God, everyone . . . Erm, shhh, He's a bit racist. Sorry. Oh, and for Christ's sake, don't get him going on slavery or poofters.'

Whoever it was who thought the flood story was OK to introduce to my son as a threat aimed at non-believers, you're a fucking idiot. It makes me so angry that people – Christians, believers, teachers, whoever – think this stuff is all right. Abraham trying to kill his son to please God – a horrible, twisted story. God closing the ocean over the Egyptians' heads after he'd parted the water for the Israelites – evidence of a vindictive, unforgiving and violent thug, not appropriate for children. Sodom and Gomorrah – this is not the case made against homosexuality, it's the case closed on the question of God's inability to discriminate between good and bad, it's as close to an endorsement of child rape as any book on sale might get away with. Not to mention the fact that all of the major religious texts glorify murder. The Lord giveth and the Lord taketh away, and the Lord doth enjoy the taking away a hell of a lot and does it to anyone He fancies regardless of age, race, creed, religious persuasion or shoe size. God should be on the sex offenders' register.

Is it just floods God sends or are all the foul and upsetting things encountered by people every day part of God's plan for us? A road death. Is that a punishment? Cancer? Aids? Starvation? Which of these are subtle coded messages from the forgetful rainbow God? He said He wouldn't do it again, but if we push our luck He's still capable of bringing His A-game and getting medieval on our arses. How is it that the focus of that horrific story has remained for so long on the tiny happy detail of Noah and his family? What about the follow-up stuff where the land is littered with the rotting corpses of the dead and the water turning stagnant and infected with disease? Where's that written down? That's the reality of a major flood disaster, not the 'Don't it put a smile on ya face' bullshit about a dove with an olive branch in its beak. Not even Fox News would report a story that badly. OK, maybe they would, but for almost every instance of God doing something nice for some people, someone, somewhere else was getting the shitty end of a particularly shitty stick.

14

A traditional church wedding
or

The Darling Buds of Maybe Not . . .

PERHAPS NOT SURPRISINGLY I COULDN'T GET MARRIED IN church. There are many reasons for this: not believing in God, not being good at lying, being a contrarian and an ASBO. It turns out that replacing the wafers with Berocca was not as well received as I'd hoped. My father-in-law was very keen that we get married in church. He's also keen on early nights, silence and Conservatism. It's a wonder we get along at all, but we do. He knows a great deal about old farming methods and trains – both of which have been increasingly badly managed for a long while now, so I like to hear what he has to say on those subjects. Best keep him off the topic of 'seen anything good on telly recently' though, because he hasn't. I think a lot of fathers, religious or not, dream of seeing their little girl marry in a nice old church. Proudly walking their blushing virgin child down the aisle towards a beaming vicar and entirely suitable young man. The image seems right somehow, particularly when it's followed by a huge balmy outdoor feast with blossom floating on the breeze and the rest of the details filled in by H.E. Bates. 'Perfick.' Even modern, liberal Dads like myself take a brief pause before imagining a same-sex, inner-city civil service to a Dub Step soundtrack followed by a reception in a night club with a group battle on the PlayStation, a toast made with class-A drugs and Domino's pizza and Jägermeister all round. That's what I imagine at least one of my kids will choose, and of course I'm totally fine with it. I'd also be happy to compromise and go traditional English with Ma Larkin and a vintage Rolls-Royce.

Anyway, out of respect for my soon to be father-in-law, my fiancée and I went to meet with the local vicar to see if we could secure that dream venue with a series of lies and deceptions. It was a nice meeting. He seemed to be quite a 'modern' vicar with a decent sense of humour. At least to begin with. My first question to him was, why Christianity? There are so many faiths. How do you know you've got it right and therefore the others have got it wrong? Why Christianity? Why not Buddhism? He took a moment to consider his answer.

I've always been rather drawn to Buddhism because I'm posh and I'm white. It's the perfect get-out clause for the non-committed, panicky atheist. You probably never saw a news story that ended with you thinking, 'Those Buddhists!

Bastards. Seriously, something's got to be done about them. They are out of control. All that sitting about. They're planning something, I tell you.' I like Buddhism. Fundamentally it seems to be about giving up on desire. You're not supposed to want anything, which makes starting Buddhism very difficult. It's a proper Catch 22. You find a Buddhist monk and explain, 'I want to be a Buddhist.' He says, 'Then you cannot.' You say, 'Fair enough, I'll leave it then. Thanks for your time. Wow, are you floating?' In some ways, now would be a very good time for me to become a Buddhist. If it's all about giving up on desire, now would seem to be ideal because I've already got a lot of stuff. If I got an iPhone I reckon I'd get through the first two years or so without really noticing any change at all. Just me and my pet gerbil called Zen.

I've meditated. It's difficult and it made me tense. Not entirely the point of meditation, I fear. I'm the same with massage. I really don't enjoy being touched by strangers (a boarding school thing, I suspect). I'm not very good at sitting cross-legged either, so even preparing for a meditate made me grumble and swear. The lotus position is not for humans with ordinary legs. It might work if you've had polio or something but otherwise it seems to me to be as natural as Anne Robinson's face. Sit, breathe and be present. That is the idea. I was present when I did it and became acutely aware of how uncomfortable sitting can be. Then I forgot how to breathe. Breathing is really very easy unless you're asthmatic or in Slough, but be careful, it's one of those things that if you think about it too deeply, you start to think you can't do it. After a few minutes of focused breathing I was honking like a goose and my vision went blurry. If you meditate every day it gets easier. I did it for a month, which felt good. Then I got a reworked version of Roy Castle's 'Record Breakers' song stuck in a loop in my head and every time I sat to meditate I sang, 'Meditation's what you need . . .' over and over until I wanted to smash my head against the fridge.

There are many different forms of Buddhism. The one I liked the most was Zen practice. There's no mysticism with it, no reincarnation or magic Kung Fu masters born in a lotus leaf. It's based on the idea that the Buddha was a bright sort of chap with some good ideas. He was a cosseted prince who went to see how normal people lived and was appalled by what he saw. It made him sad and frustrated. It's similar for Prince Philip, except that instead of describing a system of philosophical thought in which one aims to be present and accepting of reality, he's a bit racist. There's a saying, 'If you meet the Buddha on the road, kill him.' It's supposed to mean, don't treat the Buddha as anything other than a normal man. He's not to be revered or worshipped. That seems sensible, except that in any 'faith' an invitation to kill anyone will almost always be accepted and acted upon.

I'm not a Buddhist. I'd like to be but I'm too busy and there simply isn't time to make time. I find too many things unacceptable. Cheestrings, for a start. Acceptance isn't really the point anyway. The word 'acceptance' suggests there is something to accept, rather than the truth as explained in Zen practice, which is that the universe just 'is'. I can't even accept that. I try to be present in the moment but the idea of putting the kettle on and having a cup of tea when it's boiled takes me about three minutes forward in time and that soon becomes a fantasy about where I will be in eight hundred cups of tea's time. Asleep, is my main hope, though I'd settle for dancing, laughing, having sex or perhaps enjoying another cup of tea.

I wanted the good vicar to tell me how he knew he was right to be Christian and not Buddhist or one of the other ones. Had he looked at the other faiths and rejected them, or just taken up the faith he inherited from his parents? Most people do, which is hardly profound or sincere. I made it clear that I was asking if he'd considered the older religions. I wasn't trying to draw him on why he wasn't a Scientologist. To which the answer would seem to be: because I'm not rich, needy or easily led. If you haven't done it already and can spare an afternoon, I do recommend trying the Scientology 'personality test' they offer in their centres. It works like this: if you've got a personality, they ask you to leave. If you don't have one, you can stay and be 'worked on'; if you have several personalities, you get to meet Tom Cruise. It's not really a religion, Scientology; it's more of a savings club for people who think *Star Trek* is a documentary.

The vicar was ready with his answer. I was nervous. I repeated my question, 'How do you know you've got it right and the others, the Buddhists or whoever, have got it wrong?' He said, 'I don't.' I was surprised. 'I don't know. This is just the choice I've made. This is the path for me, it works for me.

But that's not to say that they've got it wrong.' This of course flies in the face of what's written in each of the Abrahamic holy books, which are very specific about the requirement to reject all other approaches to God. However, I liked his answer. It spoke of a more open mind than I'd expected to find. This guy's a liberal, I thought. This is all going to work out; I'll tell mother we are a go on the flowers. A sane, thinking, forward-looking, open-minded vicar with some of the same doubts and questions I have . . . I like this man. Then he sang the whole of 'The Lord of the Dance' to us. I shit you not. The whole thing in a small room, just my fiancée, him and me. He'd asked which songs we thought we might have at the wedding. I said, 'Probably nothing religious, to be honest. Sorry.' He told us that a lot of the songs he liked to sing in church were hardly religious at all. 'I like this one,' he said, and then in full voice and with a big smile he began:

> Dance, dance, wherever you may be.
> I am the lord of the dance said he,
> And I'll lead you all wherever you may be,
> For I am the lord of the dance said he . . .

I thought, well, that was unexpected. The look on my fiancée's face said she was taken aback too. She has a history of choral singing so I was looking to her for reassurance. Is this normal, for people who like singing this sort of thing? A pair of wide startled eyes told me it wasn't. And then he continued. A little louder and with swinging arms.

And he danced in the morning and he danced in the night.

He danced in his trousers and he danced in his tights.

I forget the precise words he used but there it all was. He sang the entire song. My bride-to-be and I continued to share nervous glances, thinking he's not going all the way, is he? But he was and he did. He even used the 'join in when you're ready' nod that teachers used to use when trying to encourage participation. A raised eyebrow, half a pause in the song, a big open mouth and ... The same look I used to use to trick my brother into launching into a hymn one bar too soon. I whispered to Sophie during round three of the chorus, 'We must leave, we're in very real danger.' And then he stopped and was calm, mild-mannered and smiling again. I was freaked out and making plans for a wedding in a cave.

He read some bits from the Bible. Which just like the Torah and the Qur'an is full of beautiful, positive, affirming, well-thought-out and well-written ideas ... and quite a few other things too. But there are beautiful ideas in all of these books; they're well worth reading and considering before moving on to a nice bit of Philip Pullman or a Jilly Cooper. He read out some kindly thoughts on how to live, how to love and being together, and it felt good. After the singalong, anything would have been a relief. He could have done fifty pages from *Mein Kampf* and I'd have been smiling. Quite suddenly his eyes lit up. He reached a passage and told me that this bit might answer my question about other religious groups. 'This is one of my favourite passages,' he said, then he read, 'A man shall be judged by his faith, and not by his works.' Then he slammed his Bible shut, looked me straight in the eye and said, 'Tell that to the Buddhists.' So you see, if you leave it long enough, say, the duration of one toe-curlingly awkward rendition of 'Dance, dance wherever you may be', it turns out you can't be a liberal and a Christian preacher. The two things are mutually exclusive. You can only be good at one if you're shit at the other. Which is what I explained to him, then stole a candle and we left as fast as we could.

I spent an afternoon with a seemingly delightful vicar in Surrey once. (Another christening: this time I was invited to anoint my Godson's head with holy water. The font boiled when I touched it. That's not normal, right?) The vicar seemed kindly and was sincere, unabashed and thoughtful in his faith. I liked him. Then he asked one of the other Godparents if he had children yet. The man (another atheist, who'd found the ceremony about as comfortable as a body cavity search) told him yes, he had two children. The vicar then pressed on and asked if there were plans for any more. The father of two said, 'Yes, quite possibly, we might have another.' To which the vicar replied, 'Oh good, we need more white children in this country.' Welcome to the church of This is ENGLAND, you know!

My wife and I got married outside. We had a Humanist celebrant. You have to be careful with the word 'Humanist'. Especially when you say it out loud. If you don't watch yourself it can sound awfully similar to humourless, and they're anything but that. No, really. They don't take themselves too seriously *at all* … It's probably because a church wedding already has gravitas whereas the non-religious ceremony is competing with some element of doubt that it is sincere or proper. There's often a whiff of cynicism that the happy couple might well be divorced before the cake's been cut.

We had a beautiful wedding. It was important for us to get married outside. We wanted to make that promise to each other in the presence of something bigger, grander and altogether more impressive than us. So we chose to do it on the side of a magnificent hill in Somerset. We needn't have bothered because my uncle Nige came and he's bigger, grander and altogether more impressive than us on his own. Getting married outside instinctively felt right and meant that a huge number of people neither my wife nor I really knew could come to the wedding. There's such a fine balance between the impersonal nature of a marquee filled with strange faces on an otherwise intimate and special day versus the extra gifts from the list at John Lewis. Go with the numbers, you won't remember much of it anyway.

We chose to go on honeymoon to South Africa. We went on safari. In the presence of nature on that scale you feel humbled and quite quickly it begins to feel like a thing to believe in. There's something comforting about realizing your place in nature and becoming aware that it could devour you if it chose to. This was a subject I had more enthusiasm for than my new wife, who found most of it bloody terrifying. South Africa and Botswana are truly amazing places. It's hard to imagine God wishing to cover all that up with water and drown every living creature on it. I mean, He'd have had to be really seriously pissed off at somebody.

My wife puts up with a lot. No more than most partners in a long-term relationship but enough for me to feel grateful that she hasn't as yet kicked my head in or turfed me out. I have a selfish streak and can be boorish and sulky. I am rarely wrong and when I am there's usually someone else to blame for the mistake. I refuse to engage in arguments most of the time but am intractable on many subjects. I'm staggeringly hairy (there's no doubt about the evolution debate once you've seen my back). I am a big mouth and often a cynic and I don't do dental hygiene to the extent that I probably should. I feel ashamed of these parts of myself whilst recognizing they are also part of what makes me interesting and funny. Our honeymoon was a mixed bag. Mostly it was divine and we had a lot of fun and saw a lot of wonderful things . . . but there was an incident.

Having not spent any time in Africa before, I was unfamiliar with a 'delicacy' of the region called biltong. I'd eaten jerky and liked it but I'd never had biltong before. It's dried bush meat, so in fact the term 'delicacy' is a massive overstatement. It's chewy old meat made from dried antelope or buffalo or ostrich or similarly strong-flavoured beasts. I really took to the stuff and ate loads of it. What I didn't realize is that when you eat biltong and then have a drink, the dried meat rehydrates and takes on its original size and shape. Essentially I re-formed an entire antelope in my stomach. I swear I could feel horns sticking out of my side too. Then I got the biltong farts. Now, under any other circumstances, I'd have been very happy with this hilarious result. I am a man, and a childish one at that, not to mention a comedian. Yes, I find blowing off funny. Had my brother been there, hilarity would have ensued all round and quite possibly some sort of league table. However, two days into your honeymoon, it's not exactly what you're looking for. When the bridal suite smells suspiciously of safari Bovril, it will test a new marriage.

This situation might have been forgivable if opening a window hadn't massively increased the chances of nocturnal visits from various creatures from the bush. I acknowledge that a more sincere apology and some committed clenching would have gone some way towards rectifying the rectal situation, but it got worse and it was too late to correct it as I'd failed to link the cause with the result and merrily went on gnawing away at various sun-dried beasties with the same appetite and enthusiasm as a vulture.

We went on a dawn game drive to look at the animals. These set off at five o'clock in the morning. You wake early, dress in khaki (unless you're from America, then it's something bright and practical) and sneak into a drab vehicle as early as the sun permits in order to see the animals when they are really active. We were in an open-top jeep with a guide driver named Peter in the front, a young family in front of us and another couple in the rear who were either on honeymoon or had their faces stuck together in some sort of unfortunate incident at a glue factory. The roads are potholed and rough;

they cut through the bush and over very wild terrain. We were being jiggled about like khaki ragdolls with binocular-shaped bruising forming on our chests. We went over a particularly large bump and a huge and unfortunate biltong-based blow-off fell out of me. No one heard it. The vehicle was open-topped and noisy enough. I've got away with that, I thought for the briefest of moments. The driver of our open-topped vehicle then brought it to a sudden halt and after two small sniffs and then one slow deep inhalation, he asked in his beautiful South African accent, 'Can everybody smell that? That's lion. You can tell because it's very meaty. It's quite fresh as well; they've been through here recently.' At this point everybody in the jeep got up, fumbling with readied cameras, and joined Peter in his sniffing. 'Yes, yes, I smell it. Come on, darling, up you get.' And, 'Get the camera, I think they've made a kill.' Needless to say I was the only one still sitting, and the more I laughed, the more the biltong made its deadly presence felt. At one point Peter, after a particularly deep sniff, advised us: 'Be careful, I think one of them might be injured.' My poor wife eventually noticed my apparent lack of interest in the king of the beasts and the fact that my shoulders were vibrating with suppressed laughter. She soon figured out what had happened and she hit me so hard that another one came out. We were there for almost forty minutes. I still can't look at the pictures without giggling and feeling a strange expanding gripe in my tummy. The whole thing would have been a lot funnier had it not been our honeymoon treat. I let my wife down. It's only guilt, but I do it all the time and that's hard to live with. By do it all the time I mean let her down, not stop an entire safari with my bum.

Theologically and spiritually speaking, my wife and I are pretty much on the same page, I think. We believe in broadly the same things. There are some differences, of course. She enjoys a star sign whereas I'm a Taurus, which means I don't really believe in that sort of thing. Earth sign, cynical, stubborn – reads books and thinks. She believes in ghosts. I've never seen one and am so enraged by the exploitative liars who make a living from upsetting recently bereaved families that I'm disposed against the whole notion of ghosts and spirits and all that nonsense. She believes in a sort of universal connected-ness that I don't really buy into. For example, if I phone her when she was just about to phone me, then we always have a couple of minutes of sheer unbelieving shock and awe at how unlikely a situation that is. She asks, 'How weird is that? I mean really, how weird is that? I was *just* about to phone you. Amazing. How weird is that?' I then have to resist the urge to smugly answer, 'It's moderately weird at *best*.' I phone my wife a lot. We speak often. Several times a day I call her just to tell her I love her and I'm thinking about her and to ask about her day. I'm not telling you that to try to redeem myself from the pits of shame surrounding both the fact of the biltong incident and that I still clearly find it so very amusing. I love my wife and I call her to say so. I am genuinely baffled by those old comedians. You know the ones who used to come on stage and open their set with: 'My wife's so fat and miserable, she's basi-cally a bastard.' Really? Do her a favour then. Go and bury your head somewhere, you dull insensitive prick. I phone my wife several times a day just to tell her I'm thinking about her, and several more times to ask where my things are. I phoned her once to ask where my phone was. That was a tense conversation. She didn't know.

It's not that I beat myself up for being a crap husband or an inadequate father or a flawed human being, not exactly. I do feel bad about myself sometimes but in the scheme of things I see myself as somewhere in the middle of the human scale. It runs from 100 per cent arsehole all of the time up to 100 per cent Michael Palin most of the time. I'd like to think I occupy a space somewhere near the middle. I'm not extraordinary like Gandhi or Martin Luther King. (I'm entirely the wrong colour to save my people from that kind of oppression – so unfair!) Neither am I dreadful like Fred West or Liam Gallagher. I'm about average. I am a humanitarian. I love my family and friends. I am generous when it suits me, though never wholly anonymously. I am selfish and callous sometimes and funny and kind for the rest. But humans are flawed, sometimes very – look at Robert Kilroy Silk. Husbands are crap, fathers inadequate and life is a series of challenges met to the best of our ability with the skills and experiences we acquire as we grow older. The trick, it seems to me, is to try to learn from those experiences and use them not to punish ourselves but to better prepare ourselves for the next challenge. If you've mastered that, you're a better person than me. It's hard not to become disheartened or bitter. I am a slow learner and often repeat the same mistake and fully expect a different result. (I believe that is the very definition of insanity.) It's harder still to remember to stay open to new ideas as we grow older. That kind of conservatism is hard-wired into the human being. Your skin sags, your organs tire and one day you know for sure that music's not as good as it used to be and that young people need some of whatever it was that made you unhappy as a child.

Essentially, I need to toughen up. I need to learn how to dial down my empathy or dial up my practical responses to the demands of my emotions. At present I feel a lot and do very little about it. When people are cruel or uncaring to each other, or when we choose to look the other way when even a glance in the right direction would show us people very close to ourselves suffering terribly, I struggle with it and feel a sense of despair hovering over my head. I can't help but think this might be a feeling that God could help to disperse or enable me to philosophize about more effectively. Maybe with God in my corner I would be able to turn the middle-class hand-wringing guilt I feel into something more useful. It doesn't make a scrap of difference to someone drowning in their bed-room in Bangladesh, or scratching for grains behind an aid truck in Ethiopia, or hiding from a tyrannical drunken partner in Peckham to know that I feel bad for them. It's use-less in real terms and yet most people empathize, sympathize and recognize the condition of our fellows without even trying to. We feel for each other, but we are usually powerless to do anything to help. It's human, we can't stop it, and for me it's often close to unbearable. God must be more than just a callous murdering shit toying with his human project. He must be, because I've seen people who believe in him and they seem from the outside to be more at peace in their heads and in their hearts than I am. Did God do that? Or did they just stop asking the questions?

15

Saying Goodbye

THERE ARE SO MANY THINGS FROM FAITH I THINK ARE beautiful and worth preserving. Religious music for a start. I find classical choral music extraordinary and moving . . . for the first few hymns, then I wonder why it all sounds the same and has to be so high in the register and creepy. Gospel at its best feels like a hurricane and the passion that inspires it has spread beyond the confines of singing in church. It's everywhere in modern popular music and enriches everything it touches. The sound of a great gospel choir is so powerful that even the most arrhythmic white conservative can't resist clapping on the downbeat and bouncing his knees up and down as if all he can hear is a buggered metronome. Even if lyrically it amounts to little more than harmonious repetition of how much God and Jesus are still really very popular down here on Earth, it feels like it must be saying something much bigger. Sincerity, passion and the power of the human voice to make us feel like we are more than ourselves are bound up in gospel music. I don't believe in God but I hope someone somewhere continues to sing amazing songs to Him. As long as someone has a little light, I hope they continue to let it shine, let it shine, let it shine!

Science and the natural world have not as far as I know inspired the same level of soaring musical expression as religious devotion. Love has, but it shares with God a mystical, ungraspable quality. The power of it moves us far beyond the realm of just feeling something. It devours us and before you know it you have lyrics like 'If I could save time in a bottle, the first thing that I'd like to do, is to save every day 'til eternity passes away, just to spend them with you' from 'Time In A Bottle'. There's a line at the end of the musical *Les Misérables*: 'To love another person is to see the face of God'. Maybe that's it. Maybe love is the great power and that is all we need. I believe in love. I've felt it from and for other people. There's plenty of experience that we can see, feel and be inspired by without the need to dedicate our art to the Lord but I'm very glad that people have done so none the less.

It is impossible to imagine a world without religion (with apologies to John Lennon, I've tried and it certainly wasn't easy). I am not convinced the world would be a better place without religion anyway. Although I'd be willing to try it. Who's with me? Religion has permeated every aspect of the world we inhabit. It has been corrosive, divisive, constructive and unifying all at once. You couldn't rip it from the world and make it never have existed. Even the most committed secular campaigners can see that its contribution has been of tremendous value. But at what cost? This is an urgent question and one that needs an answer. Religion has its past, good, bad, murdery, rapey, kindly and inspiring; but what is the future for a system of thought so resistant to change that even a new cover on a hymn book is enough to spark a civil war? Where can religion go from here?

The world is changing fast. The only thing that can truly be described as consistent is that the pace of change is accelerating. The major faiths have a series of well-constructed anchors set deep into the bedrock of the past and the solid chains that keep them from moving forwards look as sturdy as they ever did. When one chain seems unlikely to resist the strain put upon it by the fast-flowing river of progress, another is ready to be relied upon. If any part of the raft of faith strains too much in the current, then it is divided and the strong bit stays where it is with as many people as possible encouraged to climb aboard and help prevent any drift in the direction of the unrelenting flow of progress. Even if it were possible to undo the chains that bind religion to an idealized and largely fictional past and set the faiths free to move with the current, I doubt they'd survive the many twists and turns in the rapids ahead. The river has Rock and Roll in it, drugs, booze, sex, TV, films, radio, literature, philosophy, democracy, journalism, the internet and whatever's left of our libraries when the coalition government have finished attacking them for the small change it'll save. It has scientists who are hungry for knowledge and for whom change and constant questioning and reappraisal are not obstacles or inconveniences but rather the fuel that drives them. The water is filled with people connected to each other not by the enduring fear of an eternity in Hell, but in a much more immediate sense by ISDN cables, firewire, satellites, dongles, dishes, USB ports, wi-fi and even dial-up if you're with BT Broadband. Those are some large and unforgiving rapids for a vessel that hasn't moved downstream for a couple of thousand years and is beginning to creak.

You can't change history. You can lie about it and misrepresent it. Certainly, you can convince a great many people that things that did happen didn't and things that didn't did. That's why Bush and Blair still appear in public with smiles on their faces. If the three major religious texts were subjected to the same scrutiny as most other books relied upon to instruct our children in their education, they'd have been handed to the school janitor to be hidden in the back of a cupboard along with stories about Golliwogs and asbestos shorts for fat kids. The fact of religion and its place in our story should be respected where that is appropriate. Where it's not, a sincere attempt at truth and justice should be striven towards with courage and humility as its guiding principles. As to religion's future, the Tarot cards I always rely on in these matters suggest the road ahead is not an easy one. The age of communication is setting hearts and minds ablaze in parts of the world where even a secretive muttering of the word 'change' is enough to win you a free S+M session with no safe word.

If religion were to alter itself or begin to take a backseat in the affairs of men and women, what might be worth preserving? Desmond Tutu, I would hope. Architecture, art, music, sculpture and literature, of course. Only a cultural vandal or a fool (or member of an opposing theological system) would seek to destroy any of those things or to downplay the contribution some aspects of religion have made to our culture. But what else? Ritual is important to us. We are pattern-seeking and draw comfort from the familiar. That is not to say that tradition for its own sake is worth preserving. There have been thousands of corrupt and silly ideas manacled to notions of tradition and on they go because, well, they've always been there so we'd probably better not bugger about with them. Every new guardsman (a short period of service in the career of many soldiers) gets a brand new bearskin hat. Each one requires the death of a bear. A dead bear provides an impractical, pointless, funny-looking, traditional hat. Bearskin that would do well keeping a bear warm in Canada's winter, but perched on the head of a soldier makes them pass out and be ignored by the Queen in London's summer. Traditional and stupid.

Religion plays a vital role in community. We need each other, we need contact, fellowship and to know we are not totally alone. That's why people go to Ikea. We don't need tea lights, we need each other ... and meatballs. The church, mosque and temple bring people together. What they do when they assemble may not meet with everyone's approval, but the act of assembly is important. We work long hours, travel further from home and communicate remotely around the world. Many of our children have a telly in their bedroom and the idea of eating or talking together is tolerated only at Christmas, with plenty of alcohol to make it bearable and always on the understanding that there will be presents. Christmas – it's all about the getting. This is not so in religious communities. They spend time with each other and there is support and friendship facilitated by the commonality of belief. Sure, they have their problems, like hiding sex crimes, beatings, gossip, administering medieval justice and teenagers not being allowed out after 8 p.m. for fear they might meet someone with genitals, but these religious assemblies fulfil a fundamental human need to share time with other people.

The Natural History Museum in London also brings people together. They stand in awe before the wondrous collection of exhibits seeking to further our understanding of the world we share, and eat a slice of their rather good cafeteria carrot cake. But is it communion? In a sense I think it is. It's good to know that other people want to understand like I do, even if the other people are a school party whose main interest is to see who can nick the biggest rubber from the gift shop or sneak round the back of the Triceratops for a fag and a snog. But it's unstructured compared with religious assembly and no one would notice if you didn't turn up. Even if you pre-book you'd be very surprised to get a call from a museum saying, 'Some of us noticed you didn't make it to the Mammals of Africa wing this morning and we wanted to check you were OK . . .' There are many other places where we get together – swingers' parties, public swimming pools and Marks & Spencer's to name but three – but with the exception of organized clubs and societies, which go some way towards genuine community, none of these places meets the quality of coming together like religion does. Perhaps this doesn't matter and we'll evolve (we do that, you know) into beings who are less dependent on other beings. Maybe we will but, at the risk of sounding needy, I don't want to. I like you guys. Let's all meet up. 'Who's with me?' Seriously though, who is?

There are clearly a great many things, simple and complex, that faith provides which we need and will therefore be preserved. Some of them have already been absorbed into what we do without us even noticing. We don't accidentally fall to our knees, face east and pray without being aware of it, or sing a butt-kissing song to the Lord unawares, but we do say goodbye. I love the fact that we say goodbye to each other. 'Goodbye' came from 'God be with you'. We said 'God be with you' to each other at a time when there wasn't enough science. Not enough medicine, so people just died a lot. People fell down dead at the drop of a hat. Granted the head was often in the hat and had been severed in one of history's decisively important wars, but that's not the dying I mean. I mean the dying we did when we didn't know how not to, from all manner of ailments that are easily survived today. In the 'olden days' if you went outside and it was raining, you would probably die. That's how it worked. 'Oops, spot of rain on the way home this evening, darling, sorry, I'm going to die now, because my chest became moist.' In Jane Austen's stories, no one went down to the kitchen in the winter. It was too cold, you would die. 'I'm just going to get some cheese, do you want anything? Uh oh, hello? It's a mite chilly in here, Mr Darcy. Blast, it's given me consumption. Bye bye.' Thud. It was a time when a strong fart could kill you. One of mine within seconds I'm sure.

When people parted company they said, 'God be with you.' What they meant was, 'Try not to die. We don't have enough science yet so I'm not sure how this will work. But I'm guessing you'll be dead by the next time I see you. Sorry about that, but in the meantime the best I have to offer you is "God be with you".' I like that we still say that. We didn't have enough information so superstition stepped in and became a means by which we could wish the best for a friend and comfort ourselves that it was somehow going to be OK. It's a sweet and very human thing to do. I also like it because it means we crossed the linguistic bridge between 'God be with you' and 'goodbye'. At various stages in history people must have been saying (this is more fun if you read it aloud): 'God be with you', 'God be with yee', 'God be we-ye', 'Good be wey', 'Goobe-weye', 'Goobyweyee', 'Good bywye' and eventually 'Goodbye', which we now know and trust and use every day. I'd like to have been alive at the halfway point in that linguistic leap. When people parted company and simply made noises at each other. 'Goooobeeeweeeeyaaeee', a dialect still spoken in some parts of Glasgow.

I think that the final 'God be with you', the one that comes when we die, is the thing that draws more people to faith than perhaps anything else. Death is the absolute unknown and even the most ardent thrill-seekers are afraid of it. If they offered 'Actual Death' at Alton Towers there'd be no queue. Until many of the visitors had been there for half a day, when instant death would come as a blessed relief. 'To die would be an awfully big adventure,' said Peter Pan, his jaw set in defiance of the fear it holds for us all. A big adventure, we can imagine, but what if it's not? What if it's all pain and confusion or, worse still, nothing? Pain and confusion we can imagine and brace ourselves for, but we never feel truly nothing, apart from when we listen to Simply Red.

My grandmother is dying at the moment. She's very, very old. You could argue that it's her time. That may well be true. Certainly the perverse obsession with the preservation of life no matter what quality it holds is one I am horrified by. The real sadness of it all is that it's happening very slowly and each day she survives is not so much a gift from God as a sentence from humanity. When my wonderful grandmother is lucid enough to understand it, she is facing death with an idea in her head. Perhaps 'a hope' would be a better description of what she feels. She's facing the end of her life hoping she'll see my granddad again . . . Which is odd because he's still alive. Sorry, I couldn't resist honouring that ancient joke which is found in amber in certain parts of the world. He's not alive, he died almost fifteen years ago, and she's missed him. Now she is looking forward to seeing him again. And I don't know if she will. I don't think so, but I hope she does.

My grandparents were fantastic together. I don't think I've ever known a couple more demonstrably in love with each other than my Nana and Papa. They were beautiful, devoted, funny and they knew how to live. It's my understanding that they had a lot of sex. They weren't unpleasant or unnecessary about it, but neither did they see a need to conceal a genuine lust for intimate relations with each other. I think they continued to do it quite late in life. It may have been what killed him.

I remember, as children my sister and I used to go away on family holidays with them. My parents would drive us all down to the south of France, to stay in a tiny little villa. My grandparents slept in an old caravan out in the garden. At siesta time, my sister and I would sneak out from our stiflingly hot ground-floor bedroom, slip unheard through the window and hide, smiling, in the cool black shadows of the garden. This devious avoidance of an afternoon kip meant that we would often witness our grandparents' caravan heaving to and fro with enough creaking and squeaking to silence even the relentless chirrup of the cicadas, who I suspect were pretty impressed. The energetic momentum of the caravan was a mystery to us at the time, but we figured it out later. It was the hypnotic rhythm of my septuagenarian grandparents enjoying a bit of 'afternoon delight' in the full heat of the day. On occasion my sister and I would crouch beneath the curved end of the caravan and we'd talk about what would happen if on the upwards rock of the suspension springs we whipped the chocks out from underneath the wheels. Our villa was in the mountains, so with that much elderly sexual dynamism, they would have descended the steep Provençal hillside enjoying the shag of their lives and arrived in a tiny French village in time for pastis and pétanque.

Good for them. I think that's wonderful and I hope that whatever sort of apple I am, I haven't fallen too far from that tree. My granddad had a great sense of dignity accompanied by a wicked sense of humour. He was funny and he was clever, a GP who used Brylcreem and Grecian 2000 and made my grandmother very happy. We knew they were having sex; and he knew that we knew they were having sex. Everyone knew they were having sex. The next village knew they were having sex. In the middle of an afternoon in August in the late 1970s in southern France, there were men in berets carrying baguettes in their baskets telling each other, 'Mais oui, ce sont les vieux Anglais … Ils baisent encore dans l'après-midi. C'est trop chaud pour l'amour, mais les Anglais n'arretent pas. Bravo, les vieux Anglais. Bravo. Moi, je respecte ce commitment.' Every day after their siesta bonk, my grandfather would emerge, red-faced, from the caravan with a fly swat in his hand, swinging it from side to side whilst casually noting, 'A lot of flies in there today. Pretty vigorous chase this afternoon.' And we'd say, 'Yeah, there must have been some big ones too because when you hit them they sounded just like Nana!'

She'd tease him too. She had large breasts, my grandmother. She was at that age where she wouldn't get them out any more. I don't even know if that was legal in the 1970s. Not during the day anyway, but after dark she would get her breasts out and she'd tease him with them. They were, if memory serves, that extraordinary colour that old lady English tits go. An incredible, almost luminescent white. Like marble. When the moon hit them they looked almost magical. Quite incredible. I remember one night she got into the pool and swayed in the water saying, 'Look, Mervin, they're floating.' He'd dive in and we'd be dragged off to bed saying, 'What's going on, they're only having a swim?' He went in off the board, for goodness' sake, and he was in his seventies. I so hope she sees him again.

At family lunches, when I was young, my grandmother would occasionally leave the room after the main course to freshen up. Then, just before pudding was served, she would pop a freshly lipsticked face round the door and simply utter, 'Mervin . . . a word.' Upon which he would blush and scurry from the room with a slightly bashful smile; only to return a while later with a twinkle in his eye and a renewed appetite for dessert.

There's no one in the world who can sit me down and tell me that the idea of her being reunited with my grandfather in some sort of afterlife is a bad thing. The hope she hangs on to, as more and more of her days here with us are marked by only fleeting moments of comfort and calm, is beautiful and benign and it's my fervent wish that it comes true for her.

But I have a problem ... the idea of a person, beloved by any of us or not, moving on to some other afterlife existence comes from the same set of ideas that made it OK for those men to get into airplanes on 9/11 and fly them into the Twin Towers and the Pentagon. The same set of ideas that makes it OK for people to treat this life as little more than a test, because they're sure they're going somewhere better afterwards.

Those particular people who 'martyred' themselves on 9/11 were poor. They'd had their education hijacked by religious fundamentalists. The act of them hijacking planes completed that terrible circle. They'd been lied to by people who had attained enough information from the real world to know that dying and killing for Allah would be stupid, painful and frightening, so they got someone else to do it. 'All bullies are cowards' might be a cliché but in the case of suicide killings there is always a better-informed mind convincing those without that to die would be an awfully big adventure. It's easy, we did it at school, we were children and were waiting for better information, so in the meantime we told the hyperactive thick kid that he was the only boy in the school who could jump off the science lab roof and not hurt himself. Danny had over twenty stitches that day. Not difficult. It's hard to convince an educated person to commit murder or suicide. Many do, of course, because of mental illness, but to convince someone sane to do it becomes harder with every book they read. If they've only read the Qur'an, it's not too tricky, it seems. This lethal and divisive narrowing of educational focus is something we seem keen to bring about in this country with the ghastly spread of faith schools. A vile legacy left behind from the secret Catholic Tony Blair. 'We don't do God,' said Alastair Campbell, his spin doctor. Possibly not, but it seems God was pretty busy 'doing' us.

Islamic suicide bombers are made promises. They're befuddled with obscure interpretations of Mohammed's writing, they are pumped full of easy-to-package mis-information and then sent on their way with the promise of glory, the old lie that is 'Dulce et decorum est pro patria mori' (Wilfred Owen). Joining any fighting force follows a similar process. The severity of the lie depends on how well advanced and accessible education is in that country. The forces don't function too well if the ground soldiers know too much. Ask any officer and they'll tell you the same thing. I say this not to disrespect the undoubtedly brave men and women who fight for their countries, but to shame those who would seek to deceive them. Islamic jihadist murderers are told amongst other things that if they martyr themselves and take infidel lives with them, their reward in the afterlife will include seventy-two virgins, to do with as they will. I had no idea that Heaven was so heavily marketed on the promise of hot orgy action. It makes the Islamic afterlife sound more like an 18–30 holiday. I wonder if they do inflatable banana rides round the bay too. It's all very tempting ... until you think about it. Seventy-two virgin girls would be like being awarded the chattering, shrieking, terrified lower school of an all-girls madrassa. No thank you. What a bloody nightmare. What these boys thought they'd do with seventy-two virgins, I don't know. As I understand it the boys were all virgins as well. There'd just be seventy-two blushing, sticky apologies and a lot of mopping up as far as I can tell. 'Hello, are you a virgin? Oops, sorry, I've gone off. I'm not used to this. Ooh, look at that one. Shit, it's happened again. Right, how many of you are left? Hands up if you're still a virgin. Oh bloody hell, I'm on a hair trigger here. I wish I'd read more books. This is awful.' Many Islamic scholars will tell you that if you translate that part of the Qur'an directly, it isn't seventy-two virgins they are promised at all, it's seventy-two raisins. Which is pretty disappointing for your recently martyred Islamic jihadist, I think you'd agree. Seventy-two dried white grapes. Sultanas. Wow, you'd be gutted, wouldn't you? You kill yourself and several hundred other people, you arrive in the afterlife full of pride, hope and backed-up semen, only to find there's barely enough there to make a Chelsea bun. The most you can have sex with one of those is twice.

I'm not suggesting that my dear grandmother has any more in common with the 9/11 killers than to have shared in the collective need to create something we can be less afraid of when we step into the last great unknown. She hasn't been got at by an insane Mullah and is as we speak planning to blow the dining room of the care home she's in sky high, shrieking Allah-e-akbah! There'd be tiny portions of apple crumble and custard all over the walls and the *Daily Mail* would conclude that no one is safe. These stories of what happens after we die are there to comfort the living and embolden the dying. They carry the power within them (like any good story) to encourage action that might not otherwise take place. For many that action is the positive, well-meant response to the promise of eternal life at God's side and a fear of spending the rest of time in Hell. For others it's a trivialization of this life and an excuse to act with barbarism and cruelty towards those who don't agree with you.

I simply don't know if there's an afterlife of any kind. I don't wish to let go of the hope that there is one. It scares me that there might not be. I realize, thanks to David Eagleman's exquisite book *Sum*, that our imagination as far as what happens next has been stifled by the constraints of religious doctrine. He suggests forty possible explanations, including reliving your life with all the common experiences grouped together. Every shower, every cup of tea, all the pain, all the sex, all the love, lumped together into chapters of experience, as if you had just had one experience of each, and then being asked if it made any more sense that way round. I loved that idea and *Sum* made me realize just how hemmed in by conventional religious teaching our thinking on possible afterlives is. The box containing ideas about the afterlife is sturdy and has a heavy lock; it's very hard to think outside it. The atheist will tell you that when you die, that's it. You die and there is no more and it all stops. The zealot will tell you about being judged for the life you've led and going on for ever in Paradise or in Hell or in Purgatory, which is Hell Lite and where unbaptized babies go if they die before they've had a decision about their beliefs made for them by people they can't communicate with. I think in some ways that Purgatory is the hardest of all states to imagine. Unless you've ever been to Woking in Surrey, in which case I suspect it's pretty similar to that.

I hope something else happens after we die.

My best friend died a few years ago. His name was James; he was an amazing guy. Whenever I talk about him or think about him, I feel a kind of dull ache inside. The space he left in my life had no choice but to flood itself with sadness. There is also happiness, as I remember how much fun we had, but mostly it's sad now because there won't be any new experiences to enjoy with James. That's as it should be, he was my friend, I miss him. I don't mind feeling sad about James, although I have stalled, procrastinated and distracted myself in the run-up to writing this chapter so maybe in reality I do.

James died much too soon. He was in his thirties. A husband, a father, a son and my friend. He'd have lived a lot longer if he'd known how to. He didn't give up, but his heart stopped working and that meant he had to go whether he wanted to or not. He was a little older than I was and had been a friend of my sister's when we grew up. Then after rehab I became very interested in dancing. I went night-clubbing as often as I could. Clean and sober but looking to all who saw me throw shapes as if I was guzzling ecstasy tablets like Smarties. James had a severe heart condition so, despite loving dancing, he too avoided the chemicals that went with that scene. We both just loved the music and on one occasion were asked to leave a club because we were 'too far gone'. I suppose the way we danced made it look like we must be on something pretty extreme and possibly dangerous. We became very close and had silly names for each other, which came from a Vic Reeves and Bob Mortimer sketch. I called him Gattman. We went on holidays together. I was proud to be his best man when he got married and he was my head usher when I did. I paid for him when I had money and he paid for me when I was broke. I suspect if you did the maths I owe him about thirty pounds.

He'd have found the idea of his silly, dancing friend writing a book about God and religion preposterous and exciting. He wouldn't have liked it because he only ever read books whose back-cover blurb included the phrase 'Trapped behind enemy lines'. He dug McNab and got cross with me for being a pacifist wuss and refusing to watch past season two of 24 on the grounds that it's a manifesto for torture. I'm tempted to put 'Marcus Brigstocke is trapped behind enemy lines as he finds himself caught in the crossfire of atheism and faith. Only more reading and a chopper full of wry sarcastic cynicism will save him now . . .' just in case he can see what I'm up to and has time to read.

James got me my first ever stand-up gig. He started my career in comedy. He wasn't a comedian either, or a promoter. He had nothing to do with entertainment, though he did once DJ at the Ministry of Sound. What a night. He was just a friend of mine who thought I was funny. I tried to get into drama school and failed. I was heartbroken. So he took me out for lunch. As I was sitting down, he said, 'So, you failed to get in, eh? Wanker.' You know, bloke stuff, it's what friends do, it's supportive. It's how we men look after each other. There's a code, we all understand it, nothing's totally sacred. As long as no one ruins it by crying, it all works. I was gutted, and he said, 'Well, you're a shit actor anyway. Don't go to drama school. You're funny, be a comedian.' I told him I thought that was frightening and I wouldn't know how to do it. Then I made him laugh by pretending to be a stand-up and using a spoon as a microphone. He phoned me the next day and said, 'You'd better write something, I've booked you a gig and it's next week . . .'

My first ever stand-up appearance was in a comedy competition for new acts in Holborn in London. James drove me to the bar and he made me go inside. He stood and he waited with me in the wings watching as I stuffed notes and small props into various pockets about my person. He held my shaking hand as I stood, dreading the moment my name was called out. It never was, the compere said, 'Marcus Pig-snot'. I guess he thought I was a character act. It didn't matter. I wasn't sure I wanted anyone to know my real name anyway. James pushed me out there and I walked out on stage as a stand-up comedian for the first time ever.

What a thrill. It was so exciting. I died on my arse. I played to embarrassed, coughing silence. It was miserable for the first six minutes. A few people chuckled sympathetically as I fumbled with paper and a rubber chicken (true). Then, when I'd run out of props and had two minutes to go, it began to come together. People started laughing. By the end they were really laughing a lot and then clapping. I still remember exactly how I felt. I'd never been more proud or felt more like I counted in my life. After rehab and obesity and not a qualification to my name and drifting and not being sure, I suddenly felt there was a thing for me to do. I was so excited. I still feel like that about comedy. It's the best job I could ever imagine anybody having. Every time I do it, I love it, and I know I'm lucky to have had the chance to find that thing. I came second in the competition on my first ever gig. I walked off stage, still shaking, smiling and a bit emotional, and there he was. James was waiting for me, smiling, shaking and a bit emotional. As soon as I came off he said, 'Aaahhhh, you died on your arse for six minutes. Wanker.' Bloke stuff, you know, supportive. It's what we do.

He had a beer. I had a juice. We were excited. He continued to take the piss, until I got defensive, then he giggled and got his penis out to cheer me up. He wasn't gay and I'm not yet either, but he did get his penis out a lot. Too much, some said, but it's easy to judge these things in hindsight, isn't it? He had a heart condition, that's what killed him in the end. But it did a number of other things along the way. One thing it did was it excused a huge amount of otherwise quite unforgivable behaviour. He'd get his penis out, and I'd say, 'Come on, mate, put it away, it's horrible,' he'd smirk and shake his head, then look sad and point to his chest. 'I've got a heart condition.' 'Well, all right then, keep it out, but just for a minute.'

James loved rugby. He was quite posh and we went to Twickenham to watch England play as often as we could. We wore berets when we played France and put them on with shrugs and silly faces every time England scored. Because of his broken ticker he couldn't play rugby. So he made a decision early in life to do all the things that go with the game without actually playing it himself. As many boorish rugger lads know, the things that go with rugby, other than beer, cheering and yelling at the ref, often involve getting your penis out and putting it in other people's drinks. A game James liked to call Dippy Dippy Sip Sip. Not nice, but there it is. I rarely fell foul of this; as a non-drinker, I was on my guard. But I saw it happen. Up would go the cry, 'Come on, who's done that?' and he'd point to his chest, we'd laugh and all would be forgiven.

He came to see me when I was at university. He got drunk and we ended up in a kebab shop in the middle of the night. It was one of those ones with the glass-fronted chiller cabinet, where the raw meat is kept perilously close to the chilled drinks. So that even if you just have a can of something, you could easily catch E. coli. The kebab shop equivalent of a petting zoo. We walked in there in search of food and more laughter and James pressed his naked penis against the front of the glass chiller cabinet. Now, I know this is not OK. It's not that I don't understand that this isn't an acceptable way to behave, and James knew it too. If I read about someone doing it, I'd be suitably po-faced and disapproving – but trust me when I tell you it was unbelievably funny at the time. He squashed it on there like a piece of dropped kebab meat. And then said to the poor man behind the till, 'Excuse me, mate, can I have a drink please?' and pointed down at the glass panel he was leaning on. The kebab shop owner leant forward to get a can from the chiller. 'No not that one,' said James. 'That's it, a bit further forward. Yes, past the Lilt, erm . . . that one.' And he steered the man's hand to within about two centimetres of his naked, flattened penis. I repeat, I know it's not OK. James was suitably ashamed but still laughing the next day. It was wilfully naughty, and that feeling, though it always has a 'victim', is a kind of delicious thing that's hard to resist. I know that at best what happened is unhygienic, it's unpleasant, it's thoughtless and at worst it is probably a minor sex crime, but you know what . . . that's what I miss. Stupidly. Those are the things I miss, my friend's naked flattened penis and laughing until we cried. Make of that what you will.

He came with me to Glastonbury. The first time I ever played the Glastonbury Festival was 1997. He came with me and he fell over. It was a muddy year, a really muddy year, and he tripped. There were survivors from the Somme watching news footage of Glastonbury in 1997 saying, 'Ooh, that looks a bit muddy.' When James tripped he did that wonderfully illogical thing that people do when they lose balance at speed. You trip, and then you convince yourself that if you could only run fast enough, somehow wind resistance alone would bring you back into an upright position. That's what he attempted in over a foot of thick Glastonbury mud. The physics of it are mind-boggling. All he really managed to do was to lose altitude but gain speed. He looked like a panicky jet in a Barbour going down . . . hippies were blown out of the way as the inevitable impact in the soaking-wet mire was realized. I still remember exactly how he looked down there in the mud. He was drenched; he'd hurt himself. It was Friday. There were three days of the festival left, which were now ruined for him. He'd grazed his penis, which was out. It was as bad as it could be. He sat there in the mud, he looked up at us and he smiled, because he wanted us to know it was OK to laugh. And my God did we laugh. We laughed until it wasn't funny any more, and then it was funny again. It was one of those ones that several weeks later, when you're completely on your own, you remember it and just piss yourself laughing. People walk past thinking, 'Hmm, nutter!' That's what he was like. He sat down there in the mud, blinking crap out of his eyes and he began to laugh. He wanted it to be OK for everyone else, and it was.

For that and a million other reasons I could tell you about, it's so sad that he's not here any more. He left two kids behind, two wonderful little boys. I'm Godfather to one of them. So when he died we told the boys whatever they needed to hear to get through. We said, 'When you talk, if you want, Daddy can hear you. When you do things, if you want, Daddy can see you.' Just whatever they needed to hear to get through. They were little children, lost in a sea of grief. Surrounded by pain. Watching the family around them weep and stare into the cold empty space stretched out before them. The boys were told what most of us thought was best – Daddy's there whenever you need him. They shouldn't be subjected to any more pain than necessary. Right? They were children. But I afforded myself none of those same comforts. I was at the time doggedly atheist and very impressed with Richard Dawkins and *The God Delusion*. When you're dead, you're dead and it's finished. There isn't anything else. So the intellectual side of my brain beat up the emotional and the spiritual side of my brain. Until in a massive victory for rationality, that side surrendered and I slumped into depression for a year and a half. Woo-hoo. Well done, everybody. At least we maintained intellectual rigour. That's what's important, isn't it?

I don't care about any of that. I don't care at all. I hurt. I miss James. I want him to be here. I want to tell him I'm about to finish my book. I don't know where he is and I really wish I did. He was my first ever speed dial. I've got no evidence to support the idea that he's in the afterlife. I don't know what I think. I can tell you what I want, though. I want to believe that anybody you've ever loved who's no longer here still exists somewhere else. I want to believe there's a place where they go. And it's not nothing and it's more than just the idea that they live on in your memories. It's somewhere safe and kind and wonderful. I make no request for you to agree with me. There's no test and I have no clue as to what's true. It's just what I want. I think I'm still an atheist but I'd like to believe that for all the people we know who die, the loved ones we miss and grieve for – that there is a peaceful place for them to continue to be. Somewhere magical and lovely, and I want to believe my friend James is up there with them ... with his penis out. And that none of them has seen it, because they couldn't possibly know how special and funny that is. When I get there, I'll be able to say, 'Classic. Mate, you are a dirty, inappropriate legend. Has that been out since you got here, just on the off chance I would turn up? What are the other angels saying?' He'd point to his chest and the two of us would laugh our arses off, then we'd go dancing until they kicked us out of Heaven for going too far.

Professor Richard Dawkins gave an answer to a question about human need, 'The universe does not owe us comfort.' He's right, of course. The universe does not owe us comfort. But then the internet does not owe us pornography but it keeps emailing it to me. Along with invitations to extend the length of my penis. If that's not evidence that James is up there somewhere, I don't know what is. The universe does not owe us comfort but I have not a shred of doubt that we will continue to search for it wherever we can, and where the universe fails to provide we will tell each other stories until something better comes along.

There's no conclusion to this set of ideas. There's not supposed to be. I didn't find God. Or disprove his existence. I'm no more comfortable with atheism than I was. I sincerely hope that no one's drawn any conclusion from this other than perhaps the idea that it is confusion and not certainty that binds us to each other. I hope you laughed. The aim with *God Collar* the show and now the book was to say, 'I don't know and I'm not going to be arrogant enough to presume.' But you can keep the God of Abraham, if you wish to. He's not for me, nor I for him. The only thing I'm certain of is this. I'd rather be happy than right. That's what this boils down to for me. I would rather be happy than right. I know that some atheists are so happy that they're right that the two things mean exactly the same thing. They wake up every morning and think, 'Yes, right again, brilliant.' But for me, I'm not so sure about that or anything else. The universe does not owe us comfort, you don't owe me your time, so if you've got this far, I thank you sincerely and from the bottom of my heart.

Goooooodbbeeewwweeeyyaaeee.

Postscript

Capital G

I USED A CAPITAL 'G' FOR GOD. NOT OUT OF RESPECT, AS YOU can't really respect something you don't think exists. No, I used a capital G just in case I was wrong and there is a God after all. If evidence, logic and reason are not factors in any of this, or were perhaps only put here by God as a test to see if we might be tempted towards thinking we knew better than some very old books with next to no supporting documents at all, then I'm thinking that when I get judged and it is decided where I will spend eternity, the capital G will be exhibit A in the case for my defence.

It's a shameless act of cowardice, but if it turns out there is a God, there's every chance He might mind about grammar, spelling, punctuation and those sorts of things. I'm hedging my bets because you never know when God might resume His nasty smiting habit.

He recommends the most awful punishments for wearing wool and cotton together on the same day or being a man who enjoys cuddling other men or eating lobster or bacon, so I daren't imagine what He'd do if you failed to capitalize His name. He seems fine with people capitalizing on His name for their own benefit entirely – so I doubt it matters, but you can't be too careful with God. He's fickle, vengeful and prone to flights of terrible anger.

My hope is that in the balance of things, should we all come to be judged at the gates of Heaven, a bit of poor grammar might go unnoticed, but as I say you can never be too careful when it comes to pissing God off.

Imagine the vile consequences of going for a gay date to 'Hanks Lobster N Crab Shack' in a V-neck cotton T with a lovely woollen jumper over it. This could be the event that finally brings the Lord out of smiting retirement.

'You've led the life of a sodomite, despite some very clear warnings on the subject. You dressed in mixed fibres, though this I forbade in the admittedly confusing book of Leviticus. You ate of the unclean creatures that I had specifically told you to avoid, and yes I know they're delicious, that's the trap and you fell into it. All these things I forgive my child, for I am the Lord your God and I am your father and I love men (though not in the same way you do). What I cannot and will not forgive is the missing apostrophe in "Hank's". I am your maker – we've already met but figuratively speaking – prepare to meet me!'

I suppose if God's His surname then the capital G is the

right thing to use anyway, but if God is His surname, then what's his first name? Does He have one? Is He called Geoff God? Dave? Jenny? Al?

According to the research I've done there are a great many reasons why the God I've read about might wish to turn me into a pillar of salt or drown me, burn me, blow me up, crush me or dismember me, so it would be tremendously disappointing if a mixture of my failed education (my responsibility, not the system), some laziness and some dyslexia were the main factors in my violent demise and eternity spent in Hell's fire.

I don't much like the versions of God I've been presented with in my life to date, so if it transpires that He's anything like that awful grammar bully Lynne Truss and her poisonous army of pernickety pedants, then I suspect He and I will have to add that to the list of reasons why we don't get on. So God it is with a Great big G.

Hello, god. Oh, it's fine. I did it and nothing happ— Aaaghh! What's that noise?